ALL·IN·ONE

CC℠

Certified in Cybersecurity

EXAM GUIDE

ABOUT THE AUTHORS

Jordan Genung, CISSP, CISM, CISA, CCSK, CCAK, CCISO, CDPSE, CC, has served as an information security leader and security advisor for public- and private-sector organizations. His experience includes building and maturing security programs and practices across multiple sectors, including government, financial services, law enforcement, emergency services, IT and security services, and healthcare. He is co-author of the *CCISO All-in-One Exam Guide* and the LinkedIn Learning *CISA Online Learning Path.*

Steven Bennett, CISSP, has over 40 years of experience as an information security professional supporting organizations in nearly every major business sector as well as federal, state, and local government agencies. He is co-author of the *CCISO All-in-One Exam Guide* and the LinkedIn Learning *CISA Online Learning Path.* Steve's previous security industry certifications include CISA, CCISO, and GIAC GSEC, and he passed the CC exam in preparation for this book.

About the Technical Editor
Michael Lester has worked in the information security industry for over 25 years and is currently designing and building future services and offerings for Amazon Web Services Global Services Security. Previously, Mike was the chief technology officer for a security software company and the chief instructor and consultant for Shon Harris's Logical Security, LLC (now Human Element, LLC), where he taught and developed courses on CISSP, hacking/pentesting, digital forensics/e-discovery, CISA, and others. Mike also authors and instructs classes for LinkedIn Learning. He holds a master's degree in information systems security from Boston University (a National Security Agency [NSA] Center of Academic Excellence) as well as over 20 industry certifications.

About the Illustrator
Peter Gustafson is an independent graphic designer/illustrator specializing in the scientific environments of technology and engineering. For over four decades, he has supported both government and corporate clients throughout the United States and Canada—much of it in helping companies win government contracts through the formal request for proposal (RFP) process. His work has been presented to two U.S. presidents, among other notable officials. He enjoys music, gardening, community service, history, and environmental advocacy.

ALL·IN·ONE

CC^{SM}

Certified in Cybersecurity

EXAM GUIDE

Jordan Genung
Steven Bennett

Mc
Graw
Hill

New York   Chicago   San Francisco
Athens   London   Madrid   Mexico City
Milan   New Delhi   Singapore   Sydney   Toronto

McGraw Hill books are available at special quantity discounts to use as premiums and sales promotions, or for use in corporate training programs. To contact a representative, please visit the Contact Us pages at www.mhprofessional.com.

CC^{SM} Certified in Cybersecurity All-in-One Exam Guide

1 2 3 4 5 6 7 8 9   LCR   28 27 26 25 24 23

Library of Congress Control Number: 2023935993

ISBN   978-1-265-20381-8
MHID   1-265-20381-4

Sponsoring Editor	**Technical Editor**	**Production Supervisor**
Wendy Rinaldi	Michael Lester	Thomas Somers
Editorial Supervisor	**Copy Editor**	**Composition**
Patty Mon	Lisa McCoy	KnowledgeWorks Global Ltd.
Project Manager	**Proofreader**	**Illustrations**
Revathi Viswanathan, KnowledgeWorks Global Ltd.	Paul Tyler	Peter Gustafson
Acquisitions Coordinator	**Indexer**	**Art Director, Cover**
Caitlin Cromley-Linn	Ted Laux	Jeff Weeks

In memory of Scout Bennett.

CONTENTS AT A GLANCE

CONTENTS

ACKNOWLEDGMENTS

The authors wish to thank their family members for their support, without which this book would not be possible.

We also want to recognize the hardworking and dedicated staff at the NIST Computer Security Division, who work behind the scenes to develop the standards, guidelines, and innovative technologies that help our nation address current and future cybersecurity threats and challenges.

INTRODUCTION

When (ISC)² introduced the Certified in Cybersecurity (CC) certification, it piqued the interest of many in the cybersecurity industry. It's not like we needed yet another industry certification. With a half-dozen governing bodies creating and promoting over 40 security-related certification programs, it would seem we have enough certifications to go around. However, the CC certification fills an important role in that it is one of the few entry-level cybersecurity certifications that covers the fundamentals of cybersecurity. As a result, professionals no longer need to have years of experience in the security industry to obtain a certification that demonstrates their knowledge of the basics. For an industry that loves certifications, this is a bit of a game changer, because it opens the door for employers to establish criteria for basic foundational cybersecurity knowledge that every employee should know, and it gives employees a good starting point to learn the cybersecurity skills that have value in the marketplace.

In defining the topics to include in the CC certification, (ISC)²'s challenge was to decide what to include and what not to include, as cybersecurity is a broad and deep subject area. (ISC)² has been the author and governing body of the Certified Information Systems Security Professional (CISSP) certification, which was first launched in 1994. With well over 150,000 people holding the CISSP certification, it has become the industry standard certification for fundamental informational security knowledge. But the CISSP certification is for experienced professionals with a minimum of five years of work experience in two or more of the eight CISSP domains of knowledge. In contrast, the CC certification, being for entry-level people with no cybersecurity experience, had to cover less information. What (ISC)² came up with for CC is a subset of what is required for CISSP. Not as broad or as deep, the CC is a lightweight introduction to cybersecurity that is well-suited for entry-level workers in all kinds of roles that encounter cybersecurity challenges in modern organizations. The following table shows the five CC domains of knowledge listed alongside the eight CISSP domains.

CC Domains	CISSP Domains
• Security Principles	• Security and Risk Management
	• Asset Security
	• Security Architecture and Engineering
• Network Security	• Communications and Network Security
• Access Controls Concepts	• Identity and Access Management
	• Security Assessment and Testing
• Security Operations	• Security Operations
• Business Continuity (BC), Disaster Recovery (DR) & Incident Response Concepts	
	• Software Development Security

The CC certification does not cover the CISSP domains of Security Assessment and Testing, Asset Security, Security Architecture and Engineering, and Software Development Security, although some subjects within these topics are covered in a limited fashion within the CC domains. In addition, for topics common to both certifications, the CC certification does not require the candidate to have the same depth of knowledge as a CISSP candidate. For instance, while both certifications cover cryptography, the CC focuses on what cryptography is used for and how it is implemented, while the CISSP covers this information as well but also dives deep into how various types of cryptographic algorithms and protocols work. This is the case of many of the CC topics. They are addressed in terms of their purpose, function, and real-world usage, while not requiring the candidate to learn about the underlying historical, engineering, mathematical, or theoretical concepts of the topic. Therefore, the CC certification is elementary and is intended to be a starting point for anyone seeking to understand security threats and the best practices organizations use to defend against them and recover from cyberattacks.

(ISC)² says the CC certification is for people who are seeking an entry-level or junior-level role in the cybersecurity field. That's true; however, the authors of this book feel the CC certification may also have a broader use and greater value. Security threats are everywhere, and being security-aware is everyone's job. Therefore, the CC certification may not be just for people entering the cybersecurity field. Any worker is a potential victim of a cyberattack, and they, and the organization they work for, can benefit from acquiring the CC certification. Imagine if everyone in the workplace knew about cybersecurity to the extent the CC certification requires. The potential benefit to an organization's ability to manage its risk could increase greatly. This is why we have great hope for the widespread use and adoption of the CC certification.

Our approach to this book was to keep it simple by focusing on the information required for the CC exam while minimizing extra information. We try to explain the topics thoroughly by providing sufficient detail and background information for people to remember the essential information. However, we avoid providing extra information so the reader will not have to study information they are not likely to encounter on the CC exam. As a result, the book is fairly lean. If it's in the book, you should study it, unless we tell you in an Exam Tip that you don't have to.

While there are no prerequisites for the CC certification, candidates are expected to have a general knowledge of computing and information systems. This book is intended for people who have such a general understanding. We don't teach what a computer is, what memory is, and what e-mail is and what it's used for, as you are expected to know that. Most people have a sufficient understanding of information technology such that understanding this book should be easy. But if you don't have any basic computing knowledge, there are plenty of "computing for beginners" books out there that you can use to help bring you up to speed. One book we recommend is the ITF+ *CompTIA IT Fundamentals All-in-One Exam Guide, Second Edition (Exams FC0-U61)* (McGraw Hill, 2018). Even if you aren't interested in getting the ITF+ certification, the book provides a good introduction to computers, networks, and IT.

This book is organized by chapters, one for each CC domain. However, we decided not to organize the chapters in the same order as the (ISC)² domains. We decided it made more sense to move the Business Continuity, Disaster Recovery, and Incident Response domain to the last chapter. We felt this made the presentation of information flow better. Other than this change, the order of information and the topics covered within each domain are as (ISC)² defined them in their latest Exam Outline.

About (ISC)²

The International Information System Security Certification Consortium (ISC)² is an international nonprofit organization that provides certification and training for cybersecurity professionals. (ISC)² organizes industry conferences, provides cybersecurity best practice material, and offers a variety of vendor-neutral certification and training programs. (ISC)² is the certification body for the Certified in Cybersecurity (CC) certification. This means that they manage the certification process and determine the requirements and content for the exam. (ISC)² is most widely known for its Certified Information Systems Security Professional (CISSP) certification, which has become a global standard certification for experienced security professionals. In addition to those certifications mentioned, (ISC)² manages the following certifications:

- Systems Security Certified Practitioner (SSCP)
- Certified Cloud Security Professional (CCSP)
- Certified in Governance, Risk and Compliance (CGRC)
- Certified Secure Software Lifecycle Professional (CSSLP)
- HealthCare Information Security and Privacy Practitioner (HCISPP)

About the CC Certification

The Certified in Cybersecurity (CC) certification is an entry-level certification focused on foundational cybersecurity concepts from the five CC domains, which include

- Domain 1 – Security Principles
- Domain 2 – Business Continuity (BC), Disaster Recovery (DR) & Incident Response Concepts
- Domain 3 – Access Controls Concepts
- Domain 4 – Network Security
- Domain 5 – Security Operations

The certification helps provide fundamental information for newcomers to the cybersecurity industry as well as those transitioning from other industries.

(ISC)² Requirements
The (ISC)² requirements may change, so it is important for candidates to check the (ISC)² website (https://www.isc2.org/) for the most up-to-date information. The requirements listed in this section are accurate at the time of this writing.

Prerequisites

The CC certification is a foundational cybersecurity certification for newcomers in the industry. As such, it does not have a minimum experience requirement or other prerequisites that other cybersecurity certifications require. The only requirement is that the candidate must be at least 16 years of age to sit for the exam. (ISC)[2] recommends that candidates have basic information technology knowledge.

Training Options

There are two primary training avenues available to become certified:

- **Self-study**   The self-study option includes leveraging resources such as this *CC Certified in Cybersecurity All-in-One Exam Guide* to prepare for the exam.
- **Training**   CC training classes are available from training providers. This route may be preferable for CC candidates who learn best from traditional-style training.

Exam Information

The CC exam is an in-person exam proctored through (ISC)[2]-authorized Pearson VUE Test Centers. The exam consists of 100 multiple-choice questions. Candidates are given two hours to complete the exam and must achieve a minimum score of at least 700 points out of 1,000 (70%). Table 1 provides the examination weights for each domain, indicating the percentage of questions from each domain that appear on the exam.

 NOTE   Table 1 is accurate at the time of this writing. For the most up-to-date information, please visit https://www.isc2.org/.

Maintaining Certification

The learning doesn't stop once you are certified. In order to ensure certification holders keep up to date with industry knowledge, certification bodies such as (ISC)[2] have requirements that credential holders submit continuing education credits. (ISC)[2] calls them continuing professional education (CPE) credits and requires 45 CPE credits every three years to maintain the CC certification. In addition, CC certification holders must pay an annual maintenance fee (AMF) of $50 a year to maintain their certification.

Domain	Examination Weight
Security Principles	26%
Business Continuity (BC), Disaster Recovery (DR) & Incident Response Concepts	10%
Access Controls Concepts	22%
Network Security	24%
Security Operations	18%

Table 1   CC Domain Weights for the Exam

How to Use This Book

This book is organized by chapters that correspond to the CC domains as defined by (ISC)². Each chapter covers the topics required by (ISC)²'s exam outline.

Each book chapter is introduced here:

- **Chapter 1: "Security Principles,"** covers CC Domain 1, including the foundational concepts of cybersecurity. The chapter covers security fundamentals that everyone should know, the elements that comprise a typical cyberattack, and the elements of cybersecurity that are typically included in an organization's security program.

- **Chapter 2: "Access Controls Concepts,"** describes CC Domain 3 Access Controls Concepts, which are security features that permit or restrict access to information systems or facility resources. The chapter covers access control fundamental concepts, practices, administration, and both logical and physical access control methods and implementation.

- **Chapter 3: "Network Security,"** discusses a wide range of topics as defined by CC Domain 4. It covers network fundamentals, network threats and attacks, network defenses, and network infrastructure implementations.

- **Chapter 4: "Security Operations,"** covers CC Domain 5 Security Operations topics. The chapter includes discussions of data security, system hardening, best practice security policies, and how organizations go about teaching their employees about security.

- **Chapter 5: "Business Continuity (BC), Disaster Recovery (DR) & Incident Response Concepts,"** covers CC Domain 2 and discusses how organizations plan for and respond to security incidents and disasters or other incidents that impact an organization's operations. The chapter covers incident response, business continuity, and disaster recovery, discussing plans and processes for each.

Each chapter starts with a short outline and text introducing the topics covered, followed by sections corresponding to the outline. Throughout each chapter, supplemental information is provided utilizing the following features to help you understand and remember various topics:

NOTE   Notes appear throughout the book to highlight or reinforce topics or provide advice.

TIP   Tips provide information that saves you effort or time. Tips may include tricks, shortcuts, or advice to help you remember a topic. Tips may also be used to provide real-world examples of a concept or process.

EXAM TIP   These targeted tips provide key information the CC candidate should know for the CC exam. Exam Tips may include test-taking advice or warnings of exam pitfalls.

In addition to the Notes, Tips, and Exam Tips, you will encounter shaded boxes, which are used to dig deeper into a topic, present a case study, or share an anecdote that illustrates or emphasizes a subject in the chapter.

Like all McGraw Hill All-in-One Exam Guides, this book uses repetition as an aid to reinforce the information presented and to facilitate committing information to long-term memory. The end of each chapter has a "Chapter Review" section that presents a review of the essential themes of each section within the chapter. The chapter review is followed by a "Quick Review" section, which is a bulleted list of key points from the chapter that are important to remember. The "Chapter Review" and "Quick Review" sections combine to reinforce the information presented in the chapter.

Each chapter concludes with questions that test the CC candidate's retention and understanding of the topics covered. The questions contained in the book are written as another means to reinforce topics. The answers include short explanations describing why the correct answer is right and, in some cases, why the incorrect answers are wrong.

The appendix, "About the Online Content," contains instructions for accessing an online testing resource called TotalTester Online. This online tool allows the CC candidate to practice questions similar to the ones on the real exam by configuring tests by domain, number of questions, and other customizable options.

Preparing for the CC Exam

We recommend preparing for the CC exam by using a repetitive sequence as follows:

1. Read this book and try to answer the questions at the end of each chapter to reinforce comprehension of the information.

2. Use TotalTester Online to take practice tests by domain. Write down the topic of every question that you answer incorrectly or have difficulty understanding.

3. Using the list of difficult topics as a study list, go back and reread the applicable sections of the book, taking notes or using study methods that have worked for you in the past.

4. Repeat the cycle of reading, testing, and studying until you are consistently scoring above 80 percent in each domain using the TotalTester Online practice questions in Exam Mode. Using Total Tester in Practice Mode may be too easy and may result in higher scores so be sure you are practicing for the exam and recording your scores in Exam Mode.

Once you are regularly scoring 80 percent or greater in Exam Mode in each domain, you should be ready to take the CC exam with confidence.

Security Principles

This chapter discusses the following topics:
- Security fundamentals
- Elements of a typical cyberattack
- Elements of a typical security program

Cybersecurity is the practice of protecting information resources (computers, networks, and data) from unauthorized use. Security used to be as simple as locking the doors to your home and putting your money in the local bank. But today in the information age everything relies on computers and networks to perform the essential functions of almost every business and organization. From e-mail to online shopping, smartphones, social media, electronic banking, supply chain management, and critical infrastructure—you name it—everything depends on information resources that are vulnerable to attacks and therefore require protection. The goal of cybersecurity is to provide the right amount of protection to each asset based on the risks to the assets and the people who depend on them.

Cybersecurity is like a coin; it has two sides:

- On one side of the coin there are the *cyber criminals* who carry out offensive attacks against information systems and the organizations that own and operate them. Their goal is to steal assets (money or intellectual property) or disrupt the operation of information systems for personal, political, or financial gain.

- On the other side of the coin there are the *cybersecurity professionals* who carry out cyber defense. Their goal is to defend against cyberattacks, detect them when they occur, and respond to and recover from cyber incidents to minimize the impact on the organization they are protecting.

As *Certified in Cybersecurity* professionals you must have a good understanding of both offensive and defensive cybersecurity and of the techniques used by both cyber criminals and cyber defenders. At its core, information security is about protecting information *assets* from bad things. The information assets are usually data and the computing systems and networks that store, process, and transmit data. We use the term asset to refer to all three. Assets are the targets of cyberattacks or natural disasters that present risks. Assets are the things cyber professionals devote their time and resources to protecting against these risks.

Assets can be owned by anyone, but in this book, we refer to the asset owners as *organizations,* because more often than not, the targets of cybersecurity risks are businesses, governments, and private organizations. Of course, individuals are also the targets of cybersecurity threats, and many of the cybersecurity protections explained in this book apply to individuals as well. However, organizations, due to the value of the assets they are protecting and the risk that threats to those assets present to the business of the organization, require well-planned and well-executed information security programs. One of the primary purposes of the Certified in Cybersecurity certification is to describe how organizations go about creating and implementing cybersecurity programs. Therefore, the focus in this book is on securing and protecting organizations against cyber threats.

In this chapter we'll introduce the basic fundamental concepts of how cyber criminals and cyber defenders operate, and how organizations defend their information assets against threats. This chapter may introduce you to new terms and notions you may not have previously been exposed to. However, everything in this chapter will be expanded upon in the subsequent chapters in this book.

This chapter is organized in three sections as depicted in the Figure 1-1.

The first section, "Security Fundamentals," introduces topics basic to the field of cybersecurity and lays the foundation for the remaining chapters. The next section, "Elements of a Typical Cyberattack," describes what happens during most cyberattacks. Cyberattacks are what cybersecurity professionals spend most of their time defending against, preventing, and responding to. So, in this section we introduce you to what a cyber criminal typically does during a cyberattack so you can become familiar with what happens. The third section, "Elements of a Typical Security Program," describes the things most organizations do to implement cybersecurity: they perform *risk management* to understand and prioritize their risks, they use *governance and management* to lead and organize the cybersecurity operation, they implement *security controls* to meet their risk management goals, and they do all this following *professional ethics*. All of the information in Chapter 1 is foundational and is expanded upon in the subsequent chapters in this book.

Figure 1-1
Security
principles

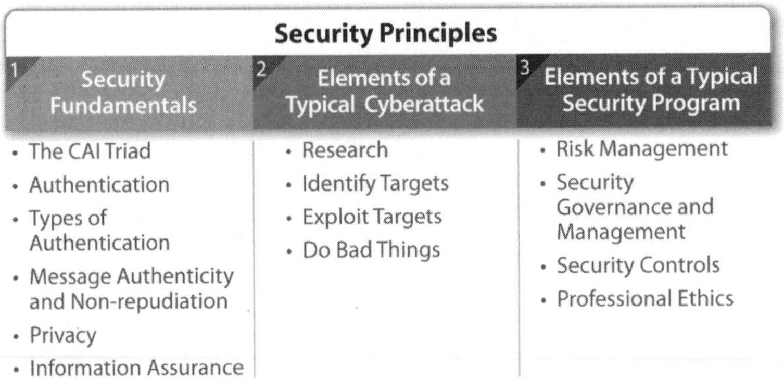

Security Principles		
1 Security Fundamentals	**2 Elements of a Typical Cyberattack**	**3 Elements of a Typical Security Program**
• The CAI Triad • Authentication • Types of Authentication • Message Authenticity and Non-repudiation • Privacy • Information Assurance	• Research • Identify Targets • Exploit Targets • Do Bad Things	• Risk Management • Security Governance and Management • Security Controls • Professional Ethics

Security Fundamentals

If you were learning to drive a car, you would probably start by first becoming familiar with the basic fundamentals of how your car operates, like using the gas and brake pedals, turn signals, and steering wheel and learning the general rules of the road. Then you would move on to more advanced concepts like actually driving the car, first in safe areas and then moving up to the highway. Cybersecurity can best be learned in a similar manner, by first learning the basic fundamentals and then graduating to more advanced concepts where those basic fundamentals are applied. This section introduces some of the fundamentals of cybersecurity.

The CAI Triad

One of the foundational concepts of cybersecurity is three core types of protection: Confidentiality, Availability, and Integrity. This is sometimes known as the *CAI triad* and is depicted in Figure 1-2.

NOTE The cybersecurity industry used to call the triad the "CIA" triad but due to confusion with the U.S. intelligence agency of the same name, the CIA moniker is no longer widely used. The name of the triad, and the order of each of the protection types, isn't important, but what is important, and what every cybersecurity professional should know, is the meaning of each leg of the triad (confidentiality, availability, and integrity), how they can be compromised, and how they are applied in cyber defense.

Confidentiality, availability, and integrity are the three tenets of security. Everything cyber attackers do are attempts to compromise one or more of these protections, and everything we do as cyber professionals is aimed at ensuring these protections are in place. Each is explained next.

Figure 1-2
The CAI triad

Confidentiality

Confidentiality is the secrecy of the information within the asset being protected. Confidentiality is the most common form of protection that cyber criminals seek to compromise. The goal of most cyberattacks is to steal data, which is a compromise of confidentiality. Cyber criminals compromise confidentiality by accessing data they are not authorized to access. Simply accessing data without proper authorization is a compromise of confidentiality.

Cybersecurity professionals can protect data against breaches of confidentiality in a number of ways. The use of *access controls* is one way to provide confidentiality. Access controls (described in more detail in Chapter 2) are processes, tools, or configuration settings that ensure that access to data is restricted to only those individuals who are authorized to access it. Another method of ensuring confidentiality is the use of *cryptography*. Cryptography (also explained in more detail later) makes data unreadable except to authorized persons and protects the confidentiality of data while the data is at rest (in storage) or while it is being transmitted.

> ### Real-World Example: Confidentiality Breach
> In 2014 a major supermarket chain was victimized by one of their own employees who leaked the personal information of nearly 100,000 employees to a file-sharing website. This deliberate breach of confidentiality by the employee was enabled by weak internal security controls on the part of the supermarket chain. The offending employee was caught and is now serving a prison sentence for his activity.

Integrity

While confidentiality is important because it ensures data is not accessed by those who are not authorized to access it, it is also important to make sure data is not being altered or corrupted in any way. Imagine if you electronically signed a contract to buy a house and when the contract is returned to you, you find the price has been increased by $100,000! Did somebody change the data? Ensuring data is not changed by unauthorized users refers to its *integrity*. Organizations and their users and customers must be assured that their data is accurate and cannot be changed. Therefore, the integrity of the data must be assured and is an important security protection.

For instance, the value of the stock of publicly traded companies depends on the accuracy of the financial information provided in their financial statements, as well as the data the financial information is based on. If a cyber criminal were able to alter any of that information, the financial statements would be unreliable, which could have serious consequences to the value of the stock and the risk of their investors. This is one reason why the U.S. Sarbanes-Oxley Act was passed. This law requires publicly traded corporations to ensure the integrity of their financial data and reporting. Cyber criminals' goals are not always stealing data—sometimes they attempt to alter data to achieve their goals to disrupt the operations of their target.

Cybersecurity professionals can use access controls to combat integrity attacks by ensuring only authorized persons can make changes to data. There are other security controls described later in this book that specifically address integrity protections. One of them is using hashes, which is a technique to detect if the contents of a data file or any data set have been altered from their original source.

Real-World Example: Integrity Breach

In 2008 media sources, including Wired News, widely reported that tree logging companies in Brazil had hired cyber criminals to compromise online systems operated by the Brazilian government. The result of these attacks was the cyber criminals altered the online records of the timber hauling quotas for these companies, allowing the companies to haul and sell more timber than they should have been allowed to. This breach of integrity resulted in an estimated 1.7 million cubic meters of timber being illegally harvested. Over 30 people were eventually caught and prosecuted for these crimes.

Availability

Data assets and information resources need to be there when they are needed. When a business publishes a website to sell their products online, the website needs to be *available* to their customers. Availability is as important as confidentiality and integrity because an organization's business depends on their systems and data being operational. Availability is a key element by which an organization's customers judge the organization's services, products, and quality.

Threats against availability are similar in nature to threats against confidentiality and integrity. Bad actors and natural disasters can threaten availability, as they can bring down systems and prevent the businesses that use them from performing essential business functions. Cyberattackers perform specific attacks to bring down websites of governments and businesses or disrupt operations of critical infrastructure entities such as electric power companies, oil and gas pipelines, financial institutions, and first responders. Availability attacks are commonly known as denial of service (DoS) attacks, which are described in greater detail in Chapter 3.

Real-World Example: Availability Breach

In 2015 the software code management site GitHub was hit by what at the time was the largest distributed denial of service (DDoS) attack ever (a DDoS attack involves multiple attacking devices working together—more about them in Chapter 3). The attack originated in China and was believed to target GitHub sites that were supporting projects that were circumventing China's government censorship efforts. The sites were unavailable for several days due to this attack until normal operations were restored.

Authentication

So far in this chapter we have learned that there are information assets and resources that are important to protect against threats. Threat actors are cyber criminals who seek to compromise the confidentiality, integrity, or availability of these information assets. And we have learned that there are security controls, or countermeasures that organizations put into place to protect the confidentiality, integrity, and availability of assets. One of the primary categories of security controls is *access controls*. Access controls are mechanisms to ensure that only those persons or resources who are specifically authorized to access an information resource are allowed to have such access. However, how can a computer system authorize a user unless it knows who the person is who is requesting access to a resource? The answer is by using *authentication*.

Authentication is the method by which systems verify that a user who is requesting access to a resource really is who they claim to be. In cybersecurity there is the concept of "need to know," which means only those persons with a legitimate need should be able to access a specific resource such as a system or data. You can't enforce need to know without authentication.

In practice, many methods are used to perform authentication. In web-based applications, programs, or systems that require a user login, authentication is a two-step process. The first step is *identification,* usually requiring the user to enter a username. The second step is *verification,* which usually requires the user to go through one or more verification factors. Verification frequently includes just one factor, such as requiring the user to enter a password. This is known as *single-factor authentication (SFA)*. However, additional security can be achieved by requiring more than one factor used in combination. The use of two authentication factors in combination is known as *dual-factor authentication* or *two-factor authentication,* and the use of two or more factors in combination is *multifactor authentication* (MFA). Verification factors are commonly categorized by type, as follows:

- Type 1, *something you know* (such as a password)
- Type 2, *something you have* (such as a smart card)
- Type 3, *something you are* (such as a biometric fingerprint)

Authentication, using any of these three types, requires that the user first go through a registration process in which they assert who they are and even agree to "terms of service" for how they agree to use (or not use) a resource they are granted access to. Some organizations require physical proof such as showing an identification card and/or signing paperwork. Once registered in the organization's systems, the organization can use any of the types of verification factors to check who the person is whenever they log in and request access to a computing resource. In Chapter 2 we explore authentication in greater detail, explaining the different types of authentication factors, their features, and how they are implemented, as well as how authentication fits within the overall access control process.

Message Authenticity and Nonrepudiation

Authenticity and *nonrepudiation* are two important concepts in information security regarding the legitimacy of data transmission. If you receive a document via e-mail, how do you really know that the document came from the person you think it came from? Can you be assured of the document's authenticity? Similarly, what if the sender denies the file you received came from them? Can they repudiate they are the one who sent it to you? For data transmission to be trustworthy, users must be able to trust and verify the authenticity and nonrepudiation of the data and transmission process. Both authenticity and nonrepudiation are accomplished through processes and technologies that prove the identity of the sender of a transmission and the integrity of the message.

Authenticity

For a message to be authentic, it must have two characteristics. The recipient must be able to trust that the message came from the source it is believed to have come from, and the recipient must know that the message has not been altered or corrupted. Technologies that implement authenticity embed additional data into the transmitted message that carries information used to prove the identity of the source and the integrity of the data. *Digital signatures,* explained later in this book, are one popular method of accomplishing authenticity.

Nonrepudiation

Technologies like digital signatures are used to guarantee that a sender of a message *cannot later deny* that they sent the message. This is called nonrepudiation. Digital signatures achieve nonrepudiation because they use a specialized authentication process which ensures that the message could only have been created by the sender and could not have been created by anyone else.

> **NOTE** *Digital signatures* are further explained in Chapter 4.

Privacy

Data privacy is a concept closely related to cybersecurity, as both deal with the handling of sensitive data. However, privacy refers to the handling of someone else's personal data and often with the level of control and consent the individual should expect to have over their own personal data. Cybersecurity is more focused on protecting data from unauthorized access. Privacy expands beyond cybersecurity to ensure the organization is authorized to collect, use, process, and share the data. In most cases the data belongs to customers, but the data could belong to any party including employees or the organization. In some cases there are laws in place that require the organization to protect the privacy of data. For instance, in the United States, personal healthcare information (PHI) is protected by the Health Insurance Portability and Accountability Act of 1996 (HIPAA). HIPAA requires organizations that obtain a patient's PHI to protect that information from being disclosed without the patient's consent. Privacy is closely associated with security because the same security controls that ensure the protection of data also contribute to ensuring the privacy of the data. Confidentiality, integrity, and availability all apply to privacy.

Information Assurance

As a cyber professional you will commonly hear the terms information security, cybersecurity, and information assurance. These terms are often used interchangeably, but they have different meanings. Information security and cybersecurity are very similar—they both deal with securing information; however, cybersecurity usually is limited to the security of information within the cyber world—(computers and networks)—whereas information security can also include information that resides in noncyber media such as print, works of art, or physical media.

Information assurance refers to the *measure* of information security. The goal of information assurance is to verify and ensure the confidentiality, integrity, and availability of data and assets, and this can only be done by measuring the effectiveness of security controls. Usually, organizations follow frameworks for information assurance. These frameworks include standards and processes for implementing and measuring an organization's risk management programs. Common information assurance frameworks include

- NIST Risk Management Framework
- International Standards Organization (ISO/IEC) 27002
- ISACA Risk IT
- Payment Card Industry Data Security Standard (PCI DSS)

The information assurance frameworks listed here are just a few, but there are many others. Later in this book we describe information assurance programs that most organizations follow and the core elements they contain.

Security Fundamentals Summary

Here are some of the important topics to remember and study about security fundamentals:

- **CAI Triad** Proper security ensures only those who are authorized can impact the confidentiality, integrity, or availability of protected information.
- **Confidentiality** The secrecy of information.
- **Integrity** The accuracy, completeness, and validity of the information.
- **Availability** The property that the information can be accessed when it is needed.
- **Authentication** Verifying who someone is.

- **Types of authentication factors:**
  - Type 1, something you know
  - Type 2, something you have
  - Type 3, something you are
- **Authenticity**   Ensures a message came from the source it is believed to have come from and the message has not been altered.
- **Nonrepudiation**   This applies to technologies like digital signatures, which ensure the message could only have been created by the sender and could not have been created by anyone else.
- **Privacy**   Refers to the handling of personal data with the level of control and consent the individual should expect to have over their own personal data.
- **Information assurance**   The measure of information security and the effectiveness of security controls.

 EXAM TIP   CC candidates should be familiar with the fundamentals of information assets, the CAI triad, authentication, nonrepudiation, privacy, and information assurance.

Elements of a Typical Cyberattack

Cybersecurity professionals devote most of their attention to preventing, defending against, and responding to *cyberattacks*. In this section we examine what a typical cyber-attack looks like. Cyberattacks are actions by cyber criminals to gain access to or disrupt information systems with the intent of causing damage or harm. Cyberattacks can take many forms but they generally involve the following steps:

1. Conduct research
2. Identify targets
3. Exploit targets
4. Do bad things

1. Conduct Research

The first step the cyber criminal performs in an attack is to gather as much information as possible about the target to be able to carry out the attack. To do this, the attacker performs a variety of research activities including performing web searches; examining social media accounts of the organization and its employees; reading blogs and media articles; attending conferences, symposia, or trade shows; or even physically observing the organization's employees or facilities. During this research, the attacker attempts to learn information about the victim such as

- Domain names
- Corporate and financial information
- Names of employees and key managers
- E-mail addresses and phone numbers
- Social media activity and friends
- Facility locations and layouts
- Ingress/egress details

Once this information is gathered, it forms the basis of the other steps in the attack.

2. Identify Targets

During this phase the attacker tries to identify the organization's information assets as well as their corresponding *vulnerabilities* that can be *exploited* (more on vulnerabilities and exploits later in this chapter). Based on data gathered from the research activities, the attacker attempts to identify specific targets such as people, organizations, departments, facilities, capabilities, data, vendor names, and information systems. To accomplish this, the attacker may use automated tools to probe the target network to produce lists of target computer systems and then probe further to discover vulnerabilities that could possibly be exploited.

3. Exploit Targets

Once the targets are identified, the attacker can design and execute the attack. This involves probing and taking advantage of specific vulnerabilities with the goal of gaining unauthorized access to the enterprise. Many times, this involves designing and creating tools to aid in the attack. Here are some common examples of methods used by attackers—all of these are explained further later in this book:

- **Phishing**   Obtaining sensitive information by disguising oneself as a trusted entity, usually via e-mail
- **Fake websites**   Used for harvesting sensitive information (credentials)
- **Malware**   Software that intentionally is harmful or malicious
- **Virus**   A type of malware that is usually hidden inside another application
- **Trojan**   A virus disguised as something useful
- **Worm**   A virus that propagates itself to other systems
- **Rootkit**   A virus that hides itself by modifying the operating system
- **Social engineering**   Tricking someone into doing something that is not in their best interest

- **Scripting** Manipulating data entered into fields to produce unintended results
- **Vulnerability-specific attacks** Exploiting software defects

The ultimate goal of this phase is to gain unauthorized access to systems and data.

4. Do Bad Things

Once the attacker gains access, they can do a variety of things to achieve their objective. Usually, the attacker attempts to expand access laterally throughout the network to explore and discover more systems and data to gain deeper access and perform more attacks. The attacker may have a specific goal in mind such as stealing personal information or credit card data, or they may just be hunting within the network for things that attract their interest. Any attack will include one or more of the following:

- Stealing data (a compromise of *confidentiality*)
- Modifying data (a compromise of *integrity*)
- Destroying data or disrupting the environment (compromises of *availability*)

Frequently, the attacker attempts to cover their tracks to avoid detection. They may use common applications and protocols, so their activity looks normal to the victim organization's intrusion detection systems (more on intrusion detection systems in Chapter 3). Or they may erase error messages or log entries that their activities may have generated. And they may be careful to remove any files and not leave behind any data that may show their identity or what they have done.

Cyberattack Models

In this book we present a picture of what happens during a typical cyberattack using a four-step model. However, there are numerous models used by cybersecurity professionals to learn about and study cyberattacks. They are simply different ways of viewing and breaking down the same problem. Some popular models used for understanding cyberattacks are the Cyber Kill Chain framework developed by Lockheed Martin and the ATT&CK knowledge base developed by MITRE.

Elements of a Cyberattack: A Summary

A cyber criminal typically performs the following actions during a cyberattack:

1. **Conduct research** Gather as much information as possible about the target organization.
2. **Identify targets** Identify target assets such as people, systems, servers, websites, databases, etc., and their vulnerabilities that could be exploited.

(continued)

3. Exploit targets   Use tools such as malware to exploit vulnerabilities to gain unauthorized access to systems and data.

4. Do bad things:

- Steal data (a compromise of confidentiality)
- Modify data (a compromise of integrity)
- Destroy data or disrupt the environment (compromises of availability)

EXAM TIP   CC candidates should know what generally happens during a cyberattack, but it is not important to memorize the specific steps used in any specific attack model.

Elements of a Typical Security Program

In the previous sections of this chapter, we introduced security fundamentals such as the CAI triad, authentication and authorization, and information assurance, and explained the basic steps a cyber criminal takes to conduct a cyberattack. All of the various security activities that an organization undertakes to protect and defend the organization against cyberattacks are often referred to as components or elements of its security program. Most organizations implement an organization-wide security program consisting of core security activities. Security programs generally include the following core elements:

- **Risk management**   The first thing an organization must do to implement cybersecurity is to understand the threats it faces and set its own priorities based on those threats and their own unique situation. Organizations follow a risk management process to identify and prioritize risks so they can make security decisions appropriate to their business environment.

- **Security governance and management**   Organizations set up their own security program, governed by external drivers such as laws and regulations and internal drivers such as business goals and operations. The security program is staffed, managed, and organized using subprograms or functions to address each area of cybersecurity based on the organization's needs. These activities are documented and managed through policies, procedures, and internal standards.

- **Security controls**   Based on the results of security governance and *risk management* activities, the organization selects and implements appropriate security controls used to protect their information assets.

- **Professional ethics**   All activities carried out by the organization follow standards of professional ethics, ensuring that each individual does what is best morally following ethical guidelines.

Each of these elements is explained herein, in its own subsection.

Risk Management

Imagine you are shopping for a new lock to install on the front door of your home. You consider whether to install a deadbolt, a chain lock, or one of those fancy digital locks with a built-in camera. You decide that based on your situation and your home, a simple doorknob lock is best for you. You may not realize it, but you just practiced *risk management*. In the fields of security and cybersecurity, *risk management* is the term used to describe the discipline of how an organization chooses and implements the right level of security that is appropriate for them and their situation or business.

One might observe that a local bank branch is not constructed in the same manner that the U.S. Bullion Depository at Fort Knox is constructed—and rightly so! This is because the local bank and Fort Knox are protecting very different assets against very different threats. The local bank may be built with a steel safe inside a building protected by a security alarm system, whereas Fort Knox is a fortified vault constructed with virtually impenetrable walls hidden deep inside tons of granite and steel protected by fences, defensive structures, and advanced technology monitoring systems and staffed by an army of armed guards. The local bank is designed appropriately to protect the value of the assets within it (millions of dollars) against the most likely threats the bank may face. In contrast Fort Knox must protect billions of dollars' worth of gold bullion against its likely threats; therefore it is designed to withstand much greater threats.

The bank/Fort Knox illustration applies to cybersecurity as well. Whereas security is always implemented using basic security fundamentals, the *amount* of security or the *extent and nature* of the security vary based on the situation. The practice of studying the potential threats facing a given organization and choosing the right kind of security to protect that organization against those threats is called *risk management*. In this section we explore how risk management is practiced by organizations as part of their information security programs. All cybersecurity professionals must learn to practice good risk management.

To illustrate risk management further, consider Figure 1-3, which shows threats and vulnerabilities most people are familiar with.

In the picture, the house is the environment that we are trying to protect. It contains assets that could be stolen or damaged if not protected against threats. In this example, the threats are burglars, car thieves, vandals, and natural disasters. Vulnerabilities are aspects of the house that could allow the threats to cause harm and expose the homeowner to risk, such as an open window and mailbox and the front door left wide open.

In the business world organizations plan for the types of risks they are most likely to face. They do this by first trying to predict what those risks might be. They also consider what the assets are they are trying to protect. Their assets and the threats to them are their *business environment*. Based on the business environment, the organization can decide what their tolerance is for risk and what they want to do about the different types of risk they face. In other words, the organization will use a *risk management process* to decide how much to spend on security and what kind of security controls are appropriate based on their tolerance for risk.

Figure 1-3   Threats and vulnerabilities

Risk Management Terminology

An important concept in understanding risk management is the relationship between vulnerabilities, threats, risks, exposures, and countermeasures. Consider these and other risk management terms:

- **Compromise**   A security incident that results in the unauthorized access of an information resource.

- **Vulnerability**   A vulnerability is any weakness that could potentially be exploited. In an information system, vulnerabilities can be in software, hardware, or even in the way humans use and interact with the information system. Here are a few examples of cybersecurity vulnerabilities that can be exploited by a cyber criminal resulting in security breaches:

  - **Application vulnerabilities**   Incorrectly designed or coded software (bugs) that result in security flaws.

  - **Unpatched systems**   Operating systems and other vendor-provided software that have known security flaws for which the manufacturer has published a patch but the patch has not yet been installed by the organization. Until the patch is installed and the bug is fixed, the software—and the organization— is vulnerable.

- **Misconfigured devices**   Misconfiguring a system, such as setting up improper file permissions or configuring administrative accounts with default passwords, leaves the system vulnerable to an attack.

- **Improperly trained users**   Human vulnerabilities are one of the weakest links in cybersecurity. Employees who do not follow security policies, break rules, or commit errors are juicy targets for cyberattackers to exploit using *social engineering* techniques.

- **Vulnerability assessment**   A planned test and review of an organization's information system or systems to uncover security vulnerabilities or weaknesses.

- **Threat**   A threat is a potentially damaging event associated with the exploitation of a vulnerability. Actors that exploit vulnerabilities are called *threat agents*. Here are a few examples of threats:

  - **Cyberattacks**   Any kind of attempt by a cyber criminal to destroy or disrupt a computer system or network. These include malware attacks, ransomware attacks, and DoS attacks.

  - **Social engineering**   Any act that attempts to influence a person to do something that may not be in their best interest. Social engineering attacks are often used as the first step in a cyberattack, often to gain a user's login credentials or other information that may help an attacker gain access to a system or network.

  - **Natural disasters**   Earthquakes, floods, fires, and inclement weather, including storms, hurricanes, tornadoes, etc., are threats that can disrupt the operations of any business and bring down computer systems and networks.

  - **Physical intrusions**   Burglars, vandals, and other bad actors threaten organizational operations by physically damaging or breaking into facilities where people are working, computers and systems are operating, or business operations are taking place.

- **Threat actors**   Actors that exploit vulnerabilities are called *threat actors* or *threat agents*. They include

  - **Cyber criminals (hackers)**   Criminals carry out exploits of security vulnerabilities to steal data or disrupt operations. These individuals do this for personal gain, to make money, for political activism, or for recognition or bragging rights within the hacker community. *Script kiddies* is another term for hackers that refers to immature and somewhat unskilled computer hackers who use programs developed by others but may not fully understand how the programs work or how dangerous they are.

  - **Criminal groups**   Groups of hackers band together to pool assets and more effectively carry out their attacks. These attacks can be well-coordinated and can result in sophisticated operations netting large amounts of money, cyber currency, or other valuable assets. Criminal groups also carry out attacks in support of political causes, or "hacktivism."

- **Nation-states**   Governments sponsor or directly perform cyber criminal activities to achieve their goals, which may be political, military, financial, or cultural.

- **Terrorist groups**   Terrorists use cyberattacks to disrupt governments or private entities or steal valuable data or money.

- **Insiders**   One of the most common, and commonly overlooked, groups of threat actors are insiders of the target organization. Insiders may be employees, contractors, visitors, or anyone who is granted access, who can then use that access to exploit a vulnerability and cause a security breach.

Insider Threats

When we perform security vulnerability assessments for private companies, one of the most common questions clients ask us is: "If you were a cyber criminal what is the first thing you would do to break into our systems and steal our data?" Our answer is: "I'd get a job here." Clients are frequently shocked to hear that one of their biggest risks is from their own employees. But employees usually have some kind of internal access, they can move around the facility or the IT systems undetected or unquestioned, and they know about internal operations. All of these things can be exploited to increase access and breach security controls. That is why employee background checks, employee security awareness training and policies, and user monitoring are important tools for cyber defenders to use to prevent security breaches.

- **Risk**   Risk is commonly defined as "the likelihood that a vulnerability could be exploited and the corresponding impact of such an event." Risk ties the vulnerability, threat, and likelihood of exploitation to the resulting business impact. Often, risk is measured, or rated. For instance, if you go on vacation, there is a risk that you could be robbed. If you leave your front door unlocked, you have a vulnerability, and your risk of a loss from being robbed is greater. However, if you lock your doors and turn on an alarm system (i.e., adding *security controls,* which we will discuss later), your risk is less. Understanding risk in a given situation and adjusting one's exposure to threats to an appropriate level is called *risk management.*

- **Exposure**   Exposure is the potential that a security breach could occur. A vulnerability can leave an organization exposed to a loss. For instance, leaving a window open in a house is certainly a vulnerability, but it is also an *exposure* to a potential loss. In an IT example, an unpatched system *exposes* the organization to a potential loss.

- **Countermeasure (or security control)**   A security control or countermeasure is anything that is put in place to mitigate a risk. In the house example, security controls include doors and locks, fences, cameras, alarm systems, etc. In information systems, security controls include the use of access controls, deployment of firewalls, enforcement of strong passwords, and the use of encryption. Security controls are discussed in much greater depth later in this book.

EXAM TIP CC candidates should have a practical understanding of foundational information security terminology such as vulnerability, threat, risk, exposure, countermeasure, and security control.

Risk Management Process

The purpose of risk management is to employ a process whereby an organization makes decisions about how much and what kind of security it needs based on the threats and risks it is most likely to face. The risk management process includes identifying and assessing risk, reducing it to an acceptable level, and implementing the right controls or countermeasures to maintain that level. Some organizations try to use risk management to strike a balance between the value of an asset and the cost of the controls to protect the asset, as shown in Figure 1-4. For instance, most organizations may find it unwise to spend $1 million to protect a $100,000 asset. A well-executed risk management process ensures the *right controls* are chosen that are appropriate to the assets and the business of the organization.

Most organizations practice some form of risk management; some use a very informal process, while others use highly structured and formal processes. In a typical organization, risk management is directed from the highest levels of the organization. Some organizations have a risk oversight board, while others may have a chief risk officer (CRO). In some organizations risk comes under the purview of the chief financial officer (CFO); in others it is the responsibility of the chief of security or the chief information security officer (CISO). Regardless of how risk management is governed and directed, the goal is to understand the risks to the business so the organization can decide how the risks should be treated, including what security controls to put in place, to defend the organization's assets against the risks.

Figure 1-4
Risk management includes choosing the appropriate controls and achieving the right balance of security versus cost.

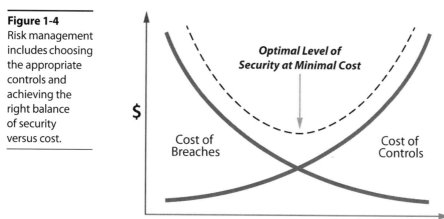

Any process that helps an organization understand its risks and decide on appropriate treatment is valuable. (ISC)² advocates a three-step risk management process as follows:

- Risk identification (framing the risks)
- Risk assessment (understanding the risks)
- Risk treatment (taking action on what to do about the risks)

These general steps are widely used in the security industry, and we examine each in this section.

Risk Identification   The first step in risk management is to identify the potential threats the organization may face. The threats are to the assets of the organization, so the threat identification begins with a thorough inventory of the assets of the organization. Each asset is identified, catalogued, and described, sometimes in a database. Then, *threat modeling* is performed. Threat modeling is the process of examining each asset, the potential threats faced by each asset, and the adverse effects caused by the threat against the asset. By modeling assets in the enterprise against all potential threats, the organization will have a good picture of what they have, the potential bad things that could occur, and the resultant impact on the business.

Risk Management Tiers

Risk management can take place at any level within an organization depending on the assets being considered. It can apply to the entire organization or to specific groups of assets. Many organizations approach risk management holistically in tiers:

- **Organizational tier**   Addresses risk by defining and implementing a holistic risk management program that applies to the entire organization
- **Mission/business process**   Addresses the risks of major functions of the business
- **Information system**   Addresses the risks of specific information systems

---

If your organization is a utility company with a datacenter located in a major metropolitan area, what kind of threats are you likely to face? Is it possible your organization may be attacked by wolves? It's possible but not very likely. For each threat, characteristics are identified, such as *likelihood of occurrence* and *potential impact to the organization*. A wolf attack may be unlikely but its impact could be severe, whereas a cyberattack that defaces the organization's charitable fundraising website may be more likely but its impact on the business may not be considered severe by the organization's leadership. Organizations may also consider the value of the asset being protected. The asset's value may be considered in either purely financial terms, such as the original or replacement cost of the asset, or the value of the asset to the business, which may be intangible.

Organizations performing risk management identify each potential threat against each asset and record factors such as severity, probability, likelihood, impact, and the value and importance of the asset to the organization's business. All of this information feeds into the next step in the process, which is *risk analysis* or *assessment*.

Risk Assessment   The exact information to be gathered during the risk management process varies based on the *risk assessment method* used. Organizations generally use either quantitative or qualitative risk assessment methods.

- **Quantitative risk assessment**   Seeks to understand risk by assigning numerical or financial values to assets along with factors with numerical weights such as threat probability, impact of loss, etc. A quantitative method may require collecting detailed financial information, including labor and materials costs or estimates from outside vendors in order to determine asset value.

- **Qualitative risk assessment**   Seeks to understand risk in non-numerical terms using ratings and priorities. Qualitative models require information about assets, threats, vulnerabilities, and the probability of occurrence of different events. Once this information is collected, an analysis is performed to capture what the threat represents to the business.

Quantitative Methods   Quantitative methods are used to calculate the monetary loss associated with a given threat. This is accomplished by assigning numeric values to each factor in the analysis. Factors may include

- Asset value
- Threat probability
- Vulnerability
- Impact of loss
- Cost of countermeasures or controls

Two frequently used quantitative methods are *single loss expectancy* and *annualized loss expectancy*.

- *Single loss expectancy (SLE)* is the potential value of a loss for a *single threat event*, such as a single cyberattack or a single physical break-in at a warehouse. Note that the event can apply to a single asset or a group of assets. The formula is

$$AV \times EF = SLE$$

  - *Asset value (AV)* is the cost of the asset or assets that are subject to the event. The AV can be simply the replacement cost of the asset, or it can include other costs that may be incurred if the asset were lost, such as labor and installation costs, costs to the business due to downtime, or even costs due to loss of business.

- *Exposure factor (EF)* is the percentage of loss that would likely occur for the subject event. For instance, if the threat being modeled is a theft and the asset is a laptop, the EF might be 100 percent (since nobody steals part of a laptop). Alternatively, if the threat is a fire and the asset is an entire datacenter, the EF may be 40 percent as an estimate for the potential loss if it's predicted that a fire in the datacenter will result in a significant loss but not a total loss. The EF is a prediction that should be backed up by data, research, or some documented reason.

- *Annualized loss expectancy (ALE)* brings in the element of time. ALE is used to predict the potential value of a loss on an annual basis. The formula is

$$SLE \times ARO = ALE$$

Annualized rate of occurrence (ARO) is an estimate of how many times the event is estimated to occur in a given year. The ALE quantitative analysis allows an organization to predict loss in terms of dollar amounts for particular events on an annual basis. Sometimes, an organization may use an ALE to establish tolerance levels; for instance, the organization may find, after analysis, that any asset that has an ALE greater than a certain threshold has the highest risk priority and should have the highest level of mitigating controls. An organization may also use the ALE to determine spending, as it may not make sense to spend $100,000 annually to protect against an asset and threat combination with an ALE of only $10,000.

Qualitative Methods   Qualitative methods do not use dollar amounts (although they may still involve performing calculations). Qualitative analysis may be as simple as an executive saying "System X is really important to us, so I designate it as high risk," or it may be a highly complex analysis with many variables. Qualitative analysis may take into account a variety of factors including

- Severity of the threat
- Likelihood of threat occurrence
- Severity of impact to the business (also known as the *consequence*)
- Effectiveness of controls

A qualitative analysis considers different threat scenarios and ranks the seriousness of each. In addition, most qualitative analysis considers the effectiveness of various controls or countermeasures.

 EXAM TIP   CC candidates are expected to understand quantitative and qualitative risk analysis and the formulas for SLE and ALE. Quantitative is all about money (which threat costs more?), whereas qualitative is about relative risk (which threat is riskier than the other?).

Quantitative vs. Qualitative Risk Analysis

Each method has its advantages and disadvantages. Quantitative analysis can be very complex and requires a great deal of data and good tools to perform it properly. However, because it is based on numbers, the results can be more objective and easier to defend. In contrast, qualitative analysis tends to be less complex and easier to implement. However, the results are subjective and are open to debate and interpretation. Some organizations rely on a hybrid approach that uses a combination of financial values and priority values to support decisions about security controls and spending.

Risk Treatment   As part of the risk management process, the possible approaches for handling specific risks are considered and recommendations are made to the decision-making authority, which we refer to as "management." The definition of who "management" is in this instance varies depending on the organization or the situation. In some organizations it is the CEO, but in others it may be the CISO, the board of directors, or a risk committee. Also, if the asset being considered is a system rather than a higher organizational tier, the risk-handling recommendation may be made to the system owner or owning organization rather than the organization's CEO or board. The key is that someone in every organization must make the decision regarding how to best handle risk for a given asset or the organization as a whole. Generally, there are four choices for how risk recommendations are made and how they are implemented:

- **Transfer** risk and make it somebody else's problem (*risk transference*). The most common form of risk transference is to buy insurance. Most people are aware of buying insurance against threats such as fire and theft, but organizations can also buy insurance against cyberattacks and even ransomware attacks.

- **Accept** the risk, which means that as long as the risk is within acceptable levels, the organization can "live with" the risk and take their chances (*risk acceptance*). For most organizations there is usually some amount of risk the organization is simply willing to accept due to its unlikeliness or the high cost of mitigation. For instance, an organization with a datacenter located on a high plateau with no history of flooding may choose to accept the relatively low risk of a flood.

- **Avoid** the risk entirely by stopping the related activity or shutting down a system entirely (*risk avoidance*). Sometimes it may be best to simply stop an activity that is too risky. The most common example of this is shutting down services or software applications that have known flaws or vulnerabilities. For instance, some organizations do not allow wireless access points on their network or do not use certain brands of products simply to avoid their potential risks.

- **Mitigate** or reduce the risk by putting in some kind of control or countermeasure (*risk mitigation*).

Security Governance and Management

Governance is the process of defining strategies to oversee the entire organization or a specific subset (such as IT governance, security governance, or financial governance) to meet organizational goals and objectives. These might include increasing profit, accountability, transparency, oversight, or value to customers or enhancing internal controls. *Security governance* is a subset of organizational governance focused on developing strategies to oversee the security program to facilitate alignment with the goals and objectives of the organization. Every organization has some type of governance in place, although some utilize more formalized processes than others. Having proper governance in place allows leadership to develop strategies that align with both the external requirements (laws and regulations, external standards, etc.) and internal requirements (organizational ethics, goals, and objectives) of the organization, as illustrated in Figure 1-5.

Where governance is all about the development of strategies that align with organizational requirements, *management* consists of the processes to execute, operate, and monitor the activities that implement the governance strategies. Governance and management are often discussed together; however, many organizations separate these functions to allow for greater accountability. Some examples of this include having a board of directors for organizational governance or having a security steering committee to govern the security program. Like anything else, a security program must be governed and managed. This section reviews the key elements of security governance, common security roles and responsibilities in an organization, as well as typical programmatic areas that make up a security program.

Security Governance Elements

Security governance is all about setting the strategy for overseeing the security program to ensure it is meeting the needs of the organization. This is shaped by a variety of factors including

- Laws and regulations
- External standards (NIST, ISO, etc.)

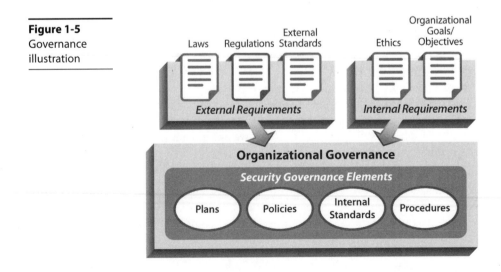

Figure 1-5 Governance illustration

- Organizational ethics, goals, and objectives

- Organizational plans, policies, procedures, and internal standards

- Risk management practices (discussed earlier in this chapter)

An organization's security program is made up of a collection of governance elements used to facilitate alignment with the requirements of the organization. These governance elements include plans, policies, internal standards, and procedures. These documents form a library of rules and practices that the organization must follow. The top-level program documents are the security policies, which define requirements that govern what will be done (but typically not how to do it). Policies are driven by requirements from laws and regulations, external standards, and other organizational requirements and are operationalized through procedures and internal standards. These elements are discussed in the following sections.

Regulations and Laws   Many organizations are subject to laws and regulations that impact the security program. *Laws and regulations* are rules typically established by a governmental body or similar agency that specify requirements that are legally enforceable. These shape an organization's behavior and often have direct implications on the security practices of the organization. Laws and regulations are often specific to a certain region, locale, industry, or data type. This is why it is important to have mechanisms in place to ensure alignment with laws and regulations relevant to the organization. Following are some examples of commonly encountered cybersecurity-related laws and regulations and the scope of the requirements:

- **Sarbanes-Oxley Act of 2002 (SOX)**   SOX is a U.S. federal law enacted to hold executives and board members accountable for the accuracy of their organization's financial statements. The law applies to all companies publicly traded on U.S. markets. The law contains requirements around internal control assessment activities that have security implications for security control review and monitoring. Executives can face prison sentences if it is discovered that their company submitted fraudulent financial reports to the Securities and Exchange Commission (SEC).

- **Health Insurance Portability and Accountability Act of 1996 (HIPAA)**   HIPAA is a U.S. federal law with requirements around protecting the security and privacy of PHI. The rules apply to healthcare providers, health plans, healthcare clearinghouses, and business associates that provide services to one of these entities that involves the use or disclosure of PHI. Noncompliance can result in civil and criminal penalties including potential fines and imprisonment.

- **Federal Information Security Management Act of 2002 (FISMA) and Federal Information Security Modernization Act if 2014 (FISMA 2014)**   FISMA is a U.S. law enacted to govern federal cybersecurity programs. The law requires U.S. federal agencies and contractors who handle federal data to implement minimum information security requirements. The standards for compliance are developed and managed by the National Institute of Standards and Technology (NIST). Failure to comply can result in loss of federal funding or contract award.

- **General Data Protection Regulation (GDPR)** GDPR is a European Union (EU) privacy law that regulates the processing of the personal data of EU citizens. GDPR applies to any organization that processes EU citizen personal data while providing services, even if the organization is located outside the EU. GDPR imposes substantial fines for noncompliance based on the nature of the infringement.

Compliance

Compliance is the process of ensuring alignment with applicable laws, regulations, external standards, ethical conduct, and other organizational goals and objectives. Compliance is often focused on legal and regulatory compliance due to the consequences of noncompliance (fines, reputational damage, and so on). However, compliance with external laws and regulations is not the only form of compliance. There are both internal and external requirements, as outlined in Figure 1-5, that drive the organization to implement plans, policies, internal standards, and procedures to facilitate compliance and support healthy governance.

Standards *External standards* are documents developed and published by external standards organizations containing best practices that may be used for the development of security program elements. Many organizations leverage external standards to help shape their security program to comply with a specific law or regulation or simply to serve as a best practice reference. Examples of standards organizations are included next:

- **International Organization for Standardization (ISO)** ISO is an independent international standard development organization that develops and publishes best practice standards on a variety of topics including information technology, information security, and other technical topics. More information is available at https://www.iso.org/.

- **National Institute of Standards and Technology (NIST)** NIST is a nonregulatory U.S. agency that publishes free standards and best practice frameworks on a range of topics including information technology and cybersecurity. Many U.S. government agencies are required to implement NIST standards to comply with federal or state laws and regulations. Other organizations voluntarily implement NIST standards as a general best practice. More information on NIST can be found at https://www.nist.gov/.

- **Payment Card Industry Security Standards Council (PCI SSC)** PCI SSC is a global organization that develops and manages standards for payment security, such as the Payment Card Industry Data Security Standard (PCI DSS), which defines security requirements for companies that handle or process credit card data or transactions. More information can be found at https://www.pcisecuritystandards.org/.

- **Institute of Electrical and Electronics Engineers (IEEE)**   IEEE is a professional organization that develops and maintains a large portfolio of standards for information technology, telecommunications, and computer networking. Information on IEEE may be found at https://www.ieee.org/.

- **Internet Engineering Task Force (IETF)**   IETF is an organization that develops technical standards around Internet protocols, network management, and other technical specifications. More information on IETF may be found at https://www.ietf.org/.

- **Cloud Security Alliance (CSA)**   CSA creates standards and best practices for cloud security for service providers as well as customers. Information regarding CSA is available at https://cloudsecurityalliance.org/.

- **Open Web Application Security Project (OWASP)**   OWASP is an international organization that develops tools, standards, and best practice documents focused on application security. Additional information on OWASP may be found at https://owasp.org/.

In some cases, an organization may be required to implement a standard to comply with a specific law, regulation, or another industry requirement. For example, compliance with PCI DSS is not required by a law or regulation. It is an example of a self-regulation standard where compliance is required and enforced by credit card companies. In other cases, the use of the standard may be optional, and an organization may voluntarily elect to use the standard as a guideline, reference, or best practice recommendation to improve security by leveraging standard practices and methodologies without "reinventing the wheel."

NOTE   In practice, the term "standard" can have different meanings within the industry. For the Certified in Cybersecurity certification, the term standard primarily refers to *external standards* developed by standards organizations such as NIST or ISO, which may be used as input in the development of organizational policies, procedures, and practices. However, the term "standard" can also refer to *internal standard* documents used to establish methods for complying with internal policies by driving a consistent approach to meeting organizational requirements by defining specific technologies, protocols, methods, or controls to be used. For example, configuration standards are used to establish specific configuration settings for hardware or software used within an organization to ensure a consistent protection level. These are often referred to as *hardening standards* or *baselines,* which are discussed in greater detail in Chapter 4.

EXAM TIP   While cybersecurity professionals should be familiar with the most common cybersecurity-related laws (e.g., HIPAA, SOX, FISMA, GDPR) and standards (e.g., NIST, ISO, PCI), specific questions about these laws and standards aren't likely to be encountered on the CC exam.

Plans   Plans are another kind of administrative governance element used by many organizations. A plan can be written for all kinds of things such as a vulnerability management plan, business continuity plan, or incident response plan. In fact, some security leaders define the organization's security governance approach in a document that is sometimes referred to as a *security program plan* or *security charter*. A security plan might be used to show how the security program aligns with the goals and objectives of the organization. As is the case with any documentation or governance element, these plans should be *living documents,* meaning they are regularly reviewed and updated to evolve over time and reflect the current approach. Plans are a good idea to write and maintain, and they may reference relevant policies, procedures, or internal standards.

Policies   *Policies* are high-level management statements providing prescriptive directives to the organization. Policies are developed based on a variety of drivers, including laws, regulations, and external standards, and other organizational requirements such as ethics, goals, and objectives. Common examples of policies include human resources (HR) policies, security policies, and so on. Policies typically avoid describing exactly how certain activities are performed (this is the function of procedures or internal standards). Instead, policies provide the framework for the development of procedures, internal standards, and controls. For example, many organizations have a data handling policy (outlining high-level data handling requirements) supported by data handling procedures (documenting specific steps and actions such as procedures for data classification, data handling, data sharing, and data destruction).

NOTE   Specific best practice security policies found in most organizations are discussed in detail in Chapter 4.

Procedures   *Procedures* are step-by-step workflows or instructions that define how a task should be accomplished. In our daily lives, we regularly interact with procedures whether we are following instructions for a Martha Stewart baking recipe, assembly instructions for IKEA furniture, or instructions for setting up a home security camera. In a typical organization, procedures are used to operationalize the vision and directives set forth in organizational policies by defining how a function is performed. Examples may include onboarding and offboarding procedures, steps for configuring or utilizing some tool or technology, and procedures that may be integrated into other plans such as a disaster recovery plan or incident response plan.

Security Roles and Responsibilities

A security program team is made up of a hierarchy of roles with various levels of responsibility. The nature and complexity of the hierarchy are typically based on the size and structure of the organization. In some organizations with smaller security teams, a cybersecurity professional may have the opportunity to touch many different areas of security. In larger organizations, the security team is typically broken down into specializations dedicated to a specific security programmatic area (compliance, vulnerability management, security engineering, etc.). Following is an overview of some of the key roles and functions seen within a typical security organization:

- **Security leadership**   Typically an organization will have a leader responsible for oversight of the information security program. The title of this role can vary based on the size and structure of the organization, but common titles include chief information security officer (CISO), chief security officer (CSO), chief risk officer (CRO), information security officer (ISO), or a vice president (VP), director, or head of information security.

- **Security management**   There may be multiple levels of security management that report up the ladder to the leader of the security program depending on the size and structure of the organization. For example, there may be a team lead, manager, senior manager, director, or VP of each security program function (security architecture, security engineering, etc.).

- **Security individual contributors**   The security professionals who serve as the "boots on the ground" performing the hands-on security work are known as individual contributors. These professionals report to security management or security leadership and can have titles ranging from security engineer, security analyst, security architect, cybersecurity specialist, and so on. Their area of focus will vary based on the size and structure of the organization but may range from compliance, security monitoring, security engineering, incident handling, or another security area.

Cybersecurity Workforce Resources

NIST, in partnership with other organizations, has developed the National Initiative for Cybersecurity Education (NICE). NICE is focused on providing cybersecurity training and workforce development resources to support organizations and individual learners in increasing the number of skilled cybersecurity professionals. As part of this initiative, the NICE Workforce Framework for Cybersecurity (NICE Framework) was developed to provide a framework to help organizations and individuals understand the various knowledge, skills, and abilities required for various roles in cybersecurity. NICE provides a plethora of resources for those interested in learning more about cybersecurity. More information can be found on the NIST NICE website (https://www.nist.gov/itl/applied-cybersecurity/nice). In addition, NICE developed the Cyberseek tool (https://www.cyberseek.org/), which provides information on the supply and demand of various cybersecurity job opportunities as well as a cybersecurity career pathway map. The career pathway map shows potential career progression and transition opportunities for various cybersecurity roles as well as details regarding salaries, skills, and credentials for each role.

EXAM TIP   Knowledge of NIST NICE or the NICE Framework is not required for the exam but is helpful for professionals entering the cybersecurity field who are interested in learning about various cybersecurity roles and training opportunities.

Typical Security Program Areas

An organization's security program is made up of numerous functions referred to as security program areas or subprograms. Organizations have their own way of naming and organizing these functions based on the nature and structure of the organization. Smaller organizations typically have smaller security teams that work in many different security areas, while larger organizations tend to have more specialized teams focused on very specific security functions. Some organizations even develop specific plans, policies, and procedures for each security program area. Following are some examples of security specializations that might be part of an organization's security program:

- **Security risk management and compliance**   This is the oversight function focused on ensuring the organization acts in accordance with its policies, procedures, and internal standards; complies with applicable external laws and regulations; and manages risk to an acceptable level as part of the risk management process.

- **Security engineering**   This is the building arm of the security program focused on the secure design and architecture of the organization's systems and technologies leveraging best security practices.

- **Security administration**   This is the operating arm of the security program focused on the administration, maintenance, and operation of various security tools and technologies. This can range from running security scans, to determining which systems have vulnerabilities or require security updates, to managing security devices and appliances on the organization's network.

- **Incident monitoring and response**   This is the investigation and response arm of the security program focused on identifying and responding to various threats and security incidents throughout the organization.

- **Security awareness**   This is the training arm of the security program focused on ensuring the people of the organization are adequately trained on the organization's security policies as well as general security best practices.

 EXAM TIP   CC candidates will likely not be tested on these exact examples of security program areas. This section serves to help the candidate understand the different functional areas of a security program and potential opportunities in the industry.

Security Controls

Everyone has assets they want to protect. This may include possessions in the home, a car, or private information stored on a personal laptop or smartphone. We want to ensure our home and car are safe from threats such as burglary, robbery, or vandalism and want to ensure private information (such as banking information) is protected from cyber threats. We protect our assets from threats by implementing security controls.

Security controls are processes or technologies put into place to protect the confidentiality, integrity, and availability of systems, assets, and information. Security controls are also referred to as *safeguards* or *countermeasures*.

Every day we interact with security controls, whether it is using a lock protecting access to a home or car, using a fingerprint to log in to access information on a laptop or smartphone, or configuring a home security surveillance system. All of these are common examples of security controls in use that protect assets of importance to us (car, house, personal information, banking information, etc.). Let's look at the security controls in place in Figure 1-6. The house has several security controls, including a lock for the front door, a security surveillance camera, a warning sign indicating the house is under surveillance, a laptop secured with a username and password used to access the camera surveillance feed, and a safe to protect valuables. Similar to the house example, a typical organization utilizes a range of common security controls such as encrypting sensitive data, requiring employees to carry ID badges, and requiring a username and password to be entered before accessing a system. These are just a few examples of common security controls.

In the previous section of this chapter, the concept of risk management was introduced, where risk is identified, assessed, and treated. An organization responds to risk through acceptance, avoidance, transference, or mitigation. An organization mitigates risk through the implementation of security controls to reduce risk to an acceptable level

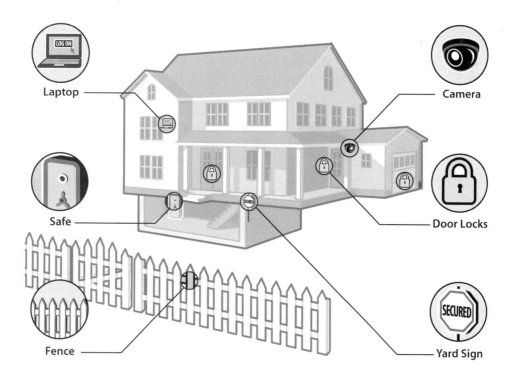

Figure 1-6   Familiar security controls

as determined by the management of the organization. This section introduces foundational details about information security controls, the concept of defense-in-depth, control types, and control functionality.

Defense-in-Depth

In practice, it is seldom that a single, stand-alone security control is used. Many security controls are typically put into place to protect a given system or asset. The use of multiple layers of security controls is referred to as *defense-in-depth* or *layered defense*. Defense-in-depth is the concept of coordinating and leveraging multiple layers of controls to increase the effort required for a potential attacker to succeed in their nefarious activity. For example, most homeowners do not want their homes to be burglarized, and a locked door alone might not be sufficient protection. Therefore, it is common for homes to have multiple layers of security controls in place. Consider the house in Figure 1-6. The house has multiple security controls in place for protection that include

- Locked external door to control access
- Surveillance camera to monitor and detect suspicious activity
- Warning sign notifying that the house has surveillance cameras in use
- Safe for additional protection of valuables

Similarly, a typical organization utilizes defense-in-depth strategies to protect systems and assets as illustrated in Figure 1-7.

This multilayered defense approach helps minimize the probability of a successful attack by forcing an attacker to go through several different protection mechanisms before gaining access to critical assets or systems

 EXAM TIP CC candidates should be familiar with the concept of defense-in-depth.

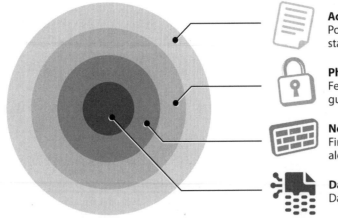

Administrative Security: Policies, procedures, standards, training, etc.

Physical Security: Fencing, locks, alarms, guards, badge readers, etc.

Network Security: Firewalls, monitoring and alerting, antivirus, etc.

Data Security: Data encryption, etc.

Figure 1-7   Defense-in-depth

Work Factor

Work factor is an important concept in cybersecurity and relates to defense-in-depth. *Work factor* is a term that describes an estimate of the effort and/or time required for a threat actor to bypass protective measures (security controls). Defense-in-depth is one strategy that leverages this concept by implementing multiple layers of defenses or controls to significantly increase the work factor for an attacker to succeed with their attack. A common control that significantly increases the work factor required for a successful attack is the implementation of MFA. Each factor (something you know, something you have, and something you are) increases the amount of work required for the cyber criminal to succeed with an attack. For instance, even if a user is tricked into giving up their password, the attacker still needs the additional authentication factor in order to gain access.

Types of Security Controls

Security controls are often grouped into categories or classes based on the nature of the control. In practice, the three categories that are most often used are administrative, technical, and physical. These are illustrated in Figure 1-8 and discussed in detail in the sections that follow.

EXAM TIP   CC candidates should know the difference between the three types of security controls (administrative, technical, and physical) and be able to identify examples of each.

Administrative Controls   *Administrative controls* are management-oriented controls that provide directives and instruction aimed at people within the organization. Administrative controls are also referred to as *soft controls* or *managerial controls*. In the home example in Figure 1-6, the warning sign indicating surveillance cameras are in use is an example of an administrative control. Other general examples of administrative controls in day-to-day life may include signing a rental agreement containing legal language and consequences for late payment, attending a driver's education course to ensure an understanding of traffic laws, or running a background check as part of screening a potential

Figure 1-8
Types of security
controls

**Administrative
Controls**   **Technical
Controls**   **Physical
Controls**

tenant for a rental property. In a typical organization, examples of administrative security controls include

- Documentation
- Training
- Human resource management

Documentation   Documentation may be one of the more commonly used administrative security controls. Documentation is used by an organization to communicate expectations and requirements to employees and other entities. These often come in the form of various legal agreements (e.g., nondisclosure or noncompete agreement) as well as other organizational documentation that employees must abide by such as organizational policies, procedures, and standards (these are discussed in greater detail later in this chapter). Organizations also develop documentation outlining their plan of action in the event some damaging event occurs, such as a business continuity plan, disaster recovery plan, or incident response plan. These plans are discussed in detail in Chapter 5.

Training   Training is another example of an administrative control. Most organizations have some training program in place to educate workers on expected behaviors or processes. Training related to complying with an organization's security requirements, protecting organizational systems or data, and general best security practices is typically known as security awareness training. Security awareness training is discussed in greater detail in Chapter 4. However, training administered by the organization often covers other areas such as ethics training, antiharassment training, and so on. Training may be delivered in multiple forms, including

- In-person training
- Computer-based video training
- Practical drills or exercises

The best training programs take advantage of a combination of training mediums and often use commercially available training courses to teach general concepts and customized training to teach concepts that are unique and specific to the organization.

Human Resource Management   Another typical example of an administrative control is the implementation of HR management practices. HR management deals with processes that an organization implements to manage the entire lifecycle of temporary or full-time employees and third-party contractors within the organization. This includes pre-employment screening, onboarding, ongoing care, and offboarding of human resources. These are typically processes managed by an organization's HR department or equivalent. While not all HR practices are security-relevant, many aspects of HR management do have security implications.

- **Hiring processes**   Hiring processes are typically the first line of defense for an organization when assessing the risk that an employee or contractor might pose.

It is important to suitably screen individuals before hiring them to ensure they are qualified and don't pose an unnecessary risk to the organization. Screening practices often include pre-employment background checks, which vary in scope and might consist of reference checks, credit checks, drug screening, criminal checks, or employment and education verification. The focus of these checks is to determine the candidate's suitability and ensure they are honest, law-abiding, and free of any undesired matters.

- **Termination processes** Termination processes occur when employment with an organization has ended. This is particularly important from an access perspective to ensure that the employee's access to systems and resources is promptly revoked. Organizations should have a defined set of procedures to follow for every termination. This may include notifying the appropriate teams to revoke access, conducting an exit interview, escorting the individual from the building, and retrieving any property belonging to the organization, such as badges, keys, computers, or other equipment.

While the security team may not be tasked with managing these processes directly, it is essential that there is a partnership between HR and security to ensure appropriate controls are in place throughout.

Technical Controls   *Technical controls* are hardware or software components that protect computing and network resources such as computers, servers, mobile devices, computer networks, or data stored within a system. Technical controls are also referred to as *logical controls*. In the home example in Figure 1-6, the laptop computer requires a logon using a password which is an example of a technical control. Other examples of technical controls in day-to-day life include using your fingerprint to unlock your phone or entering a personal identification number (PIN) when using a credit card. In a typical organization, common types of technical controls include

- Technical data security controls
- Technical access controls
- Network security controls

Technical Data Security Controls   Technical data security controls are focused on protecting information from unauthorized access, disclosure, or modification. Data is protected through encryption, ensuring data is encrypted *at rest* (data stored on computers, servers, or external media) and *in transit* (data moving between computers on a network). Data security controls are implemented by properly configuring and hardening assets that store and process information, such as servers, network equipment, applications, and so on. Data security is discussed in greater depth in the data security section of Chapter 4.

Technical Access Controls   Technical access controls (also called logical access controls) are technical systems that control access to computer resources such as computer systems, networks, applications, or databases. Typical technical access controls in an organization might include one or more of the following when authenticating with a computer, system, or application:

- Entering a username and password
- Utilizing a hardware or software MFA token
- Using biometrics (such as voice, eye, palm, or fingerprint scanner)
- Filesystem permissions on a computer

These concepts are discussed in greater detail in the "Logical Access Controls" section of Chapter 2.

Network Security Controls   An organization's network consists of a web of servers, computers, network devices, mobile devices, and so on. These network-connected assets are often referred to as hosts, endpoints, or nodes. Network security controls are controls implemented throughout the network. This includes controls implemented on the hosts themselves (such as security software installed on a computer) and on the organization's network (such as network security devices). Common examples of network security controls include

- Intrusion detection systems that detect anomalous activity on the network or endpoints
- Intrusion prevention systems that prevent anomalous activity on the network or endpoints
- Firewalls that allow or deny certain connections based on a set of rules
- Tools that collect, analyze, and centralize log data
- Antivirus/antimalware that detects and quarantines malicious software

Network security and security controls throughout a network are discussed in greater detail in Chapter 3.

Physical Controls   *Physical controls* are tangible controls put in place to protect physical resources against physical threats, including but not limited to break-ins, fires, theft, physical harm, and so on. These include protective measures for people, assets, and facilities. In the home example in Figure 1-6, the door lock, safe, and security camera are examples of physical security controls. Other examples of physical controls in day-to-day life include a lock for your bicycle, home security systems, and the fire extinguisher found in most households. In a typical organization, examples of physical controls include

- Fencing, locks, and mantraps
- Lighting
- Bollards
- Server room doors

- Alarms
- Security guards or guard dogs
- Door locks
- Stop signs
- Badge reader/badges
- Surveillance cameras
- Fire extinguisher or fire suppression system
- Biometrics to access a building or room

 NOTE Some security controls can be considered technical or physical, depending on implementation. For example, a fingerprint scanner protecting access to a datacenter is a physical control, as it protects a physical resource. A fingerprint scanner used to log in to a computer is a technical control, as it protects computing resources.

Security Control Categories

As previously discussed, the most commonly used names of control types are administrative, technical, and physical controls. However, within the cybersecurity industry, a variety of naming systems are used to describe controls. For example, NIST defines a different set of control types, which they refer to as control classes. These are management, operational, and technical. Each of these classes is defined by NIST as follows:

- **Management**   The security controls (i.e., safeguards or countermeasures) for an information system that focus on the management of risk and the management of information system security.

- **Operational**   The security controls (i.e., safeguards or countermeasures) for an information system that are primarily implemented and executed by people (as opposed to systems).

- **Technical**   The security controls (i.e., safeguards or countermeasures) for an information system that are primarily implemented and executed by the information system through mechanisms contained in the hardware, software, or firmware components.

There is no one-to-one mapping of the general control types (administrative, technical, and physical) to the NIST control classes (management, operational, and technical), except for the technical classes. Some controls, such as risk management, are administrative and management controls. Other controls, such as employee termination, are administrative and operational controls.

(continued)

EXAM TIP As a cybersecurity practitioner, you will see both the general control types (administrative, technical, and physical) and the NIST control classes (management, operational, and technical) used. You might see either or both used on the exam. Just pay attention to the context of the question, and you should be able to answer correctly.

Functions of Security Controls

The terms administrative, technical, and physical control address the type or category of the control but not how the control functions or operates. Administrative, technical, and physical security controls can be further broken down based on their functionality and the properties that describe the protection the control provides. The security functionality of a control describes what the control does for the organization. In practice, the most common functionalities of controls include the following:

- Preventive controls
- Detective controls
- Deterrent controls
- Corrective controls
- Directive controls
- Compensating controls

EXAM TIP CC candidates should be familiar with the different security functionalities and be able to identify examples of each.

Preventive Controls *Preventive controls* provide functionality that prevents or stops an adverse event or incident. In a typical household, examples of preventative controls include a door lock, gate, or fence. Preventive controls can be administrative, technical, or physical. Examples are included here:

- **Administrative** (background checks, hiring and termination processes, etc.)
- **Technical** (network intrusion prevention system, firewall, MFA, antivirus, etc.)
- **Physical** (fences, door locks, gates, etc.)

Detective Controls *Detective controls* provide functionality that helps to discover, detect, or identify when something bad might have occurred, such as an adverse activity, event, intruder, or incident. A common detective control in a house might be a security camera or a barking dog. Detective controls can be administrative, technical, or physical. Examples of each are included here:

- **Administrative** (mandatory vacation, review of access logs, etc.)
- **Technical** (a system that detects unusual activity on an organization's network)
- **Physical** (surveillance cameras, closed-circuit television [CCTV], motion sensor, etc.)

Deterrent Controls   *Deterrent controls* provide functionality that deters or discourages a potential adversary from performing an attack or engaging in unwanted behavior. Deterrent controls are generally administrative, such as a system warning banner/login banner a user might see when logging into a system notifying them that their actions on the system are being monitored, a "No Trespassing" sign you might see on private property, or a sensitive document that is watermarked with a user's name instructing them to not share the document.

Corrective Controls   *Corrective controls* provide functionality that fixes a system, process, or activity after an adverse event has occurred. A common example in a household might be using a fire extinguisher to put out a kitchen fire. Corrective controls can be administrative, technical, or physical. Examples of each are included here:

- **Administrative** (e.g., terminating an employee after an offense or implementing business continuity, disaster recovery, or incident response plans)
- **Technical** (e.g., antivirus that quarantines malicious software, restoring a system from backup)
- **Physical** (e.g., using a fire extinguisher to put out a fire, removing datacenter badge access for a lost access card)

Directive Controls   *Directive controls* provide functionality that serves to communicate expected behavior. Common examples in day-to-day life might include traffic signs that communicate expected traffic behavior such as "stop," "yield," and so on. Directive controls are generally administrative in nature such as policies, standards, procedures, training, and so on.

Compensating Controls   *Compensating controls* serve as an alternate control to a primary control, often used when the primary control is not feasible to implement due to cost, complexity, or other organizational constraints. Compensating controls include the following:

- **Administrative**   A small organization has a single employee accepting cash payments, recording deposits, and reconciling financial reports. The company may not have enough staff to fully implement separation of duties, so instead, they implement a process where leadership performs a regular review of reconciliation for additional oversight.

- **Technical**   An organization is running a critical application that relies on old software that the manufacturer no longer releases security updates for. Migrating to a new application may not be feasible, so an organization may decide to implement network isolation of the application as a compensating control.

- **Physical**   An organization determines that a full-time security guard for their office is too expensive, so instead they install fences, locks, and alarms as compensating controls.

NOTE   In some cases, a control can provide more than one control functionality. For example, antivirus could be considered preventive and corrective, and fencing could be considered preventive and deterrent.

Professional Ethics

Ethics are moral standards or principles that govern behavior with a focus on acting responsibly with integrity and accountability. It means having a moral compass to determine right from wrong even when no one is watching. We commonly face ethical dilemmas in our day-to-day life whether it's determining what to do with a lost wallet found on the street or deciding if the restaurant server should be notified that the bill is missing an item that was purchased. In some cases, the ethical or moral option is easily identifiable; however, ethical standards and everyone's own individual moral compass are often subjective and open to interpretation. This is why many organizations develop a documented code of ethics, ethics policy, and/or ethics program to set an agreed-upon standard for expected behavior for the members of the organization (employees, professional members, executives, the board, and other stakeholders). This is sometimes referred to as organizational or professional ethics.

Organizational ethics are principles put in place for creating and maintaining a culture of integrity, transparency, social responsibility, and ethical conduct within an organization based on agreed-upon standards. In some cases, ethics programs are tied into an organization's compliance initiatives. In fact, many regulations and laws require organizations to develop and adopt an ethical statement and potentially a full-blown ethics program. An organization's ethics program might consist of the following components:

- Policies, procedures, and standards for ethical conduct within the organization

- Regular ethics training for employees, staff, or members

- Consequences for noncompliance with ethical requirements

- Continuous improvement through monitoring and evaluation of program effectiveness

The security team is typically not responsible for managing the ethics program for the entire organization. In practice, this typically falls under the purview of the HR or legal department. Some organizations' security departments may even have their own specific code of ethics in addition to the organization's ethics program. Here are some examples of how ethics play a role in cybersecurity decisions:

- A cybersecurity professional discovers a security flaw in a third-party product. They may be under no legal obligation to report the flaw to the website owner; however, reporting the flaw would be the responsible thing to do.

- Cybersecurity staff believe customer data may have been compromised but are unsure. Should the customers be notified? This is an ethical decision that should not be made on the spot—there should be policies and guidelines to follow that address the situation.

As a cybersecurity practitioner, we are often entrusted with sensitive information and heightened levels of access and have a professional responsibility to act ethically and foster trust and credibility within the organization as well as in our day-to-day lives. Acting ethically and having a standard moral compass are partially what separates the cybersecurity professional from the hackers. To aid in having an agreed-upon professional standard for ethical behavior, (ISC)² has developed a Code of Ethics that all professional members must follow.

(ISC)² Code of Ethics

(ISC)² requires all certified professionals to adhere to their Code of Ethics. The (ISC)² Code of Ethics defines a fundamental professional code of conduct for (ISC)² members. If a Certified in Cybersecurity professional violates the Code of Ethics, they may be subject to a peer review panel, which will determine the appropriate consequences that might include certification revocation. The complete (ISC)² Code of Ethics is listed on the (ISC)² site at https://www.isc2.org/Ethics. Every CC candidate should review the (ISC)² Code of Ethics to prepare for the exam. As part of the process of becoming CC certified, the candidate must agree and adhere to the (ISC)² Code of Ethics.

 EXAM TIP CC candidates must review and be very familiar with the (ISC)² Code of Ethics to prepare for the exam.

Code of Ethics Preamble The (ISC)² Code of Ethics Preamble defines the high-level mission statement for the (ISC)² Code of Ethics. The following is an overview of the Code of Ethics Preamble:

- The safety and welfare of society and the common good, duty to our principals, and to each other requires that we adhere, and be seen to adhere, to the highest ethical standards of behavior.

- Therefore, strict adherence to this Code is a condition of certification.

Code of Ethics Canons   The (ISC)² Code of Ethics Canons defines four high-level requirements that represent fundamental tenets for professional conduct that all (ISC)² members should follow. An overview of these requirements is included here:

- Protect society, the common good, necessary public trust and confidence, and the infrastructure.
- Act honorably, honestly, justly, responsibly, and legally.
- Provide diligent and competent service to principals.
- Advance and protect the profession.

 EXAM TIP   CC candidates may see questions in which they are presented with an ethical situation and must make an ethical choice. For this we do not offer specific guidance; however, in general, any ethical violations observed by an (ISC)² member should be stopped and reported.

Security Program Elements Summary
Most organizations implement an organization-wide security program consisting of core security activities that generally include

- **Risk management**   Organizations follow a risk management process to identify and prioritize risks to make security decisions.
- **Security governance and management**   Organizations oversee their security program to ensure it is properly resourced (staffed, managed, and organized to address different areas of cybersecurity). These activities are documented in policies, procedures, and internal standards.
- **Security controls**   Security controls are implemented based on the results of *risk management* activities and managed as part of security program governance.
- **Professional ethics**   Activities are carried out by cybersecurity professionals following standards of professional ethics.

Chapter Review

Cybersecurity is the practice of protecting information resources (computers, networks, and data) from unauthorized use. There are two sides to the cybersecurity coin: cyber criminals carry out offensive attacks, and cybersecurity professionals defend, protect, respond, and recover from attacks. The key elements of cybersecurity are confidentiality, integrity, availability, authentication and authorization, message integrity, privacy, and information assurance.

The first step in an attack is to gather as much information as possible about the target to be able to carry out an attack. Next, the attacker tries to identify the organization's information assets as well as their corresponding vulnerabilities that can be exploited. Once the assets and vulnerabilities are enumerated, the attacker can design and execute the attack.

Organizations use a risk management process to decide how much to spend on security and what kind of controls to put in place based on their tolerance for risk. Risk management is the process of identifying and assessing risk, reducing it to an acceptable level, and implementing the right controls or countermeasures to maintain that level.

Organizations mitigate risk through the implementation of security controls to reduce risk to an acceptable level as determined by the management of the organization. Security controls are processes or technologies put into place to protect the confidentiality, integrity, and availability of systems, assets, and information.

Security governance is a subset of organizational governance focused on directing and controlling the organization's approach to security while ensuring alignment with internal and external organizational requirements. Security program governance is often shaped by laws and regulations, external standards (e.g., NIST, ISO), and organizational ethics, goals, and objectives. Organizations use a variety of governance elements to facilitate alignment with organizational requirements. These elements include plans, policies, procedures, and internal standards.

Ethics are moral standards that govern behavior. Cybersecurity practitioners have a professional responsibility to act ethically and foster trust and credibility. (ISC)² has developed a Code of Ethics that all professional members must follow to aid in ensuring there is an agreed-upon professional standard for ethical behavior.

Quick Review

- The basic principles of information security are confidentiality, availability, and integrity.

- Confidentiality is the secrecy, or privacy, of the information within the asset being protected.

- Integrity is ensuring data is not altered or corrupted in any way.

- Availability is ensuring data assets and information resources are there when they are needed.

- Authentication verifies that a user is who they claim to be.

- Multifactor authentication provides better security because it requires more than one verification factor, of different types, used in combination.

- Nonrepudiation is accomplished using technologies that ensure that a message could only have been created by the sender and could not have been created by anyone else. Therefore the sender could never deny the message came from them.

- Privacy refers to the handling and security of personal information.

- Information assurance refers to the measure of information security.
- The steps of a typical cyberattack are reconnaissance, enumeration, exploitation, and action on objectives.
- A vulnerability is a weakness that could potentially be exploited.
- A threat is a potentially damaging event associated with the exploitation of a vulnerability.
- A risk is the likelihood of a threat agent exploiting a vulnerability and the corresponding business impact.
- An exposure is an instance of being exposed to a loss or the potential that a security breach could occur.
- A countermeasure (or a control) is put into place to mitigate a potential risk.
- A threat agent is an actor that can exploit a vulnerability.
- Some organizations try to use risk management to strike a balance between the value of an asset and the cost of the controls to protect the asset.
- ISC^2 advocates a three-step risk management process as follows: risk identification (framing the risk), risk assessment (understanding the risk), and risk treatment (taking action on what to do about the risk).
- Threat modeling is the process of examining each asset, the potential threats faced by each asset, and the adverse effects caused by the threat against the asset.
- A quantitative risk assessment seeks to understand risk by assigning numerical or financial values to assets along with factors with numerical weights such as threat probability, impact of loss, etc.
- A qualitative risk assessment seeks to understand risk in non-numerical terms using ratings and priorities.
- Risk treatment options include transference, acceptance, avoidance, and mitigation.
- Governance is the set of activities by which an organization defines and controls the organization as a whole or a specific part of the organization (such as IT governance, security governance, or financial governance).
- Security governance is a subset of organizational governance focused on setting the strategies for the security program to ensure alignment with organizational requirements and objectives.
- An organization's security program is made up of a collection of governance elements (policies, internal standards, and procedures) used to facilitate alignment with external requirements (laws and regulations, external standards, etc.) and internal requirements (organizational ethics, goals, and objectives).
- Laws and regulations are rules typically established by a governmental body or similar agency that specify requirements that are legally enforceable.

- External standards are documents developed and published by external standards organizations containing best practices that may be used for the development of security program elements.

- Policies are high-level management statements providing prescriptive directives to the organization.

- Procedures are step-by-step workflows or instructions that define how a task should be accomplished.

- Security controls, also known as safeguards or countermeasures, are processes or technologies put into place to protect the confidentiality, availability, and integrity (CAI) of systems, assets, and information.

- Security controls are grouped into three main categories:

  - Administrative controls, also known as soft controls or managerial controls, are management-oriented controls that provide directives aimed at people within the organization. Examples of administrative controls include documentation (policies, procedures, standards, guidelines), training (security awareness training), and other personnel practices (hiring, firing, and so on).

  - Technical controls, also known as logical controls, are hardware or software components that protect virtual resources such as data stored within a system. Examples of technical controls are encryption, password enforcement, multifactor authentication, intrusion detection systems (IDSs), intrusion prevention systems (IPSs), and firewalls

  - Physical controls are tangible controls put in place to protect against physical threats. Examples of physical controls include fencing, lighting, locks, bollards, server room doors, alarms, and security guards.

- Security functionality of a control describes what the control does for the organization. Functionalities of controls include the following:

  - Preventive controls prevent or stop the occurrence of an adverse event or incident.

  - Detective controls discover, detect, or identify a potential adverse activity, event, intruder, or incident.

  - Deterrent controls deter or discourage a potential adversary from performing an attack or engaging in unwanted behavior.

  - Corrective controls correct adverse events that have occurred by fixing a system, process, or activity.

  - Directive controls are typically administrative controls that communicate expected behavior by specifying what actions are or are not permitted.

  - Compensating controls serve as an alternate or secondary control implementation to a primary control. These are often used when the primary control is not feasible to implement due to cost, complexity, or other organizational constraints.

- Ethics are moral standards or principles that govern behavior with a focus on acting responsibly with integrity and accountability.

Questions

1. A cyberattacker changes the website of a pharmacy so it displays incorrect information about COVID testing. This is an example of what kind of compromise?

   A. Confidentiality

   B. Integrity

   C. Availability

   D. Nonrepudiation

2. The function of a computer system that verifies the identity of a user is called _____.

   A. Authentication

   B. Authorization

   C. Authenticity

   D. Availability

3. Jane received an electronic message from Fred that was digitally signed proving it came from him. However, Fred said he never sent it. This is an example of what message integrity characteristic?

   A. Nonreputation

   B. Nonrefutability

   C. Nonrepudiation

   D. Authenticity

4. Which of the following elements do not apply to privacy?

   A. Confidentiality

   B. Integrity

   C. Availability

   D. None of the above

5. Information assurance refers to the _____ of information security.

   A. Quality

   B. Confidentiality

   C. Ethics

   D. Measurement

6. What is the first thing a cyberattacker would want to do to launch an attack against an organization?

    A. Learn about the organization's vulnerabilities.

    B. Learn about the organization's business, including domain names, corporate information, facilities, names of employees, etc.

    C. Deploy malware.

    D. Steal data.

7. An earthquake is an example of a _____ ?

    A. Threat agent

    B. Threat

    C. Vulnerability

    D. Risk

8. Which of the following statements is most correct?

    A. Security should be done the same way regardless of the situation.

    B. Security should be tailored based on the situation.

    C. It's always best to mitigate risks rather than transfer them.

    D. Risk avoidance trumps security controls every time.

9. You are asked to perform a risk assessment of an information system for the purpose of recommending the most appropriate security controls. You have a short amount of time to do this. You have information about how each asset in the system is used and its importance to the business, but you have no financial information about the assets or the information systems. Which is the most appropriate method to use for this assessment?

    A. Qualitative

    B. Threat modeling

    C. Quantitative

    D. Delphi

10. You are asked to implement a risk treatment in which your IT department is removing a server from the environment that it deems is too risky due to having too many vulnerabilities in it. You have just practiced which type of risk treatment?

    A. Risk transfer

    B. Risk avoidance

    C. Risk acceptance

    D. Risk mitigation

11. A security engineer is performing a review of an organization's datacenter security controls. They document that the datacenter lacks security cameras for monitoring the facilities. What type of control does this represent?

  A. Administrative

  B. Technical

  C. Physical

  D. Logical

12. Which of the following statements is true regarding the types of security controls?

  A. Physical controls are also referred to as logical controls.

  B. Logical controls are also referred to as managerial controls.

  C. Physical controls are also referred to as managerial controls.

  D. Administrative controls are also referred to as soft controls.

13. The senior security engineer is creating a document that provides step-by-step instructions on how to launch a vulnerability scan utilizing the organization's vulnerability scanning tool that all security engineers will be required to follow. Which of the following governance elements is this an example of?

  A. Policy

  B. Procedure

  C. Guideline

  D. Law

14. An information security policy is an example of which of the following types of controls?

  A. Administrative

  B. Technical

  C. Logical

  D. Physical

15. Sarah is a security engineer for a Software as a Service (SaaS) organization. Her friend Kyle is a systems administrator for the organization and helped her get the job by serving as a reference. While reviewing some system logs, Sarah discovered that Kyle is running a crypto-mining program on a company server for his own financial gain. How should Sarah respond to this situation?

  A. Ask Kyle to stop

  B. Ask Kyle to share the profits with her

  C. Mind her own business

  D. Escalate to senior management

Questions and Answers

1. A cyberattacker changes the website of a pharmacy so it displays incorrect information about COVID testing. This is an example of what kind of compromise?

   A. Confidentiality

   B. Integrity

   C. Availability

   D. Nonrepudiation

   B. Changing data without proper authorization is a compromise of integrity.

2. The function of a computer system that verifies the identity of a user is called _____.

   A. Authentication

   B. Authorization

   C. Authenticity

   D. Availability

   A. Authentication is the function of verifying a user's identity.

3. Jane received an electronic message from Fred that was digitally signed proving it came from him. However, Fred said he never sent it. This is an example of what message integrity characteristic?

   A. Nonreputation

   B. Nonrefutability

   C. Nonrepudiation

   D. Authenticity

   C. Nonrepudiation technologies are used to guarantee that a sender of a message cannot later deny that they sent the message.

4. Which of the following elements do not apply to privacy?

   A. Confidentiality

   B. Integrity

   C. Availability

   D. None of the above

   D. All of the items listed apply to privacy.

5. Information assurance refers to the _____ of information security.

  A. Quality

  B. Confidentiality

  C. Ethics

  D. Measurement

  D. Information assurance is the measurement of the security controls an organization has put into place.

6. What is the first thing a cyberattacker would want to do to launch an attack against an organization?

  A. Learn about the organization's vulnerabilities.

  B. Learn about the organization's business, including domain names, corporate information, facilities, names of employees, etc.

  C. Deploy malware.

  D. Steal data.

  B. While learning about vulnerabilities might seem like a good answer, the best answer is learning about the organization's business details because that will provide the basic information the cyberattacker can use to launch the attack.

7. An earthquake is an example of a _____?

  A. Threat agent

  B. Threat

  C. Vulnerability

  D. Risk

  B. An earthquake is a natural disaster that may occur and that could cause harm to an organization; therefore it is a *threat* to the organization.

8. Which of the following statements is most correct?

  A. Security should be done the same way regardless of the situation.

  B. Security should be tailored based on the situation.

  C. It's always best to mitigate risks rather than transfer them.

  D. Risk avoidance trumps security controls every time.

  B. Answers A, C, and D all contain absolute statements about applying security. But security is never absolute; it is tailored based on the situation and the organization's tolerance for risk, so the *best* answer is B.

9. You are asked to perform a risk assessment of an information system for the purpose of recommending the most appropriate security controls. You have a short amount of time to do this. You have information about how each asset in the system is used and its importance to the business, but you have no financial information about the assets or the information systems. Which is the most appropriate method to use for this assessment?

   A. Qualitative

   B. Threat modeling

   C. Quantitative

   D. Delphi

   A. Since you have no financial data, a quantitative assessment is not possible, but since you have information about how each asset in the system is used and its importance to the business, you have what you need to do a qualitative analysis.

10. You are asked to implement a risk treatment in which your IT department is removing a server from the environment that it deems is too risky due to having too many vulnerabilities in it. You have just practiced which type of risk treatment?

    A. Risk transfer

    B. Risk avoidance

    C. Risk acceptance

    D. Risk mitigation

    C. Risk avoidance is the best answer because by removing the risky server altogether, you are avoiding the risk. Answer D may have been considered because vulnerability mitigation is a type of risk treatment, but that usually involves addressing specific vulnerabilities, not removing entire systems or services.

11. A security engineer is performing a review of an organization's datacenter security controls. They document that the datacenter lacks security cameras for monitoring the facilities. What type of control does this represent?

    A. Administrative

    B. Technical

    C. Physical

    D. Logical

    C. Security cameras used for monitoring facilities are an example of physical security controls. Administrative controls are management-oriented controls such as documentation, policies, procedures, and training. Technical or logical controls are hardware or software components implemented by computer systems or network devices.

12. Which of the following statements is true regarding the types of security controls?

    A. Physical controls are also referred to as logical controls.

    B. Logical controls are also referred to as managerial controls.

    C. Physical controls are also referred to as managerial controls.

    D. Administrative controls are also referred to as soft controls.

    D. Administrative controls are also referred to as soft controls or managerial controls. Technical controls are also referred to as logical controls.

13. The senior security engineer is creating a document that provides step-by-step instructions on how to launch a vulnerability scan utilizing the organization's vulnerability scanning tool that all security engineers will be required to follow. Which of the following governance elements is this an example of?

    A. Policy

    B. Procedure

    C. Guideline

    D. Law

    B. A document containing step-by-step instructions on how to perform a vulnerability scanning is an example of a procedure. Policies are high-level management statements providing directives to the organization but do not prescribe exact steps. Guidelines serve as best practice references but are not required to be followed. While following the procedure may be a requirement of the business, the procedure itself is not a law.

14. An information security policy is an example of which of the following types of controls?

    A. Administrative

    B. Technical

    C. Logical

    D. Physical

    A. A policy is an example of an administrative control. Administrative controls are management-oriented controls that provide directives and instruction aimed at people within the organization, such as documentation, training, and other personnel management practices. Technical controls, also known as logical controls, are hardware or software components that protect virtual resources. Physical controls are tangible controls put in place to protect physical resources against physical threats

15. Sarah is a security engineer for a Software as a Service (SaaS) organization. Her friend Kyle is a systems administrator for the organization and helped her get the job by serving as a reference. While reviewing some system logs, Sarah discovered that Kyle is running a crypto-mining program on a company server for his own financial gain. How should Sarah respond to this situation?

A. Ask Kyle to stop

B. Ask Kyle to share the profits with her

C. Mind her own business

D. Escalate to senior management

D. Sarah should immediately escalate this to senior leadership in accordance with the organization's policies and procedures. This would be the ethical response to this situation.

Access Controls Concepts

This chapter discusses the following topics:
- Access control fundamentals
- Logical access controls
- Physical access controls

In Chapter 1 we introduced the concept of security controls, which are safeguards or countermeasures put into place to protect the confidentiality, integrity, and availability of systems, assets, and information. The Certified in Cybersecurity Domain 3 defines two basic types of access controls: logical (or technical) controls and physical controls. And within each of these types, controls can have various functions: preventive, detective, deterrent, corrective, directive, and compensating. Access controls are security controls that are used to control access to resources. In this chapter we explore the following aspects of access controls, each within its own section:

- Access control fundamentals, including access control concepts, practices, access control administration, and provisioning, and we examine authentication and authorization in detail.
- Logical access controls, including access control models, identity management technologies, and logical access monitoring.
- Physical access controls, including methods of preventing and controlling physical access and physical access monitoring.

Access Control Fundamentals

This section covers access control concepts that are common across all three types of access controls: logical, physical, and administrative. We cover

- Access control concepts
- Access control practices
- Identification, authentication, authorization, and accountability
- Identity and access management

- Identity and access management lifecycle
- Privileged accounts

Each of these topics is addressed in its own section.

Access Control Concepts

Access controls are security features that permit or restrict access to areas within a physical or logical environment. Access control systems can range from simple doors controlling access to physical areas like buildings or datacenters to access management systems that control access to web-based applications and databases. Access controls are the means by which we make sure that only those people who are specifically authorized can access an organization's data or other protected resources. Figure 2-1 illustrates the basic model of access control and introduces the terms *subjects, objects,* and *access.*

In our access control illustration, a *subject* is an entity that is capable of accessing an object, usually by first requesting such access. We usually think of subjects as users, but subjects can also be programs or processes that need to access an object to perform a task and do so automatically when the program is run.

An *object* is an entity, or resource, that is accessed by a subject. The object contains and/or receives data. It is through the subject's access to an object that the subject can gain access to data or perform functions. The object can be a computer, file, database, program, process, data segment, or field in a data table.

Access is the right that is granted to the subject to perform a function with the object. Functions may include operations such as read, modify, create, delete, or execute. Access is based on a set of *rules* that are established by the organization, written in a policy, and then implemented on the system that is controlling access, sometimes called an access management system (e.g., Microsoft Active Directory is a commonly used access management system).

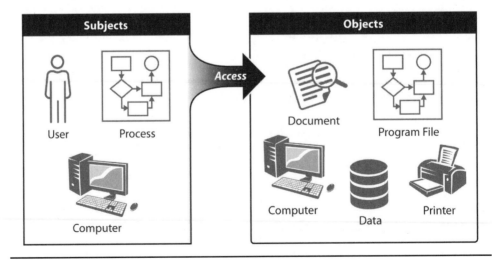

Figure 2-1   Access controls

Access control systems do more than just help the organization provision users and set up their access. The systems also keep track of users' access. The monitoring can be tuned to track which user accessed which object at what time, for how long, and what operation they performed. Granular tracking of user access allows for detailed auditing to support investigations of security incidents to understand what exactly happened and what caused an incident.

Access Control Practices

In this section we examine the following topics covering common practices in access control that CC candidates should be familiar with:

- Authorized versus unauthorized personnel
- Need to know
- Principle of least privilege
- Segregation of duties
- Two-person rule
- Memorized secrets

Authorized vs. Unauthorized Personnel

The core function of access control is allowing access to a resource (or an object) to only those subjects who are specifically authorized to access it. Likewise, if a subject is not authorized to access an object, they are prevented from accessing it. This concept of authorized and unauthorized subjects applies to users and personnel.

So, authorized personnel are those who are registered within the access management system (discussed later in this chapter) and have permissions authorizing them access to a specific resource. For that resource they are considered authorized personnel.

In present-day cybersecurity-speak, the latest buzzword is "zero trust." Zero trust simply means access to a computing, network, or data resource will not be given to any person or subject unless that access is *explicitly authorized*. In other words, in a zero trust enterprise, access controls must be used everywhere. Whether the user, or thing, making an access request is coming from across the Internet or within the same network, the same level of authorization is required.

Similar to authorized and unauthorized personnel are the concepts of authorized and unauthorized access. Authorized access takes place when an authorized user requests and is granted access to an object. Unauthorized access is when a subject gets access to a resource they are not authorized for. This can happen accidentally or maliciously. Accidental unauthorized access can happen due to a system misconfiguration, a vulnerability caused by a programming error or unpatched application, or an error by system administration or operations personnel. Malicious unauthorized access can occur if a cyberattacker obtains a user's credentials or finds a way to bypass a system's access control mechanisms.

Need to Know

Need to know is the basic premise of access control. Access to a resource should only be granted to a user who has a legitimate need to know, which means that the user requires access to the resource in order to perform a business function. In practice, when a user's permissions are set up within an information system, the user's access to systems and/or data is established based on the user's official duties. For example, if as part of a user's official duties they need to be able to edit employee personnel files, then they have a need to know and should be allowed access to the files.

In practice, employees are often reminded to be on the lookout for proper implementation of need to know in the workplace. Just because someone has been set up to access a resource, that doesn't mean they have been set up correctly. If an employee sees another employee access data and they believe the employee does not have a need to know for that data, that access should be questioned and reported according to the organization's rules or policies.

Principle of Least Privilege

The principle of least privilege is the concept that a user should only have access to the resources that they need in order to do their job but no more than that. For instance, if you are an administrator for your company's financial system, you should have administrative credentials for the financial system but not for the manufacturing system. Similarly, if a mechanic needs keys to be able to unlock the company's tool closet, those keys should not also unlock the company's safe where the money is kept. The idea is that by limiting the resources a user has access to, the risk of loss due to a compromise is reduced.

Organizations should apply the principle of least privilege whenever they grant users access to systems, data, or resources. Access should be limited to the minimum resources that a user needs in order to perform their job duties.

By applying least privilege, organizations can reap several benefits. By limiting a user's access, the risk of a compromise due to a potential vulnerability in one system can be limited to just that system. Therefore, the organization's exposure to threats is limited. Another benefit of least privilege is that it limits the organization's exposure to insider threats or employee errors. If an employee has access to resources that they don't need access to, it increases the risk the employee could, accidently or on purpose, misuse that access to compromise the confidentiality, integrity, or availability of resources that they never should have had access to in the first place.

Segregation of Duties

Also known as *separation of duties,* segregation of duties is an internal control that organizations use to prevent fraud or the likelihood of errors. The concept is that duties are assigned such that one employee does not have enough privileges that they could misuse the system or cause an error on their own. For example, if one employee is responsible for both writing checks and signing them, there is the potential for fraud or abuse. However, if one employee is responsible for writing checks and another employee is responsible for signing checks, there is much less likelihood of fraud or abuse.

Organizations use segregation of duties when they define job roles throughout the enterprise. Some organizations have policies that require segregation of duties for incompatible job functions or job functions that have the potential for fraud, mistakes, or abuse.

 EXAM TIP Exam questions regarding segregation of duties sometimes focus on its use as a countermeasure against fraud because it causes employees to collude to accomplish certain fraudulent acts. Look for the use of the words *collude* or *collusion* regarding segregation or separation of duties.

Two-Person Rule

Similar in concept to segregation of duties is the *two-person rule,* which requires certain functions to be performed by two authorized users or employees working in tandem. By requiring two people to be present, the potential for fraud, errors, or abuse is reduced. The U.S. government uses the two-person rule for nuclear weapons controls and other critical military systems operation functions. Industry widely uses the two-person rule for any function that requires such an added security measure.

One example of the two-person rule is storage areas that have two locks that require two different people to open in order to access. In fact, in response to the security breaches committed by criminal and former U.S. government contractor Edward Snowden, the National Security Agency (NSA) implemented a two-person rule for access to their server rooms.

Memorized Secrets

Memorized secrets are "something you know" such as passwords, PINs, or lock combinations used to authenticate a user to a system or a physical device. Passwords are sequences of numbers, letters, or characters entered into a computing device. Lock combinations can also be numbers, letters, or characters typed or physically manipulated into a locking device or mechanism. In either case, the memorized secret is known only to the user; therefore, the correct entry of the password or combination verifies that the authorized user is the person who is requesting access.

The use of secrets requires good practices in the following areas to avoid compromises or security issues:

- **Strength**   Memorized secrets such as passwords should not be easily guessed. This is usually accomplished by a policy that requires them to have a minimum character length and contain some combination of lowercase letters, uppercase letters, numbers, and symbols. The minimum character length is usually 8 characters, but many organizations now use 16 characters as their minimum. Combination locks usually have the type and length of characters incorporated into their design and are therefore not configurable by the organization.

- **Storage** Passwords and lock combinations can be hard to remember and easy to forget. As a result, there may be a temptation for the user to write them down or store them so they don't have to remember them. This isn't a bad idea if it is done in a secure manner, but it is a bad idea if the password or combination is stored unsecured. Writing down passwords on a sticky note or storing them in an unencrypted file on a computer isn't a good idea because the sticky note or unencrypted file can be compromised. Secrets should only be stored in a secure manner such as in a physical safe or a password manager. Password managers or vaults are software programs that store passwords or other important information in encrypted files. The passwords can only be accessed by a user with the proper credentials. Password vaults are a great way to keep passwords or other secrets secure and available for use.

- **Policy** Many organizations have password policies, which are written documents that employees are required to follow that govern how passwords or other secrets are used within the organization.

Password Rotation

Contrary to popular belief, changing passwords on a regular basis is no longer a recommended practice. Up until just a few years ago, it was common practice for organizations to require users to change their passwords frequently. The rationale was that if a password got compromised, changing it rendered the previous password useless, so requiring users to change their password frequently was considered a good thing. However, in practice organizations found that when users were required to change their password, they were likely to change it to a weak one by simply appending a letter or number to the end of their existing password. Such a password can be easily guessed by a sophisticated hacker with the right tools. As a result, password rotation (requiring users to change their passwords regularly) is no longer a common practice. In fact, NIST SP 800-63B, a popular industry guideline for authentication practices, no longer recommends changing passwords on a regular basis.

EXAM TIP CC candidates should be familiar with subjects, objects, and access as well as the concepts of need to know, least privilege, segregation (or separation) of duties, two-person rule, and password/combination practices.

Identification, Authentication, Authorization, and Accountability

In order for a subject (or user) to access an object (or resource), they must first prove who they are. Then, the access management system must be able recognize them and verify they have the proper rights to carry out the action they are requesting. The process is illustrated in Figure 2-2.

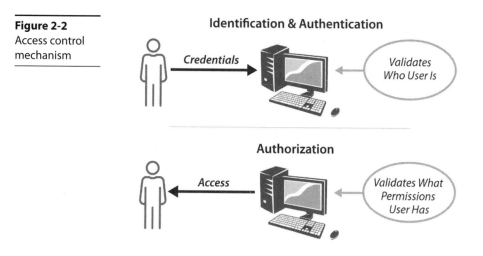

Figure 2-2
Access control
mechanism

Each aspect of the process is explained here:

- **Identification**   Identification is the act of the subject providing identifying information. In most information systems this is accomplished by the user entering in a username, user identifier (ID), or sometimes an account number. The identification usually does not change; it's like a person's name, and it exists for the life of the subject.

- **Authentication**   Authentication was introduced in Chapter 1. It is the method by which systems verify that a user really is who they claim to be. Identification and authentication are typically used in combination; together they are called *credentials*. Authentication is considered the second part of the credential, which is the verification step. This part of the credential is a *secret*: a password, PIN, cryptographic key, or a secret provided by a token or biometric device. To work, identification and authentication require a prior registration process to tell the system who the user is and what their credentials are so the system recognizes that person each time they log in or request access.

- **Authorization**   If the credentials (the username and the secret) match the information stored in the access management system, the system authorizes that the subject is who they claim to be, and access is granted. Authorization is the bestowing of a set of permissions or a level of access to objects or resources within a system.

Though not shown in the figure, *accountability* is another important feature of the process because it provides a record of the access transaction. Once a user is authenticated and granted access to a resource, they can be held accountable for their actions. If the user of credentials causes a data breach or misuses a computer system, the system not only knows who they are but since their actions are tracked and recorded using *logs*, the system has a record of what actions the user performed that led up to the security breach.

Logs are used throughout any enterprise to record actions and events and provide information to auditors and investigators. Logs are particularly useful in providing a record of access control events.

Use Unique Passwords

A few years ago, a security breach was widely reported in the news regarding an in-home security camera system that was compromised. The hacker took control of the victim's security camera and was able to not only view what was going on in the victim's home but also communicate with the victim's family members through the camera's microphone and speaker. Although the victim initially blamed the security camera vendor, the real cause was that the victim set up his camera using the same credentials (username and password) he used for many of his other online accounts. When one of those accounts was compromised by a hacker, the cyber criminal tried to use those credentials on other systems, including the security camera's website, and sure enough he got in. Once he logged in, he was able to control the camera just like a legitimate user. This is an example of why credentials should never be reused. Each system and account should have its own unique set of credentials so that a compromise of one system will not lead to a compromise of another one.

Authentication Factors

As introduced in Chapter 1, there are three ways of authenticating a subject to a system. These methods are called authentication factors, each of which is described next.

Type 1: Something You Know Type 1 verification or authentication factors require the user to know something. The most common type is a memorized secret such as a password, which is a sequence of characters known only to the user and the identity management software of the system the user is logging into. Organizations define a password policy containing the rules governing the use of passwords within the organization.

Type 2: Something You Have Type 2 verification or authentication factors require the user to have something with them. Usually, these devices are handheld tokens or smart cards. A token is a device with a digital display. The user presses a button on the token, and a number pops up on the display. The user then enters the number into the system they are logging into. The number on the token changes periodically, but the token and the system are always synchronized so the system knows what number the token should be displaying. A smart card is a plastic credit card–like device that contains memory and sometimes a microprocessor. The user inserts the smart card into a reader, and the smart card interacts with the access management system to authenticate the user. Whether a token, smart card, or another kind of type 2 device is used, the data the device produces is used by the access management system to authenticate the user.

Type 3: Something You Are Type 3 authentication factors use something the user is. Passwords (type 1) can be forgotten, and tokens (type 2) can be misplaced, but it's hard to lose your finger. Biometric devices, which read fingerprints, hand geometry, or features of the face or iris, are appealing because the user doesn't have to remember a password or carry a token. Instead, the reader examines part of the user's body to verify who the user is. Biometrics are becoming more reliable and more widespread in use. Nevertheless, biometrics can be susceptible to errors. Biometrics can falsely reject a valid user or falsely accept an unknown user. In situations where reliability is paramount and false positives and false negatives are not acceptable, biometrics should only be used in combination with other authentication factors.

Identity and Access Management

Identity management is a broad term used to describe tools and technologies that organizations use to manage access control. Identity management and access control can be managed using a centralized, decentralized, or hybrid approach as illustrated in Figure 2-3. Each of these administration types is defined and discussed here:

- **Centralized**   Most organizations use a centralized access control administration model where one department or entity is responsible for governing, managing, and configuring tools for access administration. For example, in a centralized model the IT department would manage access control for all resources (e.g., physical and all information systems). All requests for access would go through the IT department, which would manage the access to systems based on approved requests.

- **Decentralized**   In a decentralized access control administration model, access administration is managed by different departments or people for different systems throughout the organization.

- **Hybrid**   The hybrid access control administration model utilizes a combination of centralized and decentralized access control. For example, the IT department may manage access control for critical resources such as Active Directory (centralized administration), while systems belonging to individual departments, such as the sales team customer relationship management (CRM), may be managed by individual departments (decentralized administration).

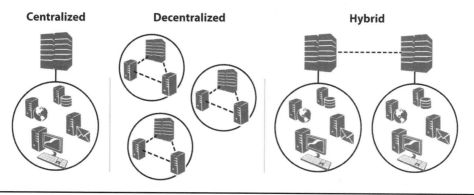

Figure 2-3   Access control administration

Each of the three methods can be implemented and managed effectively; however, success comes down to how well the organization operates. For proper access control administration, speed, accuracy, and accountability are key. When a new employee gets hired, how quickly can they get set up for the access they need? And when they are terminated, how immediately is their access turned off? Many organizations find that centralized management is best, while others claim that decentralized may be faster. However, any of the approaches can be effectively implemented with good planning, documented procedures, well-trained staff, and proper oversight.

Identity and Access Management Lifecycle

Regardless of whether an organization uses centralized, decentralized, or some other method of identity and access management, the operation follows a general lifecycle for the creation and removal of accounts that define a user's accesses. The lifecycle is depicted in Figure 2-4 and described here:

- **Provisioning** Provisioning is the creation and maintenance of user accounts as well as maintaining the correct access rights for the user. For new employees, accounts are set up upon their hire with their initial permissions defining access rights to each system and/or physical area based on their job duties and need to know. Over time a user's access requirements may change. As a result, their accounts may require updating as needed. Management approval is required for both initial account creation and account changes. In addition, care is taken to ensure that permissions and access levels are the minimum required for the user's job (using the principle of least privilege).

- **Review** Accounts are regularly reviewed and monitored to ensure that there is still a need for access over time. This is particularly important for administrator accounts and other privileged accounts with elevated access levels. When employees are transferred to new roles within the organization, their accounts and permissions are reviewed to ensure the level of access is appropriate for their role. *Privilege creep* is a term used to describe when a user gradually accrues more access rights over time beyond what is required for their role. This can occur when accounts are not properly managed or when provisioning procedures are not followed.

- **Revocation** After an employee has separated from the organization or when the employee no longer has a need for an account or access to a system, their access(es) is/are revoked. Organizations develop and follow strict procedures to ensure that when access to a resource is no longer needed, it is turned off. A good practice is for organizations to regularly review accounts and accesses to remove or disable accounts that are no longer needed.

Figure 2-4
Access control and identity management lifecycle

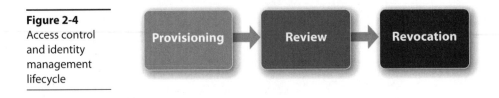

Accountability and Provisioning Example

Upon a routine review of access control logs, a U.S. federal government contractor discovered that a recently terminated employee had logged into one of their systems and had downloaded hundreds of company-proprietary and U.S. government For Official Use Only (FOUO) files. Upon further investigation it was discovered that the company's termination procedures were not followed correctly and the employee's credentials for the system in question were not revoked upon his termination as they should have been. After an internal investigation U.S. federal authorities were contacted and the stolen files were recovered from the terminated employee. In addition, the company's termination procedures were updated to implement a two-person rule to ensure that in the future all credentials for termi-nated employees for all systems would be revoked properly. In this example, routine inspection of access control logs revealed the provisioning error and the security breach, which allowed the company to resolve this security issue.

Privileged Accounts

Privileged accounts are those that have elevated privileges that allow subjects that use those accounts to make impactful changes to the organization's enterprise. Privileged accounts include system administrator accounts and can be used to make changes to systems, configurations, or other users' accounts. Privileged accounts can bypass security controls; bring systems and devices on or offline; and create, delete, or modify user accounts. Here are some examples of privileged accounts:

- **Domain administrator**   Windows Active Directory domain admin accounts can add and delete user accounts and change permissions of existing users.

- **Local administrator**   Individual computers have local administrator accounts that can be used to change configuration settings that are otherwise unavailable to regular users.

- **Superuser**   Linux or other operating systems have superuser (or "root") accounts that can have virtually unlimited privileges and functions. These users can change configuration settings, file settings and permissions, and user access rights.

- **Emergency accounts**   Some organizations have special administrator accounts that are intended to be used in the event of natural disasters or security breaches. These accounts can be used to bypass normal security controls to bring systems and accounts up faster in the event of a crisis situation.

- **Special user accounts**   Organizations may designate key personnel to get special privileges to be able to access highly sensitive systems and/or data. These accounts are usually reserved for key personnel in departments such as legal, human resources (HR), accounting, or other groups that require access to sensitive information.

- **Privileged system accounts**   In addition to privileged user accounts, applications and services use privileged accounts to run processes or programs, access databases, conduct intersystem communications, and even configure network devices or access credentials.

Because privileged accounts have a greater impact on the organization and can cause greater harm than regular accounts, they require greater attention. Best practices for privileged accounts include the following:

- Users who require privileged access should have regular accounts to use for regular access. For instance, system administrators should use administrator accounts for performing administration tasks but should use their regular user accounts to perform regular job functions. In other words, accounts should only be used for their specific purpose.

- Privileged accounts should be subject to stringent monitoring and oversight. For instance, privileged accounts should be reviewed at a greater frequency than regular accounts.

- Automated services and programs should avoid being run using privileged accounts.

- Privileged accounts should be managed separately from regular accounts.

Privileged Access Management

Privileged accounts are high risk due to the impact of their compromise. If a cyber-attacker obtains credentials for a regular account, the attacker can access only the objects available to that account. However, if a cyberattacker were to gain access to a privileged account, the impact to the organization could be much greater. Depending on the nature of the account, the cyberattacker might be able to reconfigure servers or network devices, create new user accounts, remove user accounts, reconfigure or modify databases, and otherwise wreak havoc on the enterprise. Privileged access management (PAM) is a type of access management that focuses on managing privileged accounts, usually using dedicated PAM systems and solutions.

PAM applies the principle of least privilege to decide what types of privileged accounts are absolutely necessary and who needs to have them. Organizations limit the number of privileged accounts to the minimum required to maintain proper operations, security, and recovery in the event of a disaster. Organizations also limit the number of people or subjects that are granted privileged access for the same reasons.

PAM places the management of the privileged accounts in a separate system and stores the credentials required for privileged access to systems in a separate repository. Access to the PAM system requires special credentials and access. The PAM limits what each privileged user can do to only what they need to do, enforcing the principle of least privilege at the administrator or privileged user level. Some systems now employ "just in time" access such that a user is only granted privileged access for a short window of time and then it is automatically revoked when it is no longer needed.

PAM tools and solutions also typically perform monitoring and logging of all PAM activity. This provides a resource for auditing and monitoring for compliance to regulations and other compliance drivers, as well as a tool for investigating security incidents and measuring security effectiveness.

Access Control Fundamentals Summary

To review, here are the important access control fundamental topics you may find on the CC exam:

- Access control concepts to remember are subjects, objects, and rules
- Access control practices you should be familiar with are
  - Authorized versus unauthorized personnel
  - Need to know
  - Principle of least privilege
  - Segregation (or separation) of duties
  - Two-person rule
  - Privileged accounts
  - Password and combinations
- Identity, authentication, authorization, and accountability and how they go together as a functioning process
- Identity and access management, including the different types: centralized, decentralized, and hybrid
- Identity and access management lifecycle, which includes provisioning, review, and revocation
- Privileged access management, which focuses on provisioning and managing privileged accounts

---

Logical Access Controls

In Chapter 1 the three types of security controls were introduced, which include administrative, technical, and physical. Commonly used technical controls include *technical access controls,* also known as *logical access controls.* These are technical settings in hardware and software that control access to computer and network resources (such as a computer, network, mobile device, or application). This is in contrast to physical access controls, which control access to physical resources such as datacenters and other facilities. Examples of logical access controls include

- Entering a username and password to log in to a website
- Using your fingerprint to log into a mobile phone or laptop

- Entering a username and password and a code generated from a mobile phone app to log into your bank's website (multifactor authentication)

Logical access controls are implemented by leveraging a variety of settings and technologies. This section reviews common access control models used to implement logical access rules, common tools and technologies for managing user identities, and some key considerations for monitoring logical access.

Access Control Models

Access control models are approaches to controlling how subjects interact with objects. They are rules that control the level of access and permission that subjects (e.g., users or system processes) have over objects (e.g., computers, systems). These models are implemented using a combination of features in tools and technologies such as operating systems and applications. The models allow organizations to design how access controls are implemented throughout the enterprise. The following are the primary types of access control models that are utilized:

- Discretionary access control (DAC)
- Mandatory access control (MAC)
- Role-based access control (RBAC)

Discretionary Access Control

DAC provides the owner of the resource, typically the creator, full control to configure which subjects (e.g., users, groups) can access the object (e.g., file, folder). This allows the user (object owner) the ability ("discretion") to make decisions such as what permissions other users or groups of users have over the object. The majority of modern operating systems (such as Windows, Linux, Unix, and macOS) implement DAC for their filesystems. DAC is integrated into the operating system and can be applied to individual files as well as entire file directories using access control lists.

An *access control matrix* is a table containing a set of subjects, objects, and permissions. These are used by computer systems in order to implement rules, define access control permissions, and enforce DAC. This is illustrated in Figure 2-5. An access control matrix is made up of access control lists and capabilities lists. An *access control list (ACL)* is depicted as a column in the matrix that shows an object (for example, Excel File 3) and all of the subjects that can access that object as well as their corresponding permissions (e.g., read, write, no access, full control, and so on). A *capabilities list* is represented as a row showing all of the objects a specific subject can access and their corresponding permissions over each object. For example, in Figure 2-5, Steve has Full Control over Excel File 1, No Access to Excel File 2, and Full Control over Excel File 3. This is Steve's capabilities list. While a DAC implementation in a filesystem may leverage an ACL, it is also used for other things such as firewall rules (what types of web traffic are allowed in and out).

	Excel File 1	Excel File 2	Excel File 3
Shon	Read	Read | Write	Read
Steve	Full Control	No Access	Full Control
Mike	Read | Write	No Access	Read
Lisa	Full Control	Full Control	No Access

Capabilities List

Access Control List

Figure 2-5 Example of an access control matrix

Mandatory Access Control

MAC leverages a central authority, typically a security administrator, that regulates access based on security labels, such as the clearance level that a subject (user) has been approved for, as well as the classification of the object (file, database, etc.). The subject's clearance level must be equal to or greater than the classification of the object they are trying to access. In MAC implementation, clearance levels are typically tied to the organization's data classification scheme. Data classification is discussed in greater detail in Chapter 4, but essentially it is a mapping of security requirements (secure handling, transmission, storage, sharing, etc.) to different categories of data. MAC is most commonly associated with government and military systems. There are some specialized operating systems that implement MAC (such as Security-Enhanced Linux developed by the National Security Administration [NSA] and Red Hat).

In DAC, a user who created a resource was considered the "owner" and could control access to that resource. However, in MAC this is not the case, as the user's access is based on their clearance level and the classification of the object (both assigned by the security administrator). So regardless if the user created the object, they must have a clearance level that matches the object classification level. This is illustrated in Figure 2-6.

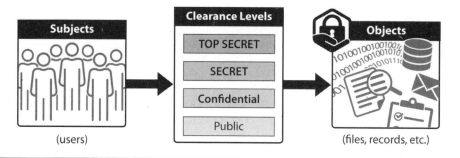

Figure 2-6 Examples of MAC clearance levels

NOTE Modern operating systems like Windows, Linux, and macOS, which are considered traditional DAC-based systems, actually implement some MAC functionality as well. They have different names in each OS; for example, Windows employs User Account Control (UAC), which is a MAC enforcement that isolates processes with different privilege levels. The MAC implementations are often used by the operating system to help mitigate the risk of malware being executed.

Role-Based Access Control

RBAC enforces access based on roles that define permissions and the level of access provided to any subjects assigned to that role. Roles are typically developed for similar users with the same access needs (e.g., HR, Sales, IT, Security). RBAC is beneficial, as it allows the organization to customize the permissions of each role instead of having to grant on-off permissions for each user, which becomes impossible to maintain. RBAC is typically centrally administered through software that allows organizations to build roles with certain privileges and provision users by assigning them to the appropriate roles.

RBAC is implemented through prebuilt roles with permissions designed around certain job functions with the same level of access requirements. Consider Figure 2-7. In this example, a Sales Role, IT Role, Finance Role, and HR Role have been established. Each role has been configured with unique permission sets and levels of access specific to the role. This allows the organization to add new employees in those business units to their corresponding access roles to ensure their level of access is consistent and based on their job responsibilities. Many organizations assign users to multiple roles and may have a general role everyone is assigned to and then more specialized roles for different functions.

Other Access Control Models

DAC, MAC, and RBAC are the commonly used access control models; however, there are other implementations as well. One example is attribute-based access control (ABAC). ABAC is also referred to as policy-based access control or claims-based access control, as it grants permissions based on a variety of attributes such as who is making the request (subject), what resource is being requested (object), environmental conditions (e.g., time of day or location), and what action is being requested (e.g., read, write). This allows access to be granted based on a combination of attributes such as date, time, Internet Protocol (IP) address, and so on.

Identity Management Technologies

Identity management is the process of identifying, authenticating, and authorizing users for access to resources. This is accomplished with a range of technologies, applications software, and solutions that facilitate the implementation of logical access controls.

Figure 2-7   Examples of RBAC roles

This section looks at some of the fundamental tools, technologies, and concepts that support identity management. These include the following:

- Directories
- Single sign-on
- Federated identity management

Directories

Most large organizations leverage some kind of directory service to manage logical access. A *directory service* stores information about users, resources, and access permissions and allows administrators to centrally configure rules to control who gets access to what in the organization's systems and network. The directory provides a means for centrally storing and managing access rules, resource information, and user credentials. The most common example of a directory service is Microsoft's Active Directory (AD).

Single Sign-On

Single sign-on, commonly referred to as SSO, is a technology that allows users to seamlessly access a range of resources after authenticating just one time. For example, let's say an organization has separate systems for e-mail, payroll, and document management. Organizations that don't leverage single sign-on require users to create and remember separate passwords for each system. With single sign-on, a user authenticates with their credentials (e.g., username and password) one time and can access all of these resources (e-mail, payroll, and document management) instead of having a separate password for each system. Single sign-on is often implemented leveraging RBAC to limit the systems that a user can use SSO with. Using the earlier example, an organization might create one standard role for the average user that allows access to e-mail and document management and another role for finance users that allows access to all three (e-mail, document management, and payroll).

Single sign-on can help encourage and promote the use of stronger passwords since users have fewer passwords they need to remember. This can also help IT and administrative staff, as it lessens the number of password reset requests they may receive.

Single sign-on is not without its downsides, though, as it can be a serious security concern because one compromised account can be used to access many resources. To reduce this risk, single sign-on is often combined with another authentication factor (such as a hardware token or mobile phone app that generates a random code) in order to leverage the benefits of good ol' multifactor authentication.

NOTE The implementation of multifactor authentication has been shown to be one of the greatest investments to increase an organization's security posture and reduce the risk of compromise. Each factor increases the work effort required for the cyber criminal to implement an attack, and even if a user is tricked into giving up their password, the attacker still needs the additional authentication factor in order to gain access.

Federated Identity Management

Federated identity management (FIM) is a variant of single sign-on that allows organizations to establish arrangements to utilize the same identification and authentication information to authenticate users across multiple different organizations. An example of this would be logging into your Spotify account with your Facebook account or logging into another third-party website with your Google Gmail account. You have likely seen and even used the "Sign in with Google" button or "Continue with Google" button to sign into a non–Google-related website (illustrated in Figure 2-8). That is FIM in action! FIM is accomplished by leveraging open protocol standards such as Security Assertion Markup Language (SAML) or OpenID Connect (OIDC).

EXAM TIP CC candidates will likely not be tested on specific federated identity management or single sign-on technologies but should be familiar with the concepts.

Monitoring Logical Access

This section is focused on techniques for monitoring logical access to computer systems. The organization should develop policies and procedures for monitoring system access. Following are some common logical access monitoring methods:

- **Account audits** Organizations should develop policies and procedures to ensure that both privileged/administrator and standard user accounts are regularly reviewed to ensure best practices are being implemented (such as need to know, least privilege, and segregation of duties). Organizations often perform annual or quarterly account audits to ensure access and permissions are appropriate. The frequency of the review is dependent on the needs of the organization. Leveraging centralized access control technologies such as directories that implement RBAC aid in making account audits simpler and more feasible.

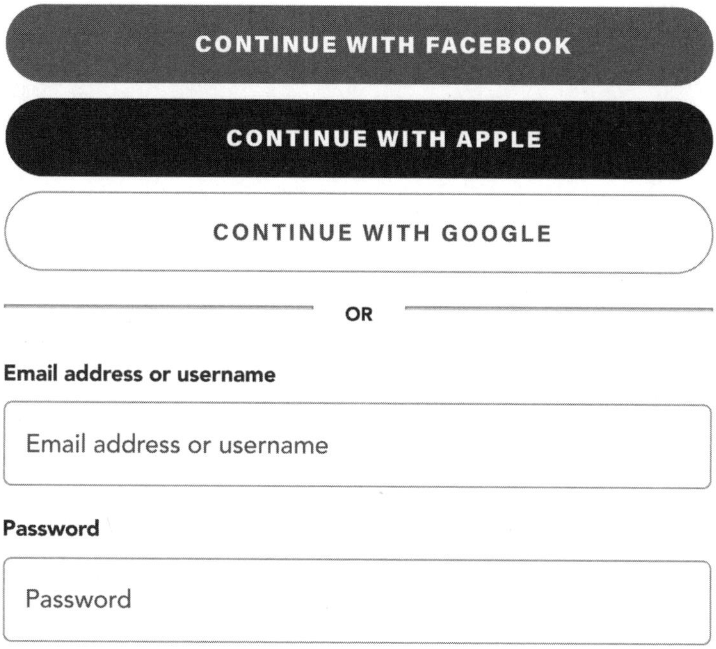

Figure 2-8 Federated identity example

- **Logs**   Logical access logs are chronicles of access events that occur on computers, networks, applications, and other systems (e.g., successful login, logout, failed login events). Organizations should have policies and procedures in place to ensure access logs are regularly reviewed in order to detect unauthorized access or other attacks. Log review may be performed manually (human reviewing the log) or automated leveraging monitoring tools and technologies. Logs are discussed in greater detail in Chapter 4.

- **Monitoring tools and technologies**   Monitoring tools and technologies are often leveraged to provide automated alerting and/or review of access logs and other events. Examples include intrusion detection tools as well as centralized logging and monitoring systems that analyze logs and alert personnel when suspicious activity or patterns are detected. Specific examples of these tools and technologies are discussed in Chapter 3.

> ### Logical Access Control Summary
> Logical access controls are technical measures implemented in hardware or software to control access to computer or network resources. Examples include using a password, fingerprint, or hardware token. Access control models are rules implemented by systems to manage access. These include DAC, MAC, and RBAC, as previously discussed.
>
> Organizations leverage various technologies to help manage user identities and authentication such as directory services, single sign-on, and federated identities.

Physical Access Control

Physical security controls are one of the three types of security controls introduced in Chapter 1 (administrative, technical, and physical). *Physical access controls* are a type of physical security control that regulates and monitors access to physical resources (such as a datacenter facility). The purpose of physical access controls is to prevent and monitor physical attacks such as break-ins, theft, and physical harm. In this section, we look at physical access controls that prevent, control, and monitor physical access to protect people, assets, and facilities.

Preventing and Controlling Physical Access

An important part of managing physical access is having proper controls in place to prevent and control access to facilities. These controls stop physical attacks from occurring by preventing intruders from being able to access key areas. In this section we review examples of the following controls that aid in managing access to physical resources:

- Perimeter and entrance protection
- Facility access
- Environmental design considerations

Perimeter and Entrance Protection

Perimeter and entrance protection measures are used to secure facilities by strategically placing physical barriers to prevent and control access. These are commonly found around the boundary of the facility to serve as the first line of physical defense. Common protection measures to restrict and control physical access include

- Bollards
- Fencing and walls
- Revolving doors and turnstile
- Mantrap

Figure 2-9 Bollards

Bollards *Bollards* are pillars or spheres often made out of concrete, metal, or other hard materials that are typically found outside of buildings between the parking lot and the entrance of the building. Bollards are commonly used to reduce the risk of someone driving a vehicle through the entrance, as the vehicle would be blocked by the bollards. Examples of bollards are included in Figure 2-9.

Fencing and Walls Fencing and walls serve as physical barriers to restrict access to an area. Access is then funneled through approved entry points such as doors and gates. The level of protection provided by these barriers is based on the strength of materials, thickness, size, and construction method utilized. For instance, a three-foot-high fence may deter casual trespassers but can easily be climbed; however, an eight-foot-high fence with barbed wire at the top is a challenge for most people. Most critical areas have fences at least eight feet high.

Revolving Doors and Turnstile Revolving doors and turnstiles are used to control access points by only allowing one person through at a time. A revolving door is something commonly seen in the entrance to a building lobby or some hotels. A turnstile is a mechanical gate with rotating arms that controls access points by only allowing one person through at a time. These are commonly seen when accessing subway stations. Figure 2-10 includes an example of a revolving door on the left and a turnstile on the right.

Mantrap A mantrap is an area that has two locked doors built in such a way that the first door must be closed before the second door can be opened and access to a secure area can be granted. This is illustrated in Figure 2-11. These are typically used in areas that require a higher degree of security (e.g., datacenter) to prevent tailgating

Figure 2-10 Revolving door and turnstile

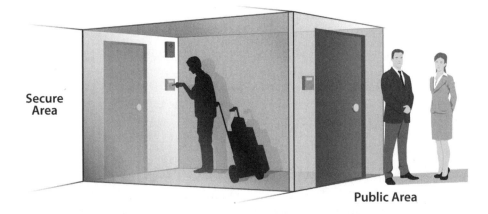

Secure
Area

Public Area

Figure 2-11 Example of a mantrap

and piggybacking (where an unauthorized person follows an authorized person inside). Mantraps may leverage revolving doors or turnstiles.

Human Safety Considerations

The most important thing is protecting the safety of employees and people within the organization. This is a particularly relevant consideration when it comes to physical access control and security. The safety of personnel even trumps security. For example, doors that have automatic locking mechanisms can be configured to fail-secure or fail-safe. *Fail-secure* (also known as fail-closed) means that during a disaster (such as a power outage) the door systems are set to automatically close and lock. *Fail-safe* (also known as fail-open) means that the doors are configured to open and remain unlocked. While a fail-secure implementation is more secure, this approach can potentially trap personnel in a building during a disaster and jeopardize human life. If there are doors that are not used for escape routes or foot traffic, a fail-secure approach may be appropriate; however, in cases where people are involved, a fail-safe approach is a must to ensure the preservation of human life.

Facility Access

In the previous section, we reviewed methods for controlling and preventing access. This section looks at ways to validate the identity of people in order to grant them access to facilities. This includes the following:

- Photo ID and sign-in sheet
- Badge systems
- Biometrics technology

Perimeter and entrance prevention controls are often combined with facility access mechanisms such as using a biometrics system with mantrap doors or using a badge system on a locked door.

MFA and Physical Access

Physical access controls can also be implemented in such a way to provide multifactor authentication (MFA) capability. For instance, MFA could be implemented using a system that requires a person to scan their badge (something you have) and enter a PIN into a keypad (something you know) in order to open a door. Similarly, a system may require a PIN (something you know) and a scan of a fingerprint in a biometric system reader (something you are) in order to access a datacenter. MFA is valuable in increasing the security for both physical and logical access.

Photo ID and Sign-in Sheet   This is likely one of the more common methods of confirming a person's identity in lower-security environments in order to control physical access. This consists of signing a sign-in sheet and confirming your identity by providing some sort of photo ID to a receptionist or security guard, who reviews it and then grants access.

Badge Systems   Badge systems are another common physical access control measure used to provide access to a facility. When leveraging a badge system, authorized personnel are issued a unique badge during enrollment when their identity is confirmed. The details of the badge are stored in a centralized system. Later, when a user swipes their badge, it compares that badge against the data in the central system to determine if access should be provided or not. There are different types of technologies that may be used in badge systems, described next:

- **Barcode**   A barcode is simply a visual representation of data. You will see these on grocery store products that are scanned at the checkout (like a can of soup). Barcodes are effective but generally not secure, as the barcode can be easily copied.

- **Magnetic stripe**   Magnetic stripe cards require the card to be physically swiped into the card reader (similar to a credit card or hotel card). Data is encoded in the dark black magnetic stripe of the card, making them more secure than barcodes; however, magnetic stripe cards can be modified by magnetism.

- **Proximity card**   Proximity cards don't need to directly touch the card reader. They simply need to be near the card reader to grant access. Unlike magnetic stripe cards, proximity cards are not affected by magnetism, and the data on the card cannot as easily be altered.

- **Smart card**   A smart card has a microprocessor in the card and is capable of both storing and processing information. A smart card can store biometric data, cryptographic keys, and other information. Smart cards can require contact with the reader or be contactless depending on the architecture. A smart card may also facilitate the implementation of MFA and require a password or PIN to activate the card.

- **RFID**   RFID stands for radio frequency identification. These cards leverage radio frequency waves instead of a magnetic stripe and can operate from a farther distance than proximity cards. RFID technology can be integrated into smart cards. A common security concern with RFID cards is that the data can be captured as it moves from the card to the card reader wirelessly over the air.

- **Hybrid**   Many of these technologies can be leveraged together. For example, a smart card could leverage RFID technology, and there are also proximity smart cards.

Biometrics Technology   The use of biometrics is one of the three types of authentication factors (something you are). Biometrics are used to identify and authenticate people using their personal attributes or characteristics to allow physical access to facilities. Biometrics confirm people's identities using physiological traits or behavioral characteristics.

- Physiological traits are unique physical attributes of the person such as fingerprints, facial structure, hand geometry, or patterns in the eye. Examples include fingerprint or palm scans, iris scans (the colored portion of the eye surrounding the pupil), and retina scans (the pattern of blood vessels on the back of the eye).

- Behavioral characteristics are characteristics based on the person's behavior such as their computer keystroke patters, pattern of their written signature, or voice print (patterns in voice tone and frequency).

Physiological traits are generally considered more accurate, as behavioral characteristics are more susceptible to forgery. Biometrics are not 100% accurate and in critical applications are commonly used in conjunction with another type of authentication factor (e.g., dual-factor or multifactor authentication).

Environmental Design Considerations

Physical security can often be addressed as part of the environmental design and construction of the facility site and location. One example of this is crime prevention through environmental design (CPTED). CPTED is a design technique focused on preventing crime by leveraging environmental design elements that discourage criminal activity by changing human behavior.

- **Natural access control**   The design of physical access in such a way that it guides people where you want them to go and prevents them from going where you don't want them to go, leveraging sidewalks, bollards, trees and shrubs, fences, and lighting.

- **Natural surveillance**   The placement of environmental features such as walkways, lighting, and so on can provide the ability to easily see people who are near the entrances and exits of buildings and facilities.

- **Territorial reinforcement**   The design of the building exterior to provide visual cues that help distinguish public and private areas. This can be accomplished by making public areas more welcoming and obvious and private areas designed to be more restrictive. For example, the design and appearance of a loading dock often conveys to people to stay away from that area if they aren't involved in loading or unloading.

Monitoring Physical Access

Physical access to facilities should be appropriately monitored. This is important in order to be able to detect physical threats as well as investigate past activity leading up to an incident. The following are some examples of detective controls used to monitor physical access:

- Security guards
- Physical access logs
- Security cameras
- Monitoring and alarm systems

Security Guards

The use of human security guards is one way to monitor physical access. Guards are often used to monitor premises as well as checking in guests or visitors by having them sign a visitor sign-in sheet and confirming their identity by reviewing their photo ID. Security guards can offer additional value, as they provide more than just detective (monitoring) capability. They can also serve to deter an intruder from performing an attack (such as a break-in, theft, or vandalism) and can delay an intruder by physically challenging them and providing an additional obstacle they must circumvent. This can help prevent the attack from occurring. Similar to human security guards, guard dogs can also perform detective functions and be a valuable part of physical security monitoring.

Physical Access Logs

Physical access should be audited and monitored through the review of physical access logs. *Physical access logs* are chronicles of events of personnel access records. These may range from sign-in sheets to software with auditing features that produce a trail of all individuals who attempted to access a room or facility using the physical access system (such as a badge reader). Physical access logs are important detective controls to maintain a record of physical access and can be used as part of an investigation to understand the events leading up to unauthorized access or an intrusion incident. It is a best practice for organizations to have a policy and procedure for regularly reviewing physical access logs and ensuring that those who have access still have a need for that access (to ensure least privilege, need to know, etc.).

Security Cameras

Security cameras can be used to take pictures of events for later viewing or to record events in real-time leveraging closed-circuit TV (CCTV) or Internet-connected cameras. These can be viewed by security guards in real time (allowing them to monitor many different areas) or simply record to capture events for later review during an investigation. Security cameras can either be hidden so attackers don't know they are being recorded or mounted in full view so attackers know they are there and potentially deter or discourage their activity. Having cameras in view can also make the area feel safer (remember CPTED). It is important that security cameras are tamper-resistant and out of reach to preserve their integrity.

Monitoring and Alarm Systems

Physical access is often monitored with additional detective controls such as monitoring and alarm systems. A physical monitoring and alarm system uses sensors that report back to a central system to alert the organization that an event has occurred and needs to be investigated. These are often referred to as physical intrusion detection systems. Systems include lasers that detect movement (think *Mission Impossible*), pressure plates, motion detectors, sensors on windows or doors that alert if they are open or broken, or other sensors that detect noise levels or heat. These systems may also be configured to deter attackers, such as a motion detector that turns on a floodlight when movement is detected.

Physical Access Control Summary

Physical access controls are steps taken to manage access to physical facilities such as datacenters or office buildings. Physical access can be prevented with bollards, fencing and walls, revolving doors and turnstiles, mantraps, and environmental design techniques. Access to facilities can be controlled using measures such as photo ID and sign-in sheets, badge systems, or biometrics. Physical access may be monitored leveraging security guards, physical access logs, cameras, and monitoring and alarm systems.

Chapter Review

Access controls are the means by which organizations ensure that only those people or entities that are authorized can access an organization's assets. Access controls can be physical or logical (technical). Access control systems are used to apply the concepts of least privilege and need to know within the organization, ensuring subjects are granted the access they require to do their jobs but no more than that. Access management systems use identification and authentication mechanisms and technologies to ensure that access is given to subjects whose identity is verified and access is correctly authorized. For subjects who require access that may carry with it the power to cause major system and resource changes and the potential to do harm, privileged access management processes and tools provide proper provisioning and accountability of those accounts.

Technical (or logical) access controls protect access to computers, network devices, applications, and other systems. Access rules and decisions are supported by the implementation of access control models such as DAC, MAC, and RBAC. DAC is implemented in most modern operating systems and allows the owner (typically the creator) of a resource to configure access rules. MAC is regulated based on the use of security labels assigned to subjects and objects by a central authority (security administrator). MAC is most commonly used in government systems. RBAC leverages roles with specific privileges, where users with similar access needs are assigned to the same role. Organizations leverage technologies to support identity management such as directory services, single sign-on, and federated identity. Logical access is monitored by performing account audits, conducting log reviews, and leveraging automated tools and technologies.

Physical access controls regulate access to physical resources such as buildings, datacenters, or other facilities. Access can be controlled through the use of protection measures such as bollards, fences, walls, doors, and mantraps. Physical access is typically managed using measures that allow the organization to identify authorized parties that should be allowed access through the use of biometrics, badge systems, or other identification (such as a license and sign-in sheet). Access can be monitored through the use of security guards, cameras, alarms, and physical access logs.

Quick Review

- Access controls are security features that permit or restrict access to areas within a physical or logical environment.
- A subject is an entity that is capable of accessing an object.
- An object is an entity that is accessed by a subject.
- Access is the right granted to a subject to perform a function with an object based on rules.

- Authorized personnel are those who are registered and have permissions authorizing access to a specific resource. Unauthorized personnel do not have such permissions.

- Access to a resource should be based on a user's need to know, which means it is required in order to perform a business function.

- The principle of least privilege is the concept that a user should only have access to the resources that they need in order to do their job but no more.

- Segregation or separation of duties means that duties are assigned such that one employee does not have enough privileges that they could misuse the system or cause an error on their own.

- The two-person rule requires certain functions to be performed by two authorized users or employees working in tandem.

- Privileged accounts are those that have elevated privileges that allow subjects who use those accounts to make impactful changes to the organization's enterprise.

- Passwords and combinations are secrets used to authenticate a user to a system or a physical device. Their use requires good practices including regular rotation, proper strength, secure and reliable storage, and a policy that governs their use.

- Identification and authentication information used together are called credentials.

- Identification is the act of the subject providing identifying information such as a username or ID.

- Authentication is the second step of the credential, which uses a secret such as a password or biometric data.

- Authorization takes place when the subject's credentials match the information in the access management system that the subject is who they claim to be.

- Accountability is accomplished using logs of access control events.

- There are three types of authentication factors:
  - Type 1: something you know (such as a password)
  - Type 2: something you have (such as a token or smart card)
  - Type 3: something you are (such as a biometric fingerprint, hand, or iris reader)

- Identity management is a broad term used to describe tools and technologies that organizations use to manage access control. Management can be implemented in a centralized or decentralized fashion or with a hybrid approach.

- The identity management lifecycle includes provisioning, review, and revocation.

- PAM is a type of access management that focuses on managing privileged accounts, usually using dedicated PAM systems and solutions.

- Logical access controls protect access to computer systems and applications.

- Logical access controls are also known as technical access controls.
- Logical access rules are implemented using access control models:
  - DAC provides the owner of the resource control to configure which subjects can access the object. Modern operating systems (such as Windows, Linux, Unix, and macOS) implement DAC for their filesystems.
  - MAC leverages a central authority that regulates access based on security labels, such as the clearance level that a subject has been approved for, as well as the classification of the object. MAC is most commonly associated with government and military systems.
  - RBAC enforces access based on roles that define permissions and the level of access provided to any subjects assigned to that role. Roles are typically developed for similar users with the same access needs (e.g., HR, Sales, IT, Security).
- An access control matrix is a table containing a set of subjects, objects, and permissions. These are used by systems to implement rules, define access control permissions, and enforce DAC. An ACL is a column in the matrix that shows an object and all subjects that can access that object as well as their corresponding permissions. A capabilities list is represented as a row showing all the objects a specific subject can access and their corresponding permissions over each object.
- Physical access controls protect access to buildings and facilities.
- Bollards are pillars or spheres made out of hard materials often placed outside building entrances to prevent vehicles from driving through the entrance.
- A mantrap is an area that has two doors built in such a way that the first door must be closed before the second door can be opened.
- Physical access to facilities is often controlled using badge access systems, biometrics, or photo ID and sign-in sheets.
- Physical access is monitored using security guards, cameras, alarms, monitors, and physical access logs.

Questions

1. Jane is a security administrator setting up access for a new employee who works in the manufacturing department. Jane makes sure to enable the employee's access for the manufacturing area but not for the parts storage area. What best describes the principle Jane is applying?

   A. Principle of authentication

   B. Two-person rule

   C. Need to know

   D. Least privilege

2. Which statement best describes the relationship between subjects, objects, and rules?

   A. A subject grants access to an object based on rules.

   B. An object is granted access to a subject based on rules.

   C. A subject is granted access to an object based on rules.

   D. An object is granted access to a subject based on credentials.

3. Credentials are composed of which of the following elements?

   A. Username and password

   B. Authorization and accountability

   C. Something you know and something you have

   D. Subjects and objects

4. Joe has to log in to many systems on a daily basis and has too many passwords to remember. What is the best way for Joe to manage his passwords?

   A. Write the passwords down on a piece of paper.

   B. Store the passwords in a text file and store it in a safe place.

   C. Use the same password for every system so he only has to remember one password.

   D. Use a password manager or password vault software.

5. Debby has been an employee of Acme Corp. for over 20 years. During that time, she has been able to access more and more systems. Now she has access to systems she doesn't even need access to in order to do her job. This is an example of what type of situation?

   A. Privilege modification

   B. Access management

   C. Privileged access management

   D. Privilege creep

6. The identity and access management lifecycle consists of which steps?

   A. Provisioning, review, revocation

   B. Setup, review, auditing

   C. Creation, monitoring, termination

   D. Identification, authentication, authorization

7. Which of the following access control models leverages roles to provision access, where users with similar access needs are assigned to the same role?

   A. DAC

   B. MAC

   C. RBAC

   D. None of the above

8. An organization is concerned about the risk of a car driving from the parking lot through the entrance of the building. Which of the following security measures would best help address this concern?

   A. Biometrics

   B. RBAC

   C. Badge system

   D. Bollards

9. The security team is reviewing the configuration of the door that serves as the only entrance or exit to the datacenter. Organization personnel commonly access the datacenter to perform their work. In the event of a fire that impacts power to the door-locking mechanism, which of the following configurations is best?

   A. The door should always remain locked.

   B. The door should fail-secure.

   C. The door should fail-open.

   D. The door should automatically lock when there is no power.

10. The security team of an organization is concerned about the physical security of datacenter access. They want the datacenter entrance built in such a way that there are two doors with locks and the first door must close before the next door can be unlocked. Which of the following is this an example of?

    A. Bollard

    B. Mantrap

    C. Fence

    D. Biometric lock

11. Which of the following access control models allows the creator of a resource the ability to assign permissions to other users?

    A. DAC

    B. MAC

    C. RBAC

    D. None of the above

Questions and Answers

1. Jane is a security administrator setting up access for a new employee who works in the manufacturing department. Jane makes sure to enable the employee's access for the manufacturing area but not for the parts storage area. What best describes the principle Jane is applying?

    A. Principle of authentication

    B. Two-person rule

    C. Need to know

    D. Least privilege

    D. Least privilege is the most correct answer. By giving the employee access to the area the employee requires access to but no more, Jane is applying the principle of least privilege.

2. Which statement best describes the relationship between subjects, objects, and rules?

    A. A subject grants access to an object based on rules.

    B. An object is granted access to a subject based on rules.

    C. A subject is granted access to an object based on rules.

    D. An object is granted access to a subject based on credentials.

    C. After first requesting access, a subject gets access to an object based on rules.

3. Credentials are composed of which of the following elements?

    A. Username and password

    B. Authorization and accountability

    C. Something you know and something you have

    D. Subjects and objects

    A. Identification (commonly a username, ID, or account number) and authentication (commonly a password, PIN, or token) are typically used in combination and are called credentials.

4. Joe has to log in to many systems on a daily basis and has too many passwords to remember. What is the best way for Joe to manage his passwords?

    A. Write the passwords down on a piece of paper.

    B. Store the passwords in a text file and store it in a safe place.

C. Use the same password for every system so he only has to remember one password.

D. Use a password manager or password vault software.

D. The best answer is to use a password manager or password vault software to manage passwords. These products require credentials to log in and protect the passwords with encryption and good access control. None of the other answers provide a secure solution.

5. Debby has been an employee of Acme Corp. for over 20 years. During that time, she has been able to access more and more systems. Now she has access to systems she doesn't even need access to in order to do her job. This is an example of what type of situation?

   A. Privilege modification

   B. Access management

   C. Privileged access management

   D. Privilege creep

   D. The situation described is an example of privilege creep, where over time a person's access increases beyond that which they require to do their job.

6. The identity and access management lifecycle consists of which steps?

   A. Provisioning, review, revocation

   B. Setup, review, auditing

   C. Creation, monitoring, termination

   D. Identification, authentication, authorization

   A. The identity and access management lifecycle consists of provisioning, review, and revocation steps.

7. Which of the following access control models leverages roles to provision access, where users with similar access needs are assigned to the same role?

   A. DAC

   B. MAC

   C. RBAC

   D. None of the above

   C. Role-based access control (RBAC) enforces access based on roles that define permissions and the level of access provided to any user assigned to that role. Roles are typically developed for similar users with the same access needs (e.g., HR, Sales, IT, Security).

8. An organization is concerned about the risk of a car driving from the parking lot through the entrance of the building. Which of the following security measures would best help address this concern?

   A. Biometrics

   B. RBAC

   C. Badge system

   D. Bollards

   D. Bollards are pillars or spheres made out of hard material used to prevent vehicles from driving through entrances. Biometrics and badge systems are measures to implement physical access control but would not prevent a car from driving through the entrance. RBAC is an access control model.

9. The security team is reviewing the configuration of the door that serves as the only entrance or exit to the datacenter. Organization personnel commonly access the datacenter to perform their work. In the event of a fire that impacts power to the door-locking mechanism, which of the following configurations is best?

   A. The door should always remain locked.

   B. The door should fail-secure.

   C. The door should fail-open.

   D. The door should automatically lock when there is no power.

   C. The door should fail-open (also known as fail-safe). While this is a less secure option, it ensures the preservation of human life, which is the number-one priority.

10. The security team of an organization is concerned about the physical security of datacenter access. They want the datacenter entrance built in such a way that there are two doors with locks and the first door must close before the next door can be unlocked. Which of the following is this an example of?

    A. Bollard

    B. Mantrap

    C. Fence

    D. Biometric lock

    B. A mantrap is an area that has two doors built in such a way that the first door must be closed before the second door can be opened.

11. Which of the following access control models allows the creator of a resource the ability to assign permissions to other users?

   A. DAC

   B. MAC

   C. RBAC

   D. None of the above

   A. Discretionary access control (DAC) provides the owner of the resource, typically the creator, full control to configure which users can access the resource.

Network Security

This chapter discusses the following topics:
- Network fundamentals
- Network threats and attacks
- Network defenses
- Network infrastructure

This chapter covers the Certified in Cybersecurity Domain 4. It starts with an overview of networking fundamentals, explaining key terminology, network devices, protocols, networking models, and how traffic moves around in a modern network. The next section provides a broad view of cyberattacks, not just network-based attacks, but many attacks an organization may face. We follow with coverage of aspects of network defenses, as (ISC)² splits network defense topics between Domains 4 and Domain 5, which we cover in Chapter 4. We finish this chapter with a discussion of how modern networks are typically implemented, describing both in-house and cloud implementations.

Network Fundamentals

Computer networks are the infrastructure that allows computers to talk to one another. They consist of hardware, software, and technologies used to allow devices and systems to communicate. In order to properly secure a network, it is important to have a fundamental understanding of how networks operate. In this section we review the following topics:

- Network types
- Wired and wireless networks
- System addresses
- Network devices and terminology
- Networking in action
- Protocols

- Ports
- OSI model
- TCP/IP
- IP addressing

Network Types

Modern computer networking occurs over two fundamental types of computer networks: local and wide area networks.

- **Local area network (LAN)**   A LAN is a computer network that covers a limited geographic area such as a home, office building, or an organization's datacenter. A LAN enables network communication between computing devices within those facilities. LANs are typically owned and operated by a single entity such as an individual home office network or an organization's enterprise network. LANs can be wired or wireless. Wireless LANs are referred to as WLANs.
- **Wide area network (WAN)**   A WAN enables communication between many remote LANs and covers a wide geographic area. WANs are networks linked together by infrastructure managed and owned by third-party telecommunication service providers.

Wired and Wireless Networks

Computer networks can be wired (devices are connected via physical cables) or wireless (leveraging wireless technologies). Historically, network communication only occurred over physical, wired connections. Every computer or system on a LAN had to, at some point, be physically connected to another system in order to communicate. *Ethernet* is a family of standards for how physical network connections are made in LANs and WANs. Ethernet is defined in the *Institute of Electrical and Electronics Engineers (IEEE) 802.3* family of standards.

Wireless technologies allow computers and other devices to communicate with other devices wirelessly using radio frequencies. One common term most have heard at some point is Wi-Fi. *Wi-Fi* is a family of wireless network protocols used for wireless communication. The most common standard is the *IEEE 802.11* family of standards, which defines the standard for wireless Ethernet. The 802.11 standards are what allow the use of wireless technology within local area networks. This is referred to as a WLAN. A common example of this is connecting to a wireless router on your home network or a wireless access point to connect to an organization's wireless network. Depending on the architecture of the network, Wi-Fi devices can connect to the Internet via a WLAN and a wireless access point. Wireless networks use a *service set identifier (SSID)* as the name of a network. The SSID allows devices to connect to and be part of the same wireless network.

System Addresses

Computers and other network-connected systems and devices have special addresses used as labels to identify them on the network and the Internet. This helps ensure network traffic is delivered to the appropriate destination, similar to how the address of a house is used for mail delivery. The two key addresses are the MAC address (also known as the physical address) and IP address (also known as the logical address) described here:

- **Media access control (MAC)**   MAC addresses are like unique serial numbers assigned to the network interface of computing devices. MAC addresses are used to uniquely identify devices on the same LAN. The MAC address is often referred to as a physical address or hardware address since it is assigned to the device's physical network interface hardware. MAC addresses must be unique to prevent conflicts on a network. They are 48-bit addresses made up of 12 hexadecimal digits. The first half of the address indicates the manufacturer of the network interface hardware as a manufacturer ID, while the last half is the device identifier. An example of a MAC address structure is 67:FC:50:B3:FC:41. MAC addresses are used at the Data Link Layer (Layer 2) of the OSI model (more on OSI later in this chapter).

- **Internet Protocol (IP)**   IP addresses are used for identifying devices for the purpose of routing traffic on a LAN or over WANs such as the Internet. An IP address is referred to as a logical address or software address, as it is a virtual address that is not hardcoded into the hardware like a MAC. IP addresses are assigned either statically, where they are manually configured on the device by a network administrator, or dynamically, where they are automatically assigned from a pool of IP addresses using the Dynamic Host Configuration Protocol (DHCP). In addition, IP addresses can be public (meaning they can be routed over the Internet) or private (meaning they can only be used on internal networks such as a LAN). An example of an IP address is 192.168.1.1 (for a private IPv4 address). IP addresses are assigned at the Network Layer (Layer 3) of the OSI model. More on IP addresses and OSI model later in this chapter.

 NOTE   A bit is the smallest unit of information consisting of a binary 1 or 0. A byte is a collection of 8 bits.

Network Devices and Terminology

Networks are made up of various devices, with different functions and purposes used to enable communication. In this section, we review some common network devices found on enterprise networks as well as general terminology used in the industry. This includes the following list:

- Switch
- Router

- Network interface
- Security appliance
- Client and server
- Wireless access point
- Endpoint
- Internet of Things
- Hub

Switch

A *switch* is a device that is used to physically segment parts of the network. A switch has many physical ports used to connect to other devices and parts of the network. Unlike a hub, a switch has some intelligence and forwards traffic based on MAC addresses through the appropriate port. The switch is able to determine the devices that are connected to it and forwards the traffic to the correct port. When traffic comes to a switch, the switch forwards the traffic directly to the destination network or computer through the specific port it is connected to (unlike a hub, which broadcasts to all connected devices). There are many different types of switches, and newer switches can even perform functions similar to a router. In addition, certain switch technology allows organizations to logically segment their networks using virtual local area networks (VLANs). VLANs are discussed in greater depth later in this chapter.

Router

A *router* is an intelligent network device that controls and routes data between network segments. The router maintains a routing table that lists various routes to different devices and parts of the network based on the destination IP address of the traffic. There are many different types of routers. For example, the router you use in your home is not the same as the router used in a datacenter (although they perform a similar function).

The typical modern home router serves as both a modem and a router. The *modem* connects a home network to an Internet service provider (ISP), while the router performs network address translation, or NAT (discussed later in this chapter), to route traffic to and from the public Internet. While these are different devices (and historically you had both on a home network), in modern times these are combined into one device that has both modem and router functionality. Home routers often have other capabilities to enforce certain security policies or firewall rules. A typical enterprise router used by large businesses and organizations is designed to be able to handle more devices and larger amounts of network traffic and provides greater speed compared to a home router.

Network Interface

A *network interface* is a physical piece of hardware integrated into computing devices to allow them to connect to a computer network (typically a LAN). This is sometimes a network interface card (NIC), and other times the network interface is integrated into other pieces of the device hardware. The network interface is what allows wired or wireless communication depending on the specifics of the interface. For example, if you have ever plugged an Ethernet cable into a desktop computer, you are plugging the cable into a port on the NIC to allow for network access.

Security Appliance

The term *security appliance* is a general term used to describe a network device that performs some kind of security function. The most well-known security appliance is the firewall. A *firewall* is a network device used to enforce certain security rules that govern how traffic may flow, such as allowing certain types of traffic and denying other types of traffic. Other types of security appliances include an intrusion detection system (IDS) or intrusion prevention system (IPS). Network security appliances are discussed later in the "Network Defenses" section of this chapter.

Client/Server

Server is a general term used to describe a computer that serves content or provides a service to another computer on the network. An example may be a web server (serving up a web page), database server (providing database storage), file server (storing files on a file share), etc. Computers that interact with a server by initiating a connection are known as *clients.*

The terms client and server represent both the function a network device performs and a model for distributing computational workloads. This is known as the client-server model. The *client-server model* is an architectural model for how computers serve up resources. The computer requesting the service or resource is known as the client, and the computer serving up the resource is referred to as the server. This is illustrated in Figure 3-1, where the client sends a request to the server and the server responds with the resource in question (such as a web page).

Wireless Access Point

A *wireless access point (AP)* is a device that allows wireless-capable devices to wirelessly connect to a network. These are often used in enterprise networks for connecting wireless devices to the organization's LAN. In order to be wireless capable, a device must have a network interface that supports wireless.

Endpoint

Endpoint is a general term used to describe a computing device on a network (such as a laptop, desktop, mobile device, smartphone, tablet, or even a server). When one of these

Figure 3-1
Example of a client-server communication flow

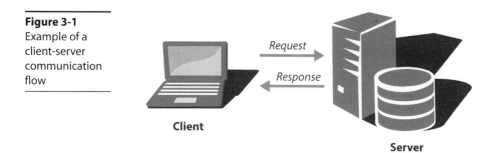

Client

Server

devices is interacting with a server, it is often referred to as a *client*. Endpoints also include things like Internet of Things (IoT) devices.

Internet of Things

Internet of Things (IoT) is a general term that is loosely used to describe devices that historically did not connect to the Internet (or a network) that now have network connectivity. These include certain sensors, wearable technology, or other "smart" devices. The term "smart" is often used when describing an IoT device such as a smart watch, smart speaker, or smart appliances. This also includes systems used for manufacturing, robots, and other infrastructure. Even some refrigerators these days have IP addresses and Internet connectivity!

Hub

A *hub* is a network device that is used to physically connect many systems and devices to the network using a wired connection. Hubs have physical ports whereby devices connect to the hub using network cables. Hubs do not have any intelligence in them to make decisions about how the traffic is routed or forwarded. Traffic comes in on one physical port and is transmitted out all physical ports on the hub to all connected devices. A *repeater* is another device that performs essentially the same function as a hub but has fewer physical ports. Due to this, a hub is sometimes referred to as a multiport repeater.

NOTE Hubs are no longer commonly found in modern enterprise networks.

Networking in Action

Now that we have gone over the different types of networks, system addresses, and common devices, let's look at how some of these devices work together. Figure 3-2 has an example of a typical home network. You likely have devices such as laptops, desktops, mobile phones, and potentially other IoT devices (e.g., home cameras or security systems).

Figure 3-2
Home network
example

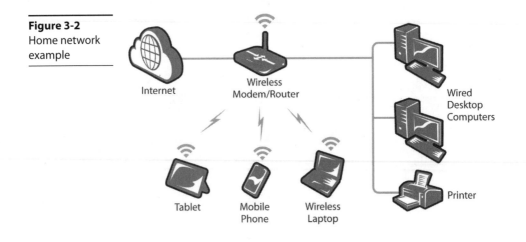

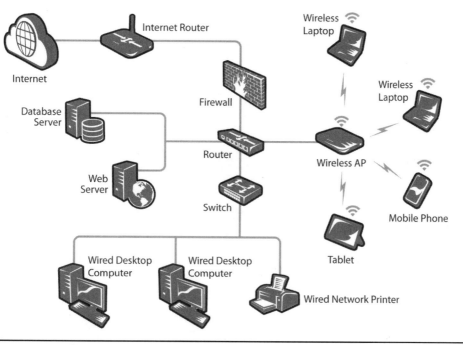

Figure 3-3   Small organization network example

These devices connect to your home network wirelessly or wired (physically plugged into the home router/modem). Devices on a home network are typically dynamically assigned private IP addresses by the home router using DHCP, often 192.168.x.x (more on DHCP and private IP addresses later in this chapter). When one of these computers needs to interact with a computer on the Internet, the home router routes that traffic and translates that private IP to a public IP assigned to the home router by the ISP.

Now let's look at a more complex network such as one found in a small organization. This is illustrated in Figure 3-3. There are many more network devices including a firewall, network switch, and routers (whereas in the home network, we only had a wireless modem/router). This network also has many more computers and devices and leverages more segmentation in its design (the wireless network is segmented from the wired desktop network, and servers are segmented from the rest of the network). The internal router sits behind the firewall and routes the traffic to the various parts of the network, and the switch is used to connect the wired desktop computers to the network.

A typical corporate network is going to be much larger and more complex than the ones previously shown. There are more switches, routers, firewalls, security appliances, network segments with various devices, and so on. The specific design varies based on the

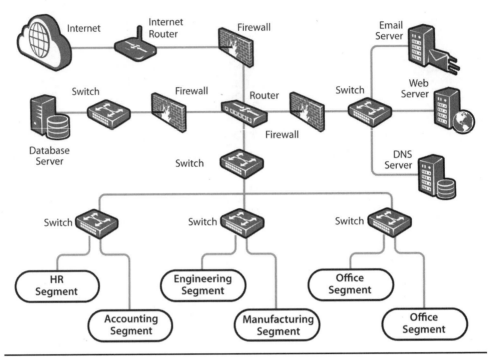

Figure 3-4 Corporate network example

size and needs of the organization. Figure 3-4 is an example of a larger network leveraging more firewalls, switches, and a segmented design to organize different areas of the network (e.g., office segment, engineering segment, accounting segment, and so on).

Protocols

Protocols are rules and standards for network communication. You can think of a protocol as a specific language that two applications use to speak to one another to ensure "Application A" can appropriately communicate with "Application B." For example, if one person is speaking French and the other person is speaking Russian, they are probably going to have a hard time communicating. This is where protocols come in to ensure a consistent standard or language is utilized. Most modern networks use protocols that are part of the Transmission Control Protocol/Internet Protocol (TCP/IP) protocols suite. Examples include network communication protocols such as the Hypertext Transfer Protocol (HTTP), which allows a web browser application and a web server service to communicate.

 NOTE We discuss the TCP/IP protocol suite in more depth later in this chapter. This section is simply to help introduce the protocol terminology.

Secure Protocols

When transmitting data across a network (and particularly across the Internet), the security of that data is a key concern. A savvy attacker with the appropriate tools and skillset can listen in and inspect network traffic as it is being sent across a network. If sensitive or confidential information is being transferred, the attacker can potentially inspect and steal that information. This is why it is essential to consider how *data in transit* (data moving from one computer to another) is protected. Data is protected in transit through the use of encryption (where plaintext/cleartext information becomes encrypted/ciphertext) by leveraging secure protocols. Protocols that encrypt data as it traverses the network are often referred to as *secure protocols* since they prevent an attacker from intercepting the plaintext information. The attacker may still be able to intercept the network traffic, but all they will see is encrypted gibberish. The two most commonly used secure protocols are

- Secure Socket Layer/Transport Layer Security (SSL/TLS)
- Secure Shell (SSH)

Protocols that send data across the network in plaintext (which means anyone can read it) are sometimes referred to as *nonsecure protocols*. HTTP is an example of an nonsecure protocol. For example, if you are logging into a website with your username and password and the website is using HTTP, your username and password will be sent in plaintext across the network (and Internet) to the web server! This means an attacker can potentially intercept that communication and steal your credentials.

SSL/TLS is often used with protocols, such as HTTP, to help secure, encrypt, and protect the integrity of communication to help prevent manipulation, eavesdropping, man-in-the-middle, and spoofing attacks. When HTTP uses SSL/TLS, it is referred to as Hypertext Transfer Protocol Secure (HTTPS). When you visit a properly configured website that is using HTTPS, the information you enter (such as the username and password) is encrypted as it is transmitted to the web server. We discuss data security and encryption in more depth in Chapter 4. For now, just remember that some protocols are considered "secure" since they transmit the data in an encrypted format and others are considered "nonsecure" since the data is not encrypted.

NOTE   CC candidates should understand the difference between secure and nonsecure protocols.

Ports

The term port can have different meanings. There are both physical and logical ports, similar to how we have both physical addresses (MAC address) and logical addresses (IP address), as discussed previously.

Physical Port

A *physical port* is a physical slot on a computer or network device that another device or cable can be plugged into. An example is an Ethernet port, which is used for LAN network communication (on a computer, router, switch, or other network device) or a USB port used for transferring data from a computer to a USB drive (or vice versa) or connecting a wired keyboard, mouse, or printer.

Logical Port

A *logical port* is a numerical identifier that is mapped to a particular protocol to tell a receiving computer what service is trying to be used. A port is similar to a phone extension, with the port being the extension number and the IP address being the phone number. For example, let's say a computer is functioning as both a web server and a file transfer server. When a client wants to interact with the web server or the file transfer server, the client needs a way to tell the server which service they want to use. This is done using ports to allow a single IP to receive different communication requests. The client calls the server using its IP address and dials the extension, which is the port. One port number is assigned to the web server service, and another port number is assigned to the file transfer service. The combination of a port and IP address is commonly referred to as a *socket*. Ports are grouped into the following ranges:

- **Well-known ports (0–1023)**   Several well-known ports are generally used for specific protocols that are part of the TCP/IP suite of protocols, such as HTTP (80), HTTPS (443), DNS (53), SMTP (25), and more (we discuss the TCP/IP suite more in the sections to follow). These mappings are set by the Internet Assigned Numbers Authority (IANA). These well-known ports range from 0 to 1023. Note that while these standard ports are commonly used for specific services, any service can run on any port. Port numbers associated with secure protocols (such as HTTPS on port 443) are often called *secure ports,* while port numbers assigned to nonsecure protocols (such as HTTP on port 80) are often called *nonsecure ports*.

- **Registered ports (1024–49151)**   Registered ports range from 1024 to 49151. These are ports that can be registered with IANA for a specific purpose. Vendors sometimes register a port for their proprietary software.

- **Dynamic/private ports (49152–65535)**   Dynamic/private ports range from 49152 to 65535. These are ports are not assigned by IANA and are used by applications as needed for customer services or ephemeral ports. Ephemeral ports are only used for a brief period of time as part of a communication session. For example, when you visit a website that is running on a web server using HTTP over port 80, an ephemeral port is allocated on your computer as the source port for the communication so that the web server knows where to reply.

 NOTE   IANA maintains a list of port numbers and their corresponding protocols here: https://www.iana.org/assignments/service-names-port-numbers/service-names-port-numbers.xhtml

OSI Model

The computer industry uses conceptual models to represent the various functions of a network. Models are used by product vendors to provide a common way of representing how network communications work, how the various devices interact, and how data is formatted when transferred from one computer to another. They break down the network into conceptual layers that make up what is commonly referred to as the network stack. The two most common models are the OSI model (discussed in this section) and the TCP/IP model (discussed in the following section). The *Open Systems Interconnection (OSI) model* is a conceptual framework that describes the functionality at each layer of a computer network. The OSI model is made up of seven layers, as illustrated in Figure 3-5.

Layers 5 to 7 (Session, Presentation, and Application) are referred to as the *upper layers*. These layers are implemented with protocols used by software applications that run on the network and interact with users. Layers 1 to 4 (Physical, Data Link, Network, and Transport) are referred to as the lower layers. These layers are more concerned with the lower-level details of how information is formatted, routed, and transmitted over the network. In the following sections, we walk through each layer of the OSI model, starting with the uppermost layer, and briefly describe the function of each.

 EXAM TIP   To remember the order and names of the layers of the OSI model, it is often helpful to come up with a mnemonic phrase such as "**A**ll **P**eople **S**eem **T**o **N**eed **D**ata **P**rocessing," with each word in the phrase starting with the corresponding first letter of the OSI model (from the top layer, Application, to the bottom layer, Physical) or vice versa, from bottom to top, using a phase such as "**P**lease **D**o **N**ot **T**hrow **S**ausage **P**izza **A**way."

Figure 3-5
OSI model layers

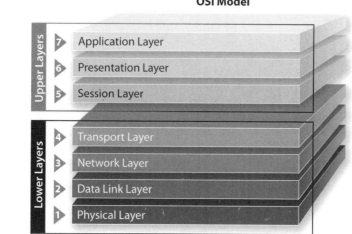

OSI Model

Encapsulation and De-encapsulation

One of the purposes of the model is to illustrate how a message or packet gets constructed and interpreted by software, using the model's protocols. When an application on a computer wants to communicate with another application on another computer, it starts building a message. Each layer of the model has its own place within the message. Layer 1 is really just the hardware layer. Layer 2 contains the part of the message that establishes the connection with the network. Layer 3 contains the part that establishes where in the network the message is supposed to go, etc. Each layer has a function that is implemented within the packet. The operation of creating the packets is called *encapsulation,* and the process of reading from the message or packet is called *de-encapsulation.*

Each layer of the network stack adds its own unique information (known as a data unit) to the message being transmitted as it travels down the network stack from the sending computer. As a result, the message grows as each layer packages up the message and adds its own information as it travels down each layer of the network stack. Similarly, as the data works its way back up the stack to the receiving computer, this process is reversed, and each layer reads each piece of information. This is known as *de-encapsulation.* The process of encapsulation and de-encapsulation is illustrated here.

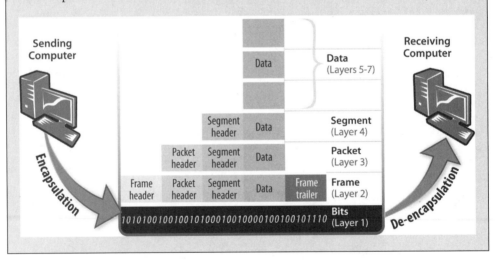

Application (Layer 7)

Although this layer is called the Application Layer, this doesn't mean application in the traditional sense such as a computer application like a web browser. Instead, the Application Layer consists of protocols used by computer applications to perform certain functions (such as a web browser using the HTTP protocol to access a website). Common protocols at this layer include Domain Name System (DNS), File Transfer

Protocol (FTP), Secure File Transfer Protocol (SFTP), Simple Network Management Protocol (SNMP), Telnet, SSH, HTTP, HTTPS, and Lightweight Directory Access Protocol (LDAP). *Data* is the term used to describe the data unit at the Application, Presentation, and Session Layers.

Presentation (Layer 6)

The Presentation Layer is responsible for translating data from something the user expects to something the network expects (and vice versa) so that it may be transferred over a network. There aren't really protocols at this layer, only services concerned with the format of the data and how it is presented. For example, if one computer using a photo editing application saves an image as a Tagged Image File Format (TIFF) or Photographic Experts Group (JPEG), the receiving computer application will be able to open and process the file even if another graphic application is being used because it is in a standard format. Common functions that occur at this layer include compression, decompression, encryption, and decryption.

Session (Layer 5)

The Session Layer is responsible for setting up, controlling, and tearing down the connection between applications communicating between two different computers. Protocols that operate at this layer include Network File System (NFS), Server Message Block (SMB), and NetBIOS.

Transport (Layer 4)

The Transport Layer handles end-to-end transport services and the establishment of logical connections between two computers (e.g., a client-server connection). Whereas the Session Layer was focused on the connection between the applications on each computer, the Transport Layer is concerned with the connection between the two computers themselves. Transmission Control Protocol (TCP) and User Datagram Protocol (UDP) operate at this layer. More on TCP and UDP to come later in this chapter. The transport layer deals with data units known as *segments* or *datagrams* (depending on if TCP or UDP is being used, respectively).

Network (Layer 3)

The Network Layer is responsible for the routing and route selection for network *packets* based on logical IP addresses. Routers are the most common network devices that operate at this layer; however, there are some network switches (referred to as Layer 3 switches) that have routing capability and operate at this layer as well. Protocols at this layer include IP, Internet Control Message Protocol (ICMP), and other routing protocols.

Data Link (Layer 2)

The Data Link Layer is responsible for transmitting and delivery of *frames* throughout a LAN based on the unique physical MAC addresses of the devices on the network. This layer is made up of two sublayers: the Logical Link Control (LLC) layer and the MAC layer. This is where physical MAC addresses are defined, which were introduced earlier in this chapter. Protocols and standards that operate at this layer include Address Resolution Protocol (ARP), Ethernet (IEEE 802.3), and wireless Ethernet (IEEE 802.11). Network devices that operate at this layer include network switches, wireless access points, and NICs on computers.

Physical (Layer 1)

The Physical Layer deals with how *bits* (binary 1's and 0's) are transmitted and received. The Physical Layer doesn't really have protocols, but instead has standards that define the physical aspects of the data transmission. Network hubs and repeaters operate at this layer.

TCP/IP

The *Transmission Control Protocol/Internet Protocol (TCP/IP) model* is an older network model developed by the Department of Defense (DoD). Whereas the OSI model is primarily a conceptual model, TCP/IP is both a model and an implementation with key network protocols. TCP/IP and its layers were designed around a suite of protocols. This is why the TCP/IP model is sometimes referred to as the *TCP/IP Protocol Suite* or *Internet Protocol Suite,* as they are the foundational protocols of most networks, including the Internet! The TCP/IP protocols also fit into various layers of the OSI model, as described earlier in this chapter. Figure 3-6 illustrates how the layers of the TCP/IP model map to the layers of the OSI model.

The TCP/IP model consists of four layers, which are (from top to bottom) the Application Layer, Host-to-Host Layer, Internet Layer, and Network Access Layer. In this section, we will walk through each layer of the TCP/IP model, discuss the functionality of that layer, and provide some key TCP/IP protocols you should be aware of.

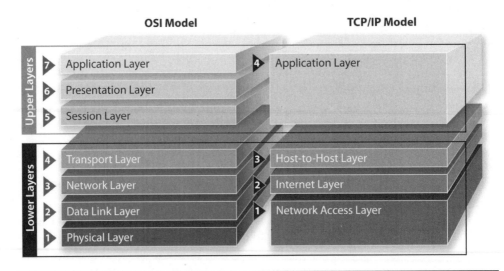

Figure 3-6 TCP/IP model compared to OSI model

EXAM TIP CC candidates should be familiar with how the OSI model layers map to the TCP/IP model layers. In addition, candidates should have a high-level understanding of the purpose of the most common TCP/IP protocol as well as the layers of the TCP/IP model and OSI model it operates at.

Application Layer

The *Application Layer* of the TCP/IP model provides various services, processes, and protocols that run on a network and are used by user applications (such as a web browser). Because of this, it is sometimes referred to as the Process Layer. This layer loosely maps to the upper three layers (Layers 5 to 7) of the OSI model (Session, Presentation, and Application, respectively). The following sections cover some of the key TCP/IP protocols that operate at the Application Layer.

Secure Sockets Layer/Transport Layer Security
The *Secure Sockets Layer (SSL)* and *Transport Layer Security (TLS)* protocols are often lumped together in conversation since the SSL protocol was the predecessor to TLS; however, they are different protocols. Both protocols use *public key encryption* (discussed in Chapter 4) to protect data communication in transit. Earlier versions of SSL and TLS had security issues, so organizations should be sure they are using TLS version 1.2 or later to ensure proper implementation. SSL/TLS does not have a specific port that is used. It is combined with other protocols such as HTTP or FTP.

NOTE Throughout this book we use the term SSL/TLS when referring to modern versions of TLS (TLS 1.2 and later).

Hypertext Transfer Protocol
Hypertext Transfer Protocol (HTTP) is a communication protocol that provides a means of transmitting and formatting messages between clients and servers. It is the primary way web browsers communicate with web servers to access web pages over the Internet. HTTP typically operates over port 80. The problem with HTTP is that information is transmitted between the client and server in plaintext. As a result, HTTP is no longer as widely used, and instead, organizations opt for HTTPS.

Hypertext Transfer Protocol Secure (HTTPS) leverages SSL/TLS with HTTP to add encryption for transmitted information. HTTPS formerly used the SSL protocol but now uses TLS as the encryption method. HTTPS ensures that once an HTTPS session is established, all traffic, including passwords and authentication information, is protected using encryption. HTTPS typically runs over port 443.

Secure Shell
Secure Shell (SSH) is a protocol used for remotely logging into and interacting with Unix/Linux computers through a text-only command-line interface. SSH is considered a secure protocol, as it encrypts the communication from the client to the server during the session. This protocol is most often used by system administrators for remotely logging into servers to perform administration functions. SSH typically runs over port 22. SSH should be leveraged over older nonsecure protocols such as *Telnet*, which transfers data in plaintext. Telnet typically leverages port 23.

File Transfer Protocol *File Transfer Protocol (FTP)* is used for transferring files between systems. The standard port for FTP is port 21. FTP transmits information in plaintext, so organizations should use a secure alternative such as SFTP or FTPS. *SSH File Transfer Protocol (SFTP)* leverages the SSH protocol to encrypt communications and, as such, typically runs on port 22. *File Transfer Protocol Secure (FTPS)* leverages TLS for encrypting communication sessions and uses port 990.

 NOTE FTP and FTPS actually each use two ports, one for commands (such as FTP commands to the client/server) and another for data transfer. FTP typically uses port 21 for commands and port 20 for data transfers, while FTPS uses port 990 for commands and 989 for data transfer. SFTP uses port 22 for both command and data transfer.

E-mail Protocols E-mail (which stands for electronic mail) is commonly used to send and receive messages (also known as e-mail) between individuals. While e-mail is not a protocol itself, it leverages other protocols for sending and receiving messages. The three common protocols for e-mail include Simple Mail Transfer Protocol (SMTP), Post Office Protocol version 3 (POP3), and Internet Mail Access Protocol (IMAP). SMTP is the standard protocol for sending e-mail (from server to server or e-mail client to server), while POP3 and IMAP are used for receiving/accessing e-mails. These are described in more detail next:

- **Simple Mail Transfer Protocol** SMTP is the protocol used for sending messages (think when you hit send on the e-mail using your e-mail client of choice). The standard port for SMTP is port 25. By default, SMTP sends communication in plaintext, so SMTP is often combined with SSL/TLS, which is called *Simple Mail Transfer Protocol Secure (SMTPS)*. SMTPS typically uses port 465 or 587.

- **Post Office Protocol version 3** The POP3 protocol is used to handle incoming e-mails (such as when you access an e-mail using an e-mail client). POP3 by default is not encrypted and uses the standard port 110. POP3 over SSL/TLS (POP3S) provides encryption of data in transit by leveraging SSL/TLS and uses the standard port 995.

- **Internet Mail Access Protocol** Similar to POP3, IMAP is also used for handling incoming e-mails but has different ways for accessing and retrieving messages from the e-mail server. IMAP does not provide encryption by default and uses port 143. IMAP over SSL/TLS (IMAPS) provides encryption and uses the standard port 993.

Network Time Protocol *Network Time Protocol (NTP)* is a protocol for the synchronization of time between the system clocks of computers. This is particularly important when it comes to logging and monitoring and investigating when a security event took place. If your systems all have different times set on their system clocks, good luck putting together a proper chain of events! NTP typically uses port 123 and has superseded the older *Time Protocol,* which leveraged port 37.

Domain Name System   The *Domain Name System (DNS)* protocol can be thought of as the address book of the Internet. It is the protocol used to translate domain names, also known as hostnames (such as www.google.com), into IP addresses. Without DNS you would need to know the public IP address of any website you wanted to visit on the Internet—wouldn't that be a pain! While DNS is used for the Internet in order to visit public websites, it is also used on private networks (such as a LAN) to name and identify computers running on the network. This allows system administrators to interact with hosts on their networks using their private domain names instead of IP addresses. DNS typically leverages port 53.

Similarly to other protocols discussed earlier, DNS queries and answers are transmitted in plaintext and are susceptible to eavesdropping and man-in-the-middle attacks. While the data being transmitted may not be as sensitive as other data types (as they are DNS queries versus the transferring of files with potentially sensitive information), it can still present a privacy concern. As such, organizations may elect to leverage DNS over TLS or DNS over HTTPS. *DNS over TLS (DoT)* encrypts DNS queries leveraging SSL/TLS and uses port 853. *DNS over HTTPS (DoH)* performs DNS queries using HTTPS and, as such, uses port 443. DoT and DoH both have their pros and cons. What is important for now is just being aware of the various protocols.

Simple Network Management Protocol   *Simple Network Management Protocol (SNMP)* is a network management protocol used to manage devices on a network. It uses a client-server architecture, where clients use *agents* running on the devices that need to be managed. These agents collect information about the device and report it back to the *manager* at the server. Early versions of SNMP provided a good way to control and obtain the status from devices on the network but had significant security flaws, including sending information in cleartext. SNMP version 3 added encryption and better authentication and should be used in lieu of older versions. SNMP uses ports 161 and 162.

Lightweight Directory Access Protocol   In Chapter 2 we discussed how large organizations use directory services to manage access and store information about users, resources, and so on. LDAP is used by subjects and applications in order to interact with the directory service. The standard port for LDAP is 389. Since LDAP sends data in cleartext, it can be susceptible to eavesdropping or other attacks. As a result, organizations should opt to leverage LDAP over TLS (LDAPS), which uses the standard port 636.

Dynamic Host Configuration Protocol   *Dynamic Host Configuration Protocol (DHCP)* is used to dynamically assign IP addresses to devices. A server (DHCP server) checks for available IP addresses from a pool and automatically assigns them to client devices. The DHCP server also takes back IP addresses when they are no longer in use and returns them to the pool for reassignment. This helps to simplify the management of larger networks (so administrators don't have to run around manually assigning an IP to every device) and prevents IP address conflicts (where two systems on the same network have the same IP address). The DHCP service typically runs on port 67 on DHCP servers.

Host-to-Host Layer

The Host-to-Host Layer of the TCP/IP model is sometimes also called the Transport Layer since it loosely maps to the Transport Layer of the OSI model. This layer is responsible for handling communication between computers (also known as hosts) across the network (hence the name host-to-host). The two most commonly used protocols that operate at this layer are TCP and UDP, described in the following sections

Transmission Control Protocol   TCP is a connection-oriented protocol used for transmitting data between hosts. It is called connection-oriented because it provides a means for reliable data transmission by periodically performing checks to make sure the connection is still established. TCP uses a three-way handshake to establish communication sessions. The *three-way handshake* is a process used by TCP for establishing connection-oriented communication sessions between computers. A high-level breakdown of this process is illustrated in Figure 3-7.

- Step 1: The first step is where the client computer wants to establish a communication session with a server. The client sends a synchronize (SYN) message to the server to let the server know that it wants to begin a communication session.

- Step 2: The server then responds to the client request with an acknowledgment (SYN + ACK).

- Step 3: The final step is where the client acknowledges the server response and responds with its own acknowledgment (ACK), which allows the transmission to proceed. Once the handshake is completed, then data transfer can begin.

This process is called a handshake, as it is similar to a typical handshake greeting. Someone reaches out their hand (SYN), the other person acknowledges this by reaching out their hand (SYN + ACK), and then they finally shake (ACK). Most protocols in the Application Layer of the TCP/IP model use TCP for connections between hosts. Examples include HTTP, HTTPS, SSH, Telnet, FTP, SFTP, FTPS, SMTP, POP3, IMAP, and LDAP.

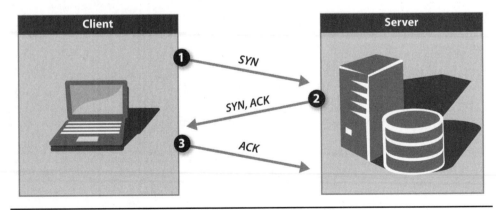

Figure 3-7   TCP three-way handshake example

User Datagram Protocol   UDP is another protocol used for transmitting data between computers. In contrast to TCP, UDP is not a connection-oriented protocol and is instead referred to as a connectionless protocol, as it does not establish a connection (three-way handshake) before transmitting data. Data is simply sent directly from one computer to another without requiring the connection to be established. This makes UDP less reliable but also faster, as it requires less overhead for the communication. UDP is used in situations where fast responses are needed (such as NTP time synchronization and DNS queries) and it is not important for the sender to know if the message was delivered (examples include voice and video data). UDP is commonly used with protocols such as NTP, DNS, DHCP, and SNMP.

   NOTE   Some protocols (such as SNMP or LDAP) can be configured to use TCP or UDP. Also, while DNS primarily uses UDP for domain name queries, it also uses TCP for specific functions.

Internet Layer

The Internet Layer of the TCP/IP model provides logical addressing and routing of IP network traffic. This layer is sometimes also referred to as the Network Layer because it loosely maps to the Network Layer (Layer 3) of the OSI model. Common protocols at this layer include IP, ICMP, and ARP. These protocols are discussed in the following sections.

Internet Protocol   Earlier in this chapter, we introduced IP addresses as one of the types of system addresses (with MAC addresses being the physical addresses and IP addresses being the logical addresses). IP addresses are used to identify devices to properly route traffic over a network. IP operates at the Internet Layer of the TCP/IP model. IP addresses are assigned statically (manually configured on devices by network administrators) or dynamically using a DHCP server (discussed earlier in this section). IP comes in two versions, IPv4 and IPv6 (discussed later in this chapter).

Internet Control Message Protocol   ICMP is a network management protocol used for error reporting, delivering status messages, and other network troubleshooting functions. The implementation of ICMP that most are familiar with is through the ping utility. The ping utility is a command-line tool that helps test the network connection between computers by sending out an ICMP request from the sending computer to the receiving computer. If the sending computer does not receive an ICMP reply within a specific time, it indicates the receiving host as unreachable.

Address Resolution Protocol   ARP is used to map IP addresses to MAC addresses (and vice versa) on a LAN. ARP serves as the bridge that connects the IP address and the MAC address. Computers on a network use ARP to learn which MAC address corresponds to which IP address and stores that information for future communication.

Network Access Layer

The Network Access Layer of the TCP/IP model loosely maps to the lower two layers (Layer 1 and Layer 2) of the OSI model (Physical and Data Link, respectively). As a result, the Network Access Layer of the TCP/IP model is sometimes called the Physical or Network Interface Layer. This layer handles the connectivity between devices using standards such as Ethernet for LANs and deals with physical MAC addresses.

IP Addressing

As discussed previously in this chapter, an IP address is a numerical label assigned to devices in order to locate them and route traffic on a network and over the Internet. IP addresses can be assigned statically by manually configuring device settings or dynamically using a DHCP server. There are two versions of IP: IP version 4 (IPv4) and IP version 6 (IPv6), and they each have different addressing characteristics. In this section we review both IPv4 and IPv6 in greater detail.

IPv4

IPv4 is used today for routing the majority of IP traffic over networks. IPv4 addresses are 32-bit numeric addresses consisting of four octets (or bytes) that each range from 0 to 255. Each bit has two possible values: 1 or 0 (remember, a bit is the smallest unit of information consisting of a binary 1 or 0, and a byte is a collection of 8 bits). This means that there are 2^32 possible addresses, which is roughly 4.3 billion IPv4 addresses. The structure of an IPv4 address is illustrated in Figure 3-8. 192.168.1.1 is an example of a private IPv4 address (public and private addresses are discussed later in this section).

IP addresses enable data to be sent and received throughout networks, similar to the address of a house for mail delivery. An address of a house has multiple elements (such as a city, state, street name, and house number), and so does an IP address. Every IP address has two components: the *network portion* (network ID) and node or *host portion* (host ID). The network portion of the address can be thought of like a street name.

Figure 3-8
IPv4 address
structure

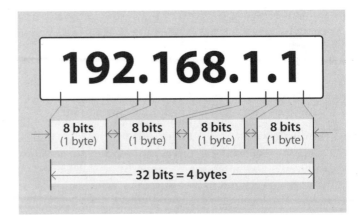

On a network, the network ID portion is the same for each device, as it tells the devices that they are all on the same network. The host portion can be thought of as the address of the house (or the device/host in this case). The host ID uniquely identifies each device on the network. Hosts/devices have different host portions of their address but share the same network portion of the address.

Due to the high demand for IPv4 addresses, there were concerns about running out of addresses. Even though 4.3 billion IPv4 addresses seem like a lot (granted not all are public addresses, which is discussed later in this section), there around 8 billion people on Earth. As a result, IPv6 addresses were created, which allow for many more addresses. IPv6 is discussed later in this chapter.

EXAM TIP   CC candidates will likely not be tested on the specific composition of IP addresses but should be familiar with what an IPv4 and IPv6 address look like as well as their purpose.

Network Address Translation

Internet routers are not configured to route private IP addresses across the Internet. However, if you check the IP addresses assigned to your home computer, you will see it is assigned a private IP address (likely something like 192.168.X.X). So, how is your computer connecting to the Internet if it's assigned a private IP? This occurs using something called network address translation (NAT). NAT is used by routers at the border of private networks (such as a LAN) to map external (public IP addresses) to internal (private IP addresses). This allows for devices assigned a private IP to connect to other networks like the Internet. NAT also helped overcome the shortcoming of the lack of IPv4 addresses.

Classful IP Addressing   IPv4 addresses have five subclasses of addresses (A through E), each with its own range of IP addresses and default subnet mask. The *subnet mask* is a 32-bit address that denotes how many bits of the IP address represent the network portion and how many bits represent the host portion. Table 3-1 provides an overview of Class A, B, and C networks. Classes D and E networks are reserved for research and other specific purposes. Networks that use this traditional method of subnetting are referred to as *classful* or *classical* networks. Classful IP addressing is no longer used today. Instead, organizations use classless IP addressing.

Classless IP Addressing   The problem with classful IP addresses is that they were very limiting in terms of how a network could be carved up, and the number of public IPv4 addresses was depleting as more organizations began to connect to the Internet (and thus need public IPs). An entire Class A network (consisting of 16 million

Class	Address Range	Description	Subnet Mask
Class A	1.x.x.x to 126.x.x.x	First octet is the network portion; the remaining three (each represented as an x) are the host portion	255.0.0.0
Class B	128.0.x.x to 191.255.x.x	First two octets are the network portion; the remaining two (each represented as an x) are the host portion	255.255.0.0
Class C	192.0.0.x to 223.255.255.x	First three octets are the network portion; the remaining 1 (represented as an x) is the host portion	255.255.255.0

Table 3-1 Class A, B, and C Networks

available host IP addresses) is too large for most organizations, while a Class C network (consisting of 254 host IP addresses) is too small for many organizations. Because of this, *classless* IP addressing and *Classless Interdomain Routing* (CIDR) was created. CIDR provides more flexibility in how class sizes are split up by no longer having to use the default subnet masks associated with the standard classes (A, B, and C). CIDR allows for customizable subnet masks. With CIDR, the subnet mask is noted after the IP address followed by a (/) and a decimal number (from 0 to 32) indicating the number of bits of the IP address that constitute the network portion of the address (network ID). For example, the address 192.168.0.10/24 indicates that the first 24 bits of the address (starting at the left) is the network address, and the remaining bits are the addresses of the node or host. Using CIDR notation, the default subnet mask of classful ranges (A, B, and C) would be notated as (/8), (/16), and (/24), respectively.

Network Segmentation

Network subnetting allows organizations to logically segment parts of their network by dividing larger IP ranges into smaller network segments. Hosts on the network are only able to communicate with other hosts that share the same network portion of the IP address (network ID). Organizations can then route tailored traffic between these segments using routers. Organizations use classless IP addressing to create subnets that do not fall into the traditional classful sizes (Class A, B, and C). Network segmentation is a network design technique that can allow organizations to logically group certain devices (such as the IT team, sales team, etc.). It can also be used to increase security by segmenting different parts of the network that may post different risks (such as segmenting the wireless network from the wired network). We discuss network segmentation and other network security design considerations in more detail later in this chapter.

Public and Private IPs IP addresses can be *public* (meaning they can be routed across the Internet) or *private* (meaning they can only be routed within a LAN and not over the Internet). *Public IP addresses* are assigned by the IANA, which is the organization responsible for managing IP addresses worldwide. *Private IP addresses* are freely assigned by any organization or individual for use on their LAN (for example, IP addresses used on a home or company network). The following are the ranges of private IP addresses that are not routable on the Internet:

- 10.0.0.0 to 10.255.255.255
- 172.16.0.0 to 172.31.255.255
- 192.168.0.0 to 192.168.255.255

NOTE   CC candidates may not be directly tested on public and private IP addresses on the exam; however, it is an important concept to understand.

Loopback Address   IP addresses in the 127.x.x.x range are reserved for loopback IP addresses. 127.0.0.1 is known as the loopback address, which is an address that allows a computer to identify and communicate with itself (e.g., using the ping utility with 127.0.0.1). The term *localhost* serves as a domain name (DNS) for the loopback address. This is often used for troubleshooting and other testing purposes. For example, if you are building a website and want to see how it looks in a web browser, you might host the website on your computer and make it available through localhost. Then you can enter localhost or 127.0.0.1 into your web browser to view the website locally without it being available to other computers on the network.

IPv6

IPv6 is the newest version of IP that was developed to help solve the concern around the depleting number of available public IPv4 addresses. IPv6 addresses are 128-bit alphanumeric addresses, which means there are 2^{128} possible IPv6 addresses, which is roughly 340 trillion trillion trillion addresses. IPv6 addresses are represented as eight groups of four alphanumeric characters ranging from 0000 to FFFF, each separated by colons (:). They can range from 0000:0000:0000:0000:0000:0000:0000:0000 to ffff: ffff:ffff:ffff:ffff:ffff:ffff:ffff. One of the clear advantages with IPv6 is the larger pool of addresses, but it also comes with other benefits such as additional security and quality of service features. Adoption of IPv6 has been slow, however, due to older networking equipment that may not support IPv6, as well as the investment organizations may need to make to reconfigure their network to support IPv6 that can make the upgrade costly and complex.

NOTE   The loopback address in IPv6 is 0:0:0:0:0:0:0:1 or ::1.

Network Fundamentals Summary

Here is a summary of the important topics covered in the "Network Fundamentals" section:

- Local area networks (LANs) and wide area networks (WANs) are the main network types.
- Networks can be wired (connected by cables) or wireless using wireless technologies.
- System addresses include the MAC address and IP address.
- The OSI model consists of the Application Layer, Presentation Layer, Session Layer, Transport Layer, Network Layer, Data Link Layer, and Physical Layer.
- The TCP/IP model consists of the Application Layer, Host-to-Host Layer, Internet Layer, and Network Access Layer.
- The two versions of IP are IPv4 and IPv6.

The following table provides an overview of the data unit, network devices, and protocols that operate at each later of the OSI model and TCP/IP model.

OSI Layer	TCP/IP	Data Unit	Network Devices	Protocol/Standards
Application				DNS, FTP, SFTP, SNMP, SSH, HTTP, HTTPS, DNS, LDAP, TELNET, SSL/TLS, DHCP
Presentation	Application	Data	Computers	ASCII, TIFF, GIF, JPEG, MPEG, MIDI, MIME
Session				NetBIOS, NFS, RPC
Transport	Host-to-Host	Segment/Datagram		TCP, UDP
Network	Internet	Packet	Router, Layer 3, Switch	IP, ICMP, ARP
Data Link	Network Access	Frame	Network Interface, Switch,	
Physical		Bit	Hub, Repeater, Cables	Ethernet, Wireless Ethernet

Network Threats and Attacks

In Chapter 1 we described the general steps that a cyber criminal carries out during a typical cyberattack. To review, they are

1. Conduct research
2. Identify targets
3. Exploit targets
4. Do bad things

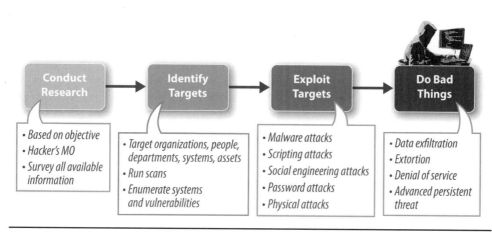

Figure 3-9 Typical network attack

In this section we explore each of the steps of an attack in more detail. The purpose of this section is for the CC candidate to gain a better understanding of the types of attacks cyberattackers perform and the methods and tools they use. Later in this chapter we explore some of the ways to go about defending against these attacks.

Consider the illustration in Figure 3-9. Each step in the diagram is discussed in its own subsection.

Conducting Research

The primary purpose of the first step in the process of planning a cyberattack is to conduct research about the planned target organization or victim. However, this can't be done without first understanding what the overall objective is. What is the cyberattacker's ultimate goal? Are they after credit card data? Are they seeking to embarrass someone? Do they want to steal trade secrets? Cyber criminals usually have a specific goal in mind, and this goal shapes the type of research they perform and the targets they are looking for.

With the goal in mind, cyber criminals, like any criminal, also each have their own modus operandi (MO), or preferred method of working. This may also shape the type of information they gather and what they do with what they find.

As stated in Chapter 1, cyber criminals survey any and all available information to learn about the victim: domain, personal and company names, addresses, phone numbers, IP addresses, names of friends, staff, departments, intelligence about the organization such as marketing, financial, political, social information, etc. All of this information informs the cyber criminal about who they are attacking and how they might plan their attack.

NOTE Not all cyberattacks are targeted ones. Sometimes the hacker doesn't care who the victim is. Instead, they launch attacks at random targets and see what they get. Many hackers successfully launch phishing, ransomware, and other attacks in this manner.

Identifying Targets

During this phase, the cyberattacker pieces together the various bits of information collected in the previous phase. This can be an iterative process as research uncovers information, which is pieced together to form a picture about the target organization, which leads to questions, which may lead to more research, and so on. The hacker's goal is to identify what organization assets to go after and what is the best first line of attack.

Many times the cyberattacker will launch automated scans against the organization's externally facing Internet assets such as web servers, e-mail servers, or any devices connected to the Internet. During research, the cyberattacker learned the domain name(s) and possibly the IP addresses of target systems of the organization. The next step is to run scans against those assets to reveal information about them.

To run scans, cyberattackers use commercially available or custom-built scanning tools. Some of these tools are available as appliances, while others are software that run on computers. Scanning can also be obtained from scanning as a service providers, although commercial scanning service providers require the target organization to grant written permission before a scan, so it's only the illicit scanners or bad guys who provide clandestine scanning as a service. There are three components of scanning:

- **Network scanning**   This seeks to enumerate (identify and list) what systems are within a targeted range of IP addresses, identifying their IP address, operating system type, and version.
- **Port scanning**   This looks at the systems found during network scanning to reveal what ports are open and therefore what services are running on them.
- **Vulnerability scanning**   This examines systems to reveal and enumerate known vulnerabilities in the operating systems and applications on the devices.

When a cyberattacker finds a system that has a known vulnerability, he does a little dance because he likely has an exploit for that vulnerability in his bag of tools that he can run. Finding systems that have known vulnerabilities is one of the goals of scanning. For instance, if a hacker runs a scan and finds a system that has the Windows ProxyLogon vulnerability (CVE-2021-26855), she can look up that vulnerability on many hacker websites and find there are several automated exploits for that vulnerability that she can run to bypass normal authentication and impersonate an administrator on that system.

> **NOTE**   CVE stands for Common Vulnerabilities and Exposures, which is a program overseen by the Cybersecurity and Infrastructure Security Agency (CISA), part of the U.S. Department of Homeland Security. The CVE program maintains a numbered list of publicly disclosed security flaws in computers and software. Information about the CVE program can be found at the CISA CVE website: https://www.cisa.gov/known-exploited-vulnerabilities-catalog

Scanning allows the hacker to build an understanding of the organization's network, assets, systems, applications, and vulnerabilities that could be exploited. All of the information discovered during scanning helps the cyberattacker plan the exploit phase of the attack.

Of course, not all first-line targets of the cyberattacker are IT assets. During the research phase, the cyber criminal may learn about physical locations that are potential targets of physical exploits or names and phone numbers of individuals or departments that are potential targets of social engineering activities.

Exploiting Targets

During the exploiting targets step of a cyberattack, the attacker takes advantage of vulnerabilities in systems or networks to gain unauthorized access. There are many types of exploits; in this section we examine the most common categories of them:

- Attacks using malicious software
- Attacks using scripts
- Attacks using social engineering
- Password attacks
- Man-in-the-middle attacks
- Physical attacks

Attacks Using Malicious Software

Malware, a contraction for *malicious software,* is software designed to infiltrate and gain unauthorized access to computer systems for the purpose of causing damage or disruption. Attackers use malware to compromise systems and carry out malicious objectives. Attackers can use malware to perform the following functions:

- Carrying out phishing attacks
- Carrying out ransomware attacks to force users to pay a ransom to prevent their data from being lost or destroyed
- Conducting denial of service (DoS) attacks to disrupt business operations
- Redirecting Internet traffic to unintended or malicious websites
- Recording users' keystrokes to capture passwords and other sensitive information
- Using spyware to collect sensitive information from users' computers

This section describes the following types of malware:

- Viruses
- Trojans, worms, and botnets
- Ransomware
- Rootkits

Viruses   A *virus* is a type of malware that is a computer program (or a portion of a program) that infects a legitimate program with a *payload*. The payload causes the legitimate program to perform a function, or functions, it was not designed to do. The payload is the portion of the virus that carries out the malicious activity, such as deleting, transmitting, or encrypting data; modifying files; or sending spam. Viruses use other programs as vehicles to deliver their payload to the intended destination. Here are a few common types of viruses:

- **Stealth virus** A stealth virus hides itself to avoid detection. It can hide its presence and also the bad things that it does to the infected file or system.

- **Polymorphic virus** A polymorphic virus is a type of stealth virus that hides itself by changing itself (actually changing the code) each time it is run. Antivirus programs designed to look for specific programs or files may not be able to detect such a virus because it never looks the same.

- **Boot sector virus** This is malicious code inserted into the boot sector of the computer's storage device. The boot sector is the portion of the computer's storage device (e.g., hard disk, floppy) that contains the machine code that starts up the computer's operating system. Upon installation, the virus either moves data from the boot sector or overwrites it with new information. Then, when the system is booted, the malicious code is executed.

- **Multipartite virus** Viruses that infect both the boot sector and other files in the system are called *multipartite*.

- **Macro virus** Many ordinary applications that users run have features that allow them to create and use macros (or scripts) that automate functions of the application. For instance, Microsoft Word and Excel are common applications that have macro capabilities. Each macro is a script that is executed to carry out a task. It is possible to write macros that perform malicious tasks. Macros can also duplicate themselves and infect other files used by the application, allowing the virus to spread to other computers if the files are shared.

- **Compression virus** Many applications compress files in order to save space for better storage or faster transmission. To do this, programs run processes to compress or decompress the file. A compression virus is one that is embedded within a compressed file. When the user decompresses the file to access its contents, the virus executes and performs its malicious task.

 EXAM TIP It's good to know about the various types of viruses, but you aren't likely to encounter questions about the different types on the CC exam.

Trojans, Worms, and Botnets Other types of malware are similar to a virus but have differing characteristics and functions. Here are a few of them:

- **Trojan** A trojan is a malicious program that tricks the user into running it because it looks like a legitimate program. Sometimes the trojan includes the actual program that the user intends to run, so it appears the program is running correctly when it is also running the malicious code. Well-designed trojans can be hard to detect because they can appear to be legitimate programs running correctly.

- **Worm**   A worm is similar to a virus but differs from a virus in that it is able to replicate itself. Unlike a virus, which requires a host program to infect, a worm can stand alone and does not require a host program to do its damage or replicate itself. Worms usually exploit known vulnerabilities in systems or software applications. Once they infect a system, the worm can scan the network for other computers that have exploitable vulnerabilities and spread to them.

- **Botnet**   A botnet is a group of infected systems that are remotely controlled by cyber criminals to perform an attack. Remote control is carried out by command and control software that enables the attackers to control the botnets as a group.

Some Well-Known and Common Computer Viruses and Attacks

There have been hundreds, if not thousands, of computer viruses written and used by hackers. Here are a few such viruses that have become well known because their impact was significant or newsworthy:

- **Storm Worm**   Discovered in 2007, Storm Worm became the largest botnet ever, infecting as many as 1 million computers. Storm Worm combined elements of different types of viruses: it was a trojan horse, a worm, and a botnet. Worse, it was also polymorphic, making it difficult to detect because it created mutations of itself. In fact, some variants of Storm Worm were capable of changing their footprint every 10 to 30 minutes. Storm Worm was traced to Russian hackers who used it to launch attacks against sites "for hire." Anyone with an axe to grind could hire and pay the cyber criminals to use Storm Worm to carry out cyberattacks against their adversaries.

- **Morris worm**   First launched in 1988, the Morris worm was one of the first virus attacks against public computer networks. Developed by a college student (named Morris) who claimed the original purpose of the worm was to determine the size of the Internet at that time, the virus quickly spread, causing widespread performance problems as the infected computers became overwhelmed or crashed entirely. Mr. Morris gained notoriety as the first person to become convicted under the Computer Fraud and Abuse Act of 1986.

- **Emotet trojan**   Emotet is a strain, or variant, of the malware called Heodo. Emotet is a trojan delivered to victims' computers via phishing e-mails or macros embedded in document files. The group of hackers behind Emotet, named Mealybug, used it to create a botnet of infected systems that they sold access to, enabling ransomware and other attacks to be launched against targeted entities. First released in 2014, it wasn't until 2021 that the Emotet botnet infrastructure was taken down by law enforcement agencies in Europe and the United States. However, Emotet remains an active threat today.

(continued)

- **Mira botnet**   Mira is a botnet used to launch large DoS attacks starting in 2016. Mira was unique in that it attacked noncomputer devices such as cameras and routers by attempting to log in to them using default usernames and passwords to take control. The Federal Bureau of Investigation (FBI) caught the creators of Mira, and they plead guilty to their crimes.

- **Sapphire (or SQL Slammer)**   Sapphire was another DoS worm. Released in 2003, it spread incredibly fast, taking only 15 minutes to spread worldwide, and eventually caused over $1 billion in damage. Sapphire takes advantage of known vulnerabilities in Microsoft SQL Server software.

NOTE   The Mira attack is an example of a common vulnerability—organizations using devices with default credentials on their networks. Many computing and noncomputing devices and software such as network devices, firewalls, and Internet of Things devices like industrial control systems are preconfigured with default credentials that are built in to the device. These default credentials are easily found in manuals or on the Internet. They are intended to be temporary and should be changed after the initial installation of the device. However, using these devices improperly can be a security risk because left unchanged, the default credentials can easily be used by an unauthorized user to take control of the device, such as in the case of the Mira attack. Organizations should always ensure that default credentials are changed and use strong passwords after device installation and after reconfiguration.

Ransomware   Ransomware is a type of malware that forces its victim to make a difficult choice: either pay a ransom or lose valuable assets. Like other viruses, ransomware is delivered through the usual attack mechanisms: phishing e-mails, social engineering tricks, or exploiting known vulnerabilities in operating systems or other programs. When the ransomware infects a system, it usually encrypts important files and notifies the user that unless a ransom is paid, the data will remain encrypted and lost to the user and their organization.

In some cases when the ransom is paid, the cyber criminals follow through on their promise to help the victim recover their data. They do this by providing decryption keys and instructions on how to restore the encrypted files.

There are variants of ransomware attacks in which the cyber criminal threatens to reveal sensitive information about the victim or even pornographic material which may have been placed on the victim's system by the attacker. But all ransomware presents the organization with the same dilemma: pay the ransom or something bad will happen.

Ransomware Examples

Here are a few examples of ransomware attacks.

- **CryptoLocker**   CryptoLocker was released in 2013 and was spread primarily by fake e-mails that looked like legitimate ones from shipping vendors UPS and FedEx. Once infected, the victim's computer came under control of the attacker and files were encrypted using asymmetric cryptography (see Chapter 4). Some victims reported that they paid the ransom but never received the decryption keys so they were unable to recover their data—a doubly cruel attack.

- **Ryuk**   Ryuk was widely prevalent in 2018 and 2019 and was used in conjunction with relatively high demands for payment by the criminals. One feature of Ryuk is that it disables the Windows System Restore feature, thereby preventing the victim organization from going back to an earlier, noninfected point in time in an attempt to recover from the attack without paying a ransom.

- **Petya**   Petya (and its variant NotPetya) is unique because it is spread using an exploit that was originally developed by, and stolen from, the U.S. National Security Agency (NSA). The exploit takes advantage of a vulnerability in Windows. The bad news is that while the virus looks and behaves like ransomware by encrypting files and demanding a ransom, there is actually no way to pay the ransom. The website provided is not valid, so there is no way to pay the ransom and recover the files.

EXAM TIP   CC candidates should be familiar with the various types of malware but do not need to remember specific examples of virus attacks and virus names.

Rootkits   Rootkits are tools that enable and maintain privileged access to an operating system. Rootkits are not always malicious (they can have legitimate uses), but this discussion covers only rootkits that carry malicious code (e.g., rootkit "malware"). Like other malware, rootkit malware must be delivered to the target in some manner. Therefore, a rootkit is always combined with some other type of exploit in order to get the rootkit installed. Once installed, the rootkit can hide itself from detection. Rootkits can be difficult or impossible to detect, especially when they reside inside the kernel. Sometimes removal can be accomplished only by reinstalling the operating system or even replacing hardware in cases where the rootkit has impacted firmware or caused damage to electronics.

Attacks Using Scripts

Scripting is like coding in that it is a way to provide instructions to a computer to make it do something. When a developer or manufacturer creates a software product or application, they usually provide one of two ways a user can give it commands: manually (using either a graphical user interface or by typing into a command line) or programmatically using programs or scripts such as with an application programming interface (API). Some products support both manual and programmatic control.

Cyber criminals use scripts to take advantage of weaknesses in products that allow them to execute commands to make the products do things the user is not authorized to do. Weaknesses may exist in operating systems or applications due to programming or configuration errors on the part of the manufacturers (in the case of commercial software) or developers (in the case of custom or in-house developed software). Certain weaknesses can be exploited by the hacker's use of scripting to conduct an attack. Several such attacks are discussed next.

Buffer Overflows When a program is expecting input, either from another program or from a user entering text into a field, it stores the data in a buffer, or area of memory. The program usually expects the data to be of a certain size and therefore creates a buffer of the correct size to accept the expected data. If the data received is greater in size than the size of the buffer, the extra data overflows into other buffers or areas of memory, which can cause erroneous operation. Cyberattackers take advantage of products that have such weaknesses. They craft attacks to take advantage of programs that do not perform proper checking of input data and are therefore vulnerable to buffer overflow attacks.

When a buffer overflow occurs, the data that exceeds the size of the buffer overflows into adjacent areas of memory. If that memory is another buffer, the data can corrupt the operation of the program that uses it. In some cases, the overflowed data is executed by the system as if it were a command or even an executable program. Buffer overflows can be used to cause a system to execute commands without the correct authorization. Often the attacker injects into the buffer malicious code that will be executed on the attacker's behalf but under the context of the program that is currently running on the system. This can lead to the attacker taking control of the system, resulting in a security breach.

Buffer overflows can be prevented during the development phase of software engineering by implementing proper input checking to ensure only the right type and size of data are accepted by the program or by preventing data from being written to certain areas of memory, thus minimizing the potential impact of an overflow.

Cross-Site Scripting Cross-site scripting (XSS) is a type of attack whereby the attacker injects a malicious script into a website that is trusted by the intended victim(s) of the attack. Then, when the unsuspecting victim visits the site, the script is executed by the victim's browser. Such scripts can access the victim's cookies, tokens, or other sensitive information.

Typical victims of this type of attack are people who visit websites like message boards, forums, or social media sites. The attacker may post legitimate information for the victim to see alongside a script that is hidden to the victim but is executed by the victim's browser to carry out the attack. Or a variant of this attack occurs when a victim receives a malicious e-mail message that entices them to click a link. The e-mail not only contains the link to a web server but also contains the malicious script that is reflected by the server to the victim's browser. The browser then executes the script, carrying out the malicious activity.

HTTP Response Splitting   *HTTP response splitting* is another type of attack where an attacker sends a malicious script to a website. In this attack the attacker crafts data that contains malformed headers by inserting a carriage return and line feed in the request, thereby splitting the request, which changes the behavior of the web application. The malformed headers allow the attacker to manipulate the behavior of the server side of the application. The result is that when a victim's browser then connects to the web server, their browser will fall under the control of the attacker. HTTP response splitting can be used to launch cross-site scripting attacks or "poison" the web cache with false data that can result in defacement of a website.

SQL Injection   Sometimes when a user visits a website and enters data into a form or web page, the data is sent by the web server to a database such as one that uses Structured Query Language (SQL). If the web server software does not properly check the data input by the user, it could allow an attacker to put *SQL commands* in the field, which are then executed by the SQL database without proper authorization. Such an attack may be used to take control of the database, escalate privileges, and modify or steal data from the database without the proper authorization.

Timing and Race Conditions   A *timing attack,* also called a *race condition attack,* is an entire family of attacks in which the attacker takes advantage of the time between a sequence of events. One example is a time of check/time of use (TOC/TOU) attack. This occurs when the system checks to see if a specific file exists for a later operation. In this case the attacker replaces that file with a malicious one in between the time of the check and the time the file is used. There are countless variations of this type of attack. Any instance where a program implements a specific sequence of events that depends on other programs or external events could be vulnerable to such an attack.

Backdoors   Although not a specific type of attack, a backdoor is a feature of many different kinds of attacks. *Backdoor* is a broad term used to describe any method whereby an unauthorized user can bypass security controls to gain access to a system or program. Backdoors facilitate communication between an infected or compromised system and an unauthorized system or user. Backdoors can be present when a system or program is not designed or coded correctly. Backdoors can also be created by a cyber criminal using malware.

 EXAM TIP   CC candidates should be familiar with the basic concepts of scripting-related attacks, including buffer overflows, cross-site scripting, SQL injection, HTTP response splitting, timing attacks, and backdoors.

Attacks Using Social Engineering

Cyber criminals know that people are the weakest link in information security. For a savvy criminal it is easier to trick someone into giving up their password than it is to hack into a system. The term *social engineering* refers to the use of deception to trick someone into doing something that may not be in their best interest. Social engineering has been used by scam artists for years and now is an integral part of cyberattacks.

Social engineering takes many forms but can be considered in three categories: pretexting, quid pro quo, and baiting.

Pretexting   *Pretexting* uses a fake scenario to deceive someone. Here are a few examples:

- A user receives a call from "Tech Support" telling them their computer has a virus and the user should give them remote access to their computer to "fix" the problem. But of course, the caller isn't really Tech Support but is instead a cyber criminal. Unfortunately, the criminal often successfully convinces the user to give them remote access or share their login credentials, and the user becomes the victim of cybercrime.

- A user receives an e-mail from their bank indicating their password has expired with a link they should click on to change it. The e-mail looks convincing, and the web page used to change the password looks real. But they are both fake, and the bad guys use the web page to steal the user's credentials. The attackers then use the credentials to access the user's bank account and steal their money.

- A company chief financial officer (CFO) gets an e-mail from the "chief executive officer (CEO)" telling her to transfer a large sum of money to a new vendor's bank account. The CFO follows the CEO's instructions, only to find out too late that the e-mail didn't really come from the CEO, but from a cyberattacker.

Quid Pro Quo   A real quid pro quo (QPQ) is an exchange of information or goods, such as a purchase. But sometimes the exchange isn't what it appears to be. If a deal sounds too good to be true, it may not be. Here are a couple of examples:

- A buyer for a company needed to buy universal serial bus (USB) drives. Most places the buyer visited sold them for $50 each, but he found a website in China selling them for only $10 each. Sounded like a bargain. Too bad the cheaper drives contained malware and infected all of the company's computers.

- Many online sites sell versions of software products for a fraction of the cost of other sites. The software appears to be the real thing. However, many of these deeply discounted products are fraudulent versions of the product and, if they work at all, contain adware and/or malware that can cause serious security breaches.

Baiting   *Baiting* is simply luring someone into a trap. We've all heard the story of the famous Trojan Horse sent by the Greeks as a gift to the city of Troy in the twelfth century BC. When the Trojans brought the giant horse sculpture into the city, it contained Greek soldiers hidden inside ready for a sneak attack. The rest, as they say, is history. Here are a few cyber examples of baiting:

- An unsuspecting person finds a keychain with a USB drive attached to it on the floor and turns it in to the front desk. The receptionist, wanting to figure out who the USB belongs to, decides to plug the drive into his computer. Big mistake. The drive contains malware and not only infects the receptionist's computer but spreads throughout the company network. Dropping USB drives onto the ground is a common method of attack by hackers.

- An employee receives an e-mail announcing that she is the lucky winner of a new computer game. But the e-mail lures the victim to a website that contains an exploit that runs from the user's browser. This is another successful attack using a combination of social engineering and cross-site scripting.

 EXAM TIP CC candidates should be familiar with the basic concepts of social engineering but do not need to know the names of specific types such as baiting, quid quo pro, and pretexting.

Phishing and Spear Phishing

Phishing is a term that refers to e-mail–based attacks in which the cyber criminal crafts and sends e-mails that look like legitimate e-mails from a real business, but the e-mail is really fraudulent. The e-mail frequently contains an attachment or a link for the recipient to click on. But selecting either of these does not download the desired attachment or take the recipient to the desired website but instead downloads malware or takes the recipient to a fraudulent website.

Phishing e-mails are usually not personalized; rather, they are sent to a large number of recipients in the hope that a few of them will fall victim to the attack and click on the link or attachment. In contrast, *spear phishing* attacks are phishing e-mails sent to specific individuals or employees of organizations. They are phishing attacks specifically targeted at a company, government entity, or financial organization, usually for financial or political gain.

One of the most important things organizations and individuals can do to protect themselves against phishing and spear phishing attacks is to validate a uniform resource locator (URL) before clicking on a link. Before selecting a link or downloading an e-mail attachment, the user should mouse over the link and carefully inspect the URL. Does it look suspicious? Does the domain name make sense? Does the link use SSL/TLS encryption (avoid links that use HTTP instead of HTTPS)? Are there any homographs in the domain name (for instance, the hacker may substitute the letters "rn" for the letter "m")? Practicing good URL hygiene and being careful about what you click on can be the best way to protect against phishing and spear phishing attacks.

Password Attacks

Since passwords are the most prevalent method used for authentication, they are juicy targets for hackers. By obtaining passwords, especially passwords for privileged accounts, cyber criminals can gain access to the data and systems that are their ultimate objective. This section explores the most common ways hackers obtain passwords. But first let's explore how passwords are stored and used.

In most modern computer operating systems (Windows, Unix/Linux, macOS, Android), and modern applications, when a user creates a password, the password itself is not stored by the operating system because, as we know, storing passwords in plaintext form is a bad practice, since anyone with access to the file or database where the password is stored could read it. Instead, an encrypted form of the password is stored. To do this, the password undergoes a one-way transformation called a hash. The mechanics of how hashing works is explained in Chapter 4 in the section describing cryptography. For now, understand that a hash is a *one-way mathematical transformation of data*. What this means is the system takes the password, transforms it, and stores the new value (the hash) instead of the actual password. If a hacker were ever able to access the hashed value, they couldn't reasonably figure out the password from it, because the hashing algorithm is one-way. If the hash is created using modern cryptographic methods, it is mathematically infeasible for someone to figure out the password from the hashed value.

When a user logs into a system and enters in their username and password, the system transforms the password using the one-way hashing algorithm. Using the username, it looks up the database record of the user to find the hash that was stored when the password was first created. It then compares the two hashed values for verification. This function is built into the operating system and can't be bypassed. If a hacker were to obtain the hash of a password, they couldn't do anything with it because the operating system has to go through its authentication function starting with the password, hashing it, and comparing it to the stored hash in order for authentication to work. This is the way authentication works in modern operating systems.

Cyber criminals go to great lengths to try to obtain or determine passwords. Here are a few methods they use:

- **Social engineering** Why perform a complicated technical attack to get a password when you can just ask someone for it? Hackers use many social engineering tricks to get people to give up their passwords, from fake phone calls from "Tech Support" asking the victim for their password due to an "emergency" to fake e-mails from people masquerading as people of authority. Organizations should have policies and training for all users to ensure they never, ever tell anyone their password for any reason whatsoever.

- **Phishing and spear phishing** As described earlier, phishing and spear phishing attacks use fake e-mails that look like legitimate business communications. They can be used to deliver malware but can also be used to entice users to give up their password. The most common method is a phishing e-mail that looks like it's from tech support stating the user's password has expired and they need to create a new one. The e-mail directs the user to a fake website, which first asks the user for their current password, then their new one, and the hacker has therefore obtained the user's credentials.

- **Brute force attack**   If a hacker has managed to capture a hashed password or an entire hashed password database from an operating system, there is no feasible way they could mathematically compute what password created which hash, but they could potentially figure it out with trial and error . . . a lot of trial and error. For instance, for a given guessed password the hacker would compute the hash, then compare it to the captured hash value to see if there is a match. This process potentially takes about one millisecond. By extrapolation the hacker could try 1 million guesses in one second and so on. This is called a *brute force attack*. With enough time and resources, passwords could potentially be guessed, depending on the size of the password and the amount of computing power the hacker has. But there is a practical limit to doing this. If the password is 16 characters or greater, no modern computer or super-computer system could possibly brute force all the possible combinations to figure out the password. However, since many organizations use less than 16-character passwords, brute force attacks can be, and have been, successful. They just take a lot of time and computing resources on the part of the hacker.

- **Dictionary attack**   This is a form of brute force attack in which the hacker creates a dictionary or list of words or character combinations that are potential passwords. The hacker then uses tools to compute their hashes. The hashes can then be compared against hashes captured from password databases during the course of cyberattack activities. Like brute force attacks, lots of computing resources are required to conduct a dictionary attack.

- **Rainbow tables**   Using a dictionary to create a list of hashes takes time and processing power. For efficiency, hackers do this ahead of time and store the results in what are called rainbow tables. They are simply stores of password and hash combinations that have already been computed that hackers can use to compare against captured password hash databases. Hackers buy and sell rainbow tables to help each other in their malicious activities.

NOTE   A brute force attack does not necessarily require that the attacker first capture a database of hashed passwords. Brute force attacks can simply be a series of guesses against the password entry field of an application or a web page. Nowadays, best security practice dictates that applications or web pages limit the number of unsuccessful password tries to only a few attempts before the application locks the user out. As a result, some applications are resilient against brute force attacks while others are susceptible to them.

Man-in-the Middle Attacks

Man-in-the-middle (MITM) are a class of attacks in which a cyberattacker intercepts communication between two entities. MITM attacks can be used just for eavesdropping and capturing data but can also be used to alter the communication in some fashion. Therefore, MITM attacks can be attacks against confidentiality, integrity, or availability depending on the exact operation.

In a typical MITM attack the cyber criminal puts themselves in-between the client and the server, or between the user's browser and the web server in a World Wide Web (WWW) Internet connection. Here are a few ways the attacker could accomplish this:

- By gaining access to a portion of the network in which the targeted communication will occur. For instance, in an Internet café or restaurant, the attacker can gain access to the local Wi-Fi and use eavesdropping tools to spy on local traffic. The attacker can capture data and even passwords which, if transmitted in plaintext, are stolen by the hacker.

- Hackers can setup their own Wi-Fi access points to trick users into connecting to them thinking they are connecting to legitimate business, organization, or public Wi-Fi access points. By doing this, hackers can capture and collect a user's data or manipulate it to their liking.

- Cyber criminals execute attacks called *DNS spoofing* or *DNS poisoning* in which they cause routers to resolve a DNS entry to the wrong web address, usually a fake one that they use to capture user data or even download malware. So, when the user wants to go to "www.my_bank.com," they are instead connecting to the hacker's web server.

Physical Attacks

Regarding cybersecurity, physical attacks are another method of gaining access to cyber assets. The physical access controls discussed in Chapter 2 are important tools for two reasons:

- To prevent criminals from directly destroying or stealing the networking and information processing equipment

- To prevent cyber criminals from physically accessing networking and information processing equipment for the purpose of carrying out a cyberattack

When cyber criminals gain physical access to IT resources, the physical and cyber worlds converge. That is why physical security is included in the Certified in Cybersecurity domain topics. Breakdowns in physical security can lead to cybersecurity exploits. Here are a few examples:

- A cyber criminal gains access to a datacenter and slips a USB drive into a slot in one of the servers. The USB drive contains malware which infects the server and the other systems on the network.

- After gaining physical access, a cyber criminal resets and reboots several servers and network devices, causing them to revert to default configurations and default passwords and leaving them vulnerable to his malicious activities.

- A cyber criminal gains access to an organization's facility not through the main entrance, which is well-protected, but through the side door near the smoking area, which is propped open during the day. He steals a laptop, which is found to have credit card and customer data on it.

- A cyber attacker gains physical access to a government facility and finds a room with an empty desk and an open ethernet wall socket. He plugs in a laptop and runs network sniffer software which allows him to capture and analyze network traffic to learn about the network and plan his attack.

- A cyber criminal gains access to a major corporation and wanders through the building, shoulder surfing, taking papers off printers, snapping pictures of desks and whiteboards, writing down passwords from sticky notes, eavesdropping on phone calls, and helping herself to lunch from the fridge. Everything she learns, except for the food from the fridge, can be used during a cyberattack.

 NOTE *Shoulder surfing* is a technique of snooping where the attacker literally looks over the shoulder of a user to see what they are doing on their computer, cellphone, or other device.

Cyber and physical assets can be targeted separately or together. As a result, cybersecurity professionals need to address security holistically and consider all possible methods of attack.

Physical Attack Example: Stuxnet and Operation Olympic Games

In the mid-2000s the governments of the United States and Israel jointly launched a historic cyberattack against an Iranian nuclear facility seeking to do harm to Iran's nuclear program. The covert program was named Operation Olympic Games by the U.S. government. The malware they developed is called Stuxnet, and it infected computers connected to specific types of programmable logic controllers (PLCs) manufactured by Siemens. These controllers were used by Iran to control centrifuges used in the process of refining uranium. The malware caused the centrifuges to spin irregularly, which caused significant damage to the refining equipment, thereby accomplishing the goal of the U.S. and Israeli governments.

The Iranian computers were "air-gapped," meaning they were not connected to the Internet or any external network. Therefore, the Stuxnet malware must have been delivered to the affected servers via a physical attack. Although it has never been proven, it is widely surmised that an Iranian worker was hired to infect one of the servers by inserting a USB drive containing the malware. Even though the systems were not connected to an external network, they were interconnected via an internal network, allowing the malware to spread to other vulnerable systems at the Iranian facility. Unfortunately, the attack would have ended there; however, Stuxnet proved how difficult it can be to prevent a virus from spreading. At some point someone connected one of the infected computers to the Internet, enabling the Stuxnet virus to spread externally. Today it is believed Stuxnet has spread to over 100 countries and thousands of systems.

Doing Bad Things

As shown in the previous sections, the cyber criminal has many methods available to them to exploit target systems and networks. These include deploying malware, writing scripts, guessing passwords, and using social engineering and MITM attacks. Once a system is exploited the hacker can then seek to carry out whatever their objectives may be. This section explores some of the cyberattacker's objectives and some of the bad things they do during a cyberattack, including

- Data exfiltration
- Extortion
- Denial of service
- Advanced persistent threat

Objectives: Monetary, Political, or Personal

Cyber criminals are motivated by many things, but cyber criminal activity usually comes down to three possible motivators: monetary, personal, or political (or some combination thereof).

Cyber criminals can monetize their activity by collecting a ransom from their victims, by stealing data that has value and selling it (such as credit card data, personal information, or company secrets and intellectual property), or by fraudulently conducting electronic financial transactions. But money isn't the only reason. There have been many instances of cyber criminals carrying out cyberattacks for personal reasons. Former and current employees of organizations have carried out cyberattacks to take revenge on their employer, cause embarrassment to supervisors, or defame coworkers. In a case in 2021 in the United Kingdom, a former school IT employee who was fired retaliated against his former employer by launching multiple cyberattacks against the school's network causing loss of data belonging to the school and students. The culprit was caught, pled guilty, and was sentenced to 21 months in prison. Personal motivation for hacking also includes doing it for the challenge and/or the bragging rights within the community of hackers or their associates.

Cyberterrorism is cyber criminal activity that is politically motivated. In recent years there has been a sharp increase in cyberterrorism. Cyberterrorist attacks are meant to cause harm to governments, organizations, or individuals based on real or perceived political views or positions. One variant of cyberterrorism is hacktivism, which is carrying out a cyber attack to bring attention to a political or social cause.

Exfiltration

Exfiltration is essentially the unauthorized transfer of data from a computer or network. This is one of the basic goals of most cyberattacks: to steal data. Most often this includes personal or corporate information that can be sold or used to extort people and organizations for financial gain. Exfiltration can be accomplished by an attacker gaining unauthorized access to a resource that stores, transmits, or processes data using any of the methods described in the previous section describing exploits. Data is most often stolen during transmission (data in transit) or from storage (data at rest) usually stored in files and databases. However, some attacks can obtain data from computer memory during processing tasks.

Typical targets of data exfiltration include

- Credit card data
- Personally identifiable information (PII), which can include names, addresses, birthdates, social security numbers, photographs, and other personal identifiers
- Usernames and passwords
- Cryptographic keys
- Company-proprietary information, including financial data, trade secrets, patents, designs, plans, procedures, etc.
- Intellectual property such as works of art, source code, chemical or drug formulas, sales and marketing plans, etc.
- Financial data, including banking data and account numbers
- National and government agency data, including classified and military data, plans, procedures, secrets, etc.
- Protected health information (PHI), a person's personal healthcare information as specified by the Health Insurance Portability and Accountability Act (HIPAA)

In other words, almost any data processed, transmitted by, and stored in information systems today is a potential target for cyber criminals.

Data is stolen during transmission (data in transit) by the use of sniffers (which capture data flowing on a network) or packet analyzers (which do the same but offer analysis capabilities as well). These and many other legitimate network tools can read the network traffic and access data as long as it isn't encrypted. For encrypted data, such as web sessions using the HTTPS protocol, cyber criminals use specific kinds of MITM attacks in which the cyber criminal sets up an "interceptor" device in between the client and the server. The interceptor acts as a proxy between the two, appearing nearly invisible but capturing the data.

Organizations protect data in transit primarily by using encryption methods (described in Chapter 4) such as encrypted protocols like IPSec, HTTPS, SSL/TLS, SFTP, and FTPS. Data at rest protections include whole disk, file, and database encryption as well as access controls and permissions.

Extortion

Earlier in this chapter we discussed ransomware, which is malware used for extortion purposes. In the case of extortion, ransomware is the mechanism for both the exploit and the "doing bad thing" part of the attack. However, ransomware attacks are not the only method of cyber extortion. Cyber extortion attacks involve the cyber criminal forcing people or organizations to pay money or release data to the cyber criminal. They do this via threats or even bullying.

Social engineering is one such method used for cyber extortion using any of the exploit methods introduced in the social engineering section (pretexting, etc.). Forcing someone into giving up their password and accessing their bank account and stealing their money is cyber extortion. So is forcing someone into giving up their *corporate* password and then threatening to report them and get them fired if they don't send the cyber criminal money.

A more direct attack is for the cyber criminal to compromise someone's computer and then find, or plant, troublesome photos or information on it that the hacker threatens to expose to third parties. The third parties may be the victim's family, employer, business partners, customers, law enforcement, regulatory agencies, or anyone, depending on the nature of the data and the situation. The victim is then faced with paying the hacker or dealing with the consequences of the data being exposed.

Denial of Service

Denial of service (DoS) attacks are attacks against availability. Any attack that causes a legitimate user to be unable to access an information system or network is a DoS attack. DoS attacks render a resource unavailable by many means, most often by overwhelming the system with requests or processing tasks such that the system is unable to do its intended job or causing it to crash due to its inability to handle the work. The term DoS attack usually refers to an attack launched from a single computer.

Distributed denial of service (DDoS) attacks are DoS attacks launched from many computers, usually in the form of a botnet, which is a group of computers infected with malware that puts them under the control of a hacker. This is illustrated in Figure 3-10. Since the goal of these attacks is to overwhelm the victim's system or systems, a DDoS can be more effective because it creates more traffic or more requests against the target, as shown in the figure.

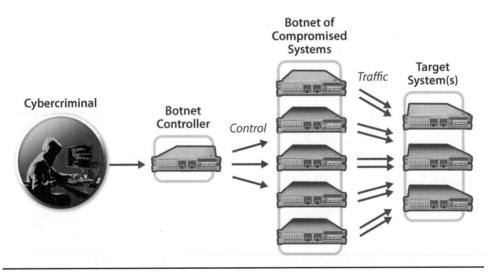

Figure 3-10   Distributed denial of service (DDoS) attack

Here are a few common types of DoS attacks which can also be launched as DDoS attacks using botnets:

- **Smurf attack**   In this attack the hacker sends specially crafted ICMP messages to a system. In normal operation the message is supposed to contain the IP address of the system that sent the message and the receiving system is supposed to send a reply to that IP address. But in the case of the attack, the message contains a false or spoofed source IP address, substituting the IP address of a system they want to attack. When used with a special type of IP traffic called a "directed broadcast," this attack can produce a large amount of network traffic at the victim system causing a DoS. Directed broadcasts, in which a sender asks a remotely located device such as a router to broadcast messages, is usually disabled on network devices nowadays, thus preventing this type of attack.

- **SYN flood attack**   This is similar to a smurf attack in that it uses a spoofed IP address to direct a flood of traffic to the victim system. The difference is the SYN attack uses TCP/IP instead of ICMP, which the smurf attack uses. Earlier in this chapter we described the three-way TCP handshake. During a SYN attack the attacker sends multiple SYN connection requests (the first phase of the three-way handshake) to overload the victim's system.

- **Ping attack**   A ping attack is another attack that uses the ICMP protocol. It involves using the ICMP ping or echo command, which is supposed to simply ask a computer, "Are you there?" by sending one ping and expecting one response back. But if an attacker floods a system with many ping requests, it can overwhelm the system and the supporting network resources. A variant of this attack is the *ping of death* attack in which the attacker creates ping requests of extremely large size. Such large ping messages can disrupt systems that are not designed to handle them.

Another form of DoS is *website defacement*. In this attack the cyber criminal changes the appearance and/or content of web pages. The purpose may be vandalism, political activism, terrorism, or as part of a social engineering scheme to trick users. In any case, if a hacker gains access to the web server and web pages with unauthorized edit privileges, they can change the content of the pages to accomplish their objective. In some cases, this can render the site unusable, which is a denial of service.

Advanced Persistent Threat

Many cyberattacks involve a quick strike in which the cyber criminal gains access to a computer system or network; accomplishes their objective such as extortion, exfiltration, or DoS; and then leaves. However, in many other attacks the cyber criminal does not leave right away. Their goal is to maintain a longer-term presence within the victim's system or network, stealthily doing malicious activities over a period of time. There are actors that perform these types of attacks who tend to be very sophisticated at what they do. Not only do these cyber criminals use sophisticated attack methods but they also use sophisticated methods to cover their tracks during the attack. Threats from these sophisticated persistent attacks are called an advanced persistent threat (APT).

During an APT the cyber criminal commonly seeks to expand the attack over time within the enterprise, probing the network, finding more systems with vulnerabilities, exploiting them, and gaining unauthorized access to more and more systems and data. APT attacks use some of the same attack methods as the normal attacks; however, APTs tend to be more sophisticated. The APT cyber criminal tends to have more expertise and resources than the average cyber criminal, and therefore the attacks usually involve a combination of attack methods, newly designed exploits, and usually more manual probing on the part of the hacker. The APT cyber criminal also takes great steps to cover up their tracks such as clearing event logs and command history files or modifying file attributes so they can continue their work for as long as possible without being detected.

APTs, due to their sophistication and use of advanced resources, tend to come from criminal organizations or nation-states. Criminal groups operating in Russia, Iran, North Korea, and China are known to be the source of damaging APT attacks around the world.

Network Threats and Attacks Summary

Here are the important topics to remember about network threats and attacks:

- Cyber criminals most commonly carry out the following types of attacks:
  - Malware
  - Scripting
  - Social engineering
  - Password attacks
  - Man-in-the-middle attacks
- There are many types of malware including viruses, trojans, worms, botnets, ransomware, and rootkits.
- Common scripting attacks include buffer overflows, cross-site scripting, HTTP response splitting, SQL injection, and timing/race conditions.
- Backdoors are a feature of many different kinds of attacks.
- Social engineering attacks use deception to trick someone into doing something that may not be in their best interest.
- Phishing and spear phishing use e-mails that look like real e-mails but are actually fraudulent.
- Password attacks are any attacks that seek to obtain a user's credentials. Methods include social engineering, phishing, brute force, dictionary, and rainbow tables.
- Man-in-the-middle attacks are attacks where a hacker inserts themselves in between legitimate communication.

- Exfiltration is the unauthorized transfer of data from a computer or network.

- Cyber extortion attacks involve the cyber criminal forcing people or organizations to pay money or release data to the cyber criminal.

- Denial of service (DoS) attacks are attacks against availability. DoS attacks render a resource unavailable, most often by overwhelming the system with requests or processing tasks such that the system is unable to do its intended job.

- Distributed denial of service (DDoS) attacks refer to DoS attacks launched from many computers, usually in the form of a botnet.

- An advanced persistent threat (APT) is an attack in which a sophisticated attacker maintains a long-term presence within the victim's system or network, stealthily doing malicious activities over a period of time.

Network Defenses

In Chapter 1 we introduced the concept of defense-in-depth, which means that rather than rely on just one control, a better strategy is to use multiple layers of security controls. In this section, we review common security elements that most organizations include in a typical defense-in-depth solution. These defense-in-depth elements are

- Firewalls
- Network security architecture elements
  - Network segmentation
  - Demilitarized zones
  - Virtual private networks
- Network access control
- E-mail and web application filtering
- Network operations elements
  - Threat intelligence
  - IDS/IPS
  - Antivirus software
- Wireless security
- IoT security
- Security assessments and testing

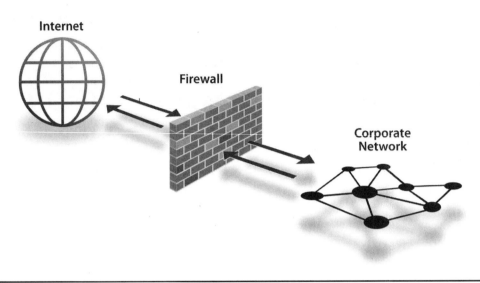

Figure 3-11 Typical firewall implementation

Firewalls

A firewall is a network device used to control access between two networks or two segments of a network. The firewall permits certain kinds of traffic to flow through it while preventing other kinds of traffic. The ability to prevent certain kinds of traffic makes the firewall a valuable security tool because it can be used to create areas of a network in which only certain types of activity is allowed and other activity is prevented. Figure 3-11 shows a typical firewall implementation.

In the figure, the firewall limits the type of traffic to and from the corporate network to only that which the corporation wants, based on the organization's security policies. For instance, the corporation may only want to allow connections from certain locations (IP addresses) or applications to connect to the corporate network. Likewise, they may want to limit the type of data that can leave the corporate network. These are some of the things that can be done with a firewall.

In this section we describe three general types of firewalls: packet filter, proxy, and stateful/dynamic packet filter, which are sometimes referred to as firewall generations 1, 2, and 3, respectively.

Packet Filter

Packet filters are the most basic and least expensive type of firewall. A packet filter is a kind of router. It screens all traffic and makes decisions as to whether to allow or deny traffic to pass from one of its interfaces to another based on the header information of each message. The firewall contains an access control list (ACL) which is configured by the organization. The ACL contains the rules upon which the firewall allows or denies what traffic can flow. The ACL contains information including

- Source and destination IP addresses
- Source and destination port numbers
- Protocol
- Direction of traffic

For example, an ACL may contain a rule that says web traffic using the HTTP protocol can enter the organization's LAN only if it contains the destination IP address of the organization's web server.

Proxy

Proxy firewalls do not allow direct communication between the networks they are installed between. Instead, they act as a middleman. The proxy hides the IP address of the devices within the network it is protecting. The proxy intercepts and repackages all traffic, applies a security policy, and prevents direct connections between the two networks. This makes it harder for cyber criminals to discover information about what is on the other side of the proxy.

Stateful/Dynamic Packet Filter

A stateful/dynamic packet filter takes the concept of a packet filter one step further. Instead of just using an ACL, they take into account the nature of the communication that is taking place to make decisions about what connections to allow or deny. They do this by examining the messages going back and forth and keeping track of what they previously learned about a conversation. They make access decisions based on the following information:

- IP address
- Protocols and commands
- Historical comparisons with previous packets
- The content of packets

A stateful firewall monitors the state of network conversations and allows packets to flow through the firewall only if they are part of existing authorized conversations. For example, if the firewall sees a computer connect to a web server and the web server replies, the firewall knows the kind of traffic that should be occurring during that kind of conversation and allows it but disallows other kinds of traffic. The firewall can log and keep track of multiple connections simultaneously.

 EXAM TIP   CC candidates should be familiar with the different types of firewalls and their functions.

Network Security Architecture Elements

Organizations commonly use network segmentation as a security control, as it allows them to group the network into segments or security zones for which rules can be defined and access controlled. One specific type of security zone is called a demilitarized zone (DMZ). Other architectural security controls are virtual private networks (VPNs) and network access controls (NACs). Segmentation, DMZs, and VPNs are discussed in the following subsections.

Network Segmentation

Network segmentation is a network design approach that allows organizations to group portions of the network into segments, each acting like a small network. Segmentation is accomplished by controlling how traffic flows to parts of the network based on policies. For example, an organization may use segmentation to create a segment of their network that is just for their financial systems and yet another segment that is just for their Internet-facing web servers. By proper design and configuration of network devices, the organization can ensure that only authorized users can access the segments of the network they need to based on the user's job function and need to know.

Segmentation has several benefits such as improving performance by limiting traffic in portions of the network to only the type of traffic required for the functions on that segment. In the example in the previous paragraph, web traffic would not adversely affect network traffic at the financial system, and vice versa, because they are on different network segments and communication between them is restricted. Segmentation is a beneficial tool for cybersecurity for several reasons:

- Segmentation helps an organization implement the principle of least privilege at a granular level on the network, enforcing the concept of zero trust.

- Segmentation creates more barriers for a hacker to go through to reach sensitive systems, thereby increasing the work factor of an attack.

- Segmentation limits how far an attack can spread throughout a network.

Segmentation can be accomplished *physically*, by separating the network into separate networks, or *logically*, by creating virtual networks or VLANs. Separate physical networks are accomplished using subnetting, as explained in the section "Network Segmentation." VLANs are a method of segmentation implemented by configuring routers and switches to associate specific nodes on the network with logical segments on a LAN (each logical segment is a VLAN). Communication between VLANs is restricted by security policy configured on the routers and switches.

Micro-segmentation takes the concept of isolating network segments and controlling who has access to what one step further: by doing it at the application level. With micro-segmentation, anything on the network, any device or any application, can be its own segment. That means access can be controlled for any device or application. With traditional networks, segmentation isolates traffic between segments, but everything within a segment, all the servers and applications, are lumped together. With micro-segmentation, isolation inside of the segment can be achieved.

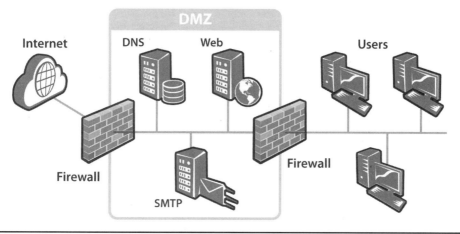

Figure 3-12 DMZ implementation

To effectively implement micro-segmentation requires software-defined networking (SDN). SDN is a networking framework that provides better and more granular control and management of the network. SDNs provide greater ability to automate, provision, control, and troubleshoot the network. From a security standpoint SDN provides great granularity in defining segments and access controls to create micro-segments to control access to applications and data.

EXAM TIP CC candidates should know the purpose and functions of network segmentation, VLANs, VPNs, and micro-segmentation.

Demilitarized Zones

One specific implementation of network segmentation is a DMZ. A DMZ is a network segment that is positioned in between the organization's connection to the Internet and their internal networks. See Figure 3-12 for an illustration of a DMZ implementation.

The purpose of the DMZ is to create a buffer zone between the organization's internal network and the outside world. The DMZ is bordered by two firewalls. Organizations usually place their e-mail, web, and DNS servers in the DMZ, as these servers require access to the Internet. Although these servers are "Internet-facing," they are still protected by a firewall. In the event of a cyberattack, if the hacker were to successfully breach the external firewall and compromise a system in the DMZ, they would still have to get through the second firewall to get to the internal network.

Virtual Private Networks

A VPN is a secure connection to a private network through a public network such as the Internet. The connection is encrypted and secured virtually, extending the organization's private network to authorized users outside of it. A VPN is illustrated in Figure 3-13.

VPNs use tunneling technology that provides an encrypted channel through an untrusted network from the user's system to the VPN server. The untrusted network is

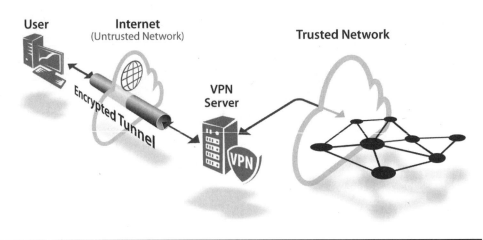

Figure 3-13 VPN illustration

most often the Internet (we call it untrusted because we cannot control the security on the Internet). Using a VPN, an organization's remote users can access resources on the internal corporate network almost as if they had a direct connection to it. We say *almost* because using VPNs can involve extra operational steps and can introduce delays in transmission, which can impact performance.

Organizations typically use VPNs as a way to allow employees to work from home, a coffee shop, or anywhere outside of the office. The VPN protects the path from the employee's computer to the office from sniffing or interception by hackers.

VPNs use tunneling protocols to protect the data and manage the connection. The protocols encapsulate the frame/packet so it can be transmitted through a network by preserving the original protocol headers so the message can be "unwrapped" at its destination while allowing the encapsulated frame to be routed as normal traffic. Older protocols include Point-to-Point Tunneling Protocol (PPTP) and Layer 2 Tunneling Protocol (L2TP); however, the de facto standard protocol for VPNs is IP Security (IPSec), which is a suite of protocols that provides data integrity, authentication, and confidentiality.

VPNs for Home Use

An alternate and popular use of VPNs for home users is as a safer way to use the Internet. In this method, shown in Figure 3-14, instead of the VPN server providing a connection to a trusted network, it provides another connection to the Internet. With this approach the VPN server acts as a proxy, hiding the user from a direct connection to Internet resources. VPNs have become a popular option for home users because it allows them to use the Internet safely and anonymously using an encrypted tunnel to the VPN server while hiding their IP address from Internet traffic. This makes it harder for cyber criminals to intercept messages on the encrypted portion of the connection and makes it impossible to track the user's activity on the Internet due to the proxy. VPNs for home use are commonly sold as subscription services.

Network Access Control

NAC is a technology that allows organizations to implement controls that limit what devices can connect to their network. For example, if you want to connect to a corporate network that is configured for NAC, the network will not allow your computer to connect until it first checks your computer to see if it meets certain criteria based on a policy. The policy may say that only computers that have specific configuration settings or have antivirus software installed or have up-to-date patches installed can connect to the network. This helps keep the network free of devices that could introduce threats into the environment such as malware, hidden scripts, or software that is otherwise not permitted on the network. Many organizations use NAC as a security control to prevent rogue devices from connecting to their network.

E-mail and Web Application Filtering

There are many specialized security appliances and services available used to defend networks. Two of the most popular are e-mail and web application filters. Either can be implemented as appliances, software running on a computer, or as services offered by vendors.

E-mail filters examine an organization's inbound and outbound e-mail traffic looking for evidence of phishing, spam, malware, suspicious links, disallowed attachments, and other threats. If a malicious e-mail is discovered, the filter blocks or quarantines the e-mail and automatically deletes it or requires it to be manually inspected depending on how the filter is configured. Web filters act as web firewalls. They monitor traffic between web applications and the Internet based on a set of rules configurable by the organization to permit benign traffic while preventing malicious traffic.

Network Operations Elements

Organizations perform actions to prevent and detect malicious activities. Many organizations, especially large ones, have security operations centers in which dedicated security staff deploy and operate security tools to protect and monitor the enterprise on an ongoing basis. Whether or not organizations have formal security operations centers, there are a few key detection, monitoring, and prevention tools and technologies they all make use of. This section discusses them.

Threat Intelligence

In Chapter 1 we discussed the risk management process in which the organization lists and characterizes the threats they are likely to face. And later in this chapter we discuss IDS/IPS and antivirus systems, all of which operate based on their understanding of threats. For these processes and systems to work effectively there must be intelligence available about what threats are out there and what they can do. Organizations shouldn't be guessing about what threats they may face. Their decisions and protections should be based on facts.

Organizations and product vendors collect information about threats from private threat subscription services such as CrowdStrike and Mandiant, open source threat intelligence exchanges such as the Open Threat Exchange (OTX), and public threat feeds such as the FBI's InfraGard. Threats include types of malware and other exploits; threat actors including nation-states, individuals, and organizations involved in hacking; and details about the methods of attack. By collecting and studying data about threats, organizations can prepare for and defend against them. Vendors that produce security products such as intrusion detection and antivirus products incorporate threat intelligence into their products so these products know what they are looking for and what they need to do to detect and/or defend against the threats. Organizations use threat intelligence to help them perform risk management and choose the right approaches to defending against threats.

Threat intelligence includes information about current and emerging threats such as

- Threat actors
- Actor's tactics, techniques, and processes
- Vulnerabilities prone to the threat
- Indicators that a compromise may have occurred
  - IP addresses of malicious sources
  - Domain names of infected sites and botnet servers
  - Malware file footprints and malware behavior signatures

Some organizations purchase subscriptions to threat intelligence feeds or services that provide them with real-time information about the latest cyber threats. Sometimes these feeds interface directly with IDS/IPS or other security products so they can protect against the latest threats. Many organizations employ *threat intelligence analysts* whose job it is to study the threat landscape and help the organization stay ahead of the curve by ensuring they can defend against the latest threats to the organization.

IDS and IPS

Organizations purchase tools that they install onto their networks that help them detect if and when they are under attack. Two of these types of tools are called IDSs and IPSs. Both deploy sensors throughout the network that communicate with a centralized control or reporting system. The centralized system allows the security staff to view indicators of malicious activity and take measures to prevent security breaches. IDS and IPS differ in that an IDS merely detects and reports on potential malicious activity, whereas an IPS not only detects and reports but also automatically takes defensive action in response to what it sees, such as blocking certain types of traffic.

A *network-based IDS/IPS (NIDS)* uses sensors deployed throughout the network in the form of specialized appliances or computers running specialized NIDS software. A *host-based IDS/IPS (HIDS)* uses software (called agents) installed on host computers that monitor for, and detect, malicious activity on the host. HIDS agents look for host- or OS-specific activities that malware or cyber criminals are known to perform, such as running processes, registry changes, file alteration, and so on. Whether network or host based, several detection methods are employed by IDSs/IPSs. Modern IDS/IPS products usually take advantage of more than one of these methods:

- *Signature-based IDS/IPSs* look for specific patterns in traffic, specific messages, or specific files on systems. These specific patterns are called *signatures*. Usually IDS/IPS product vendors use a threat intelligence subscription service whereby the products continually learn about new attacks and what kinds of signatures would be indicative of their presence. New signatures are downloaded to the IDS/IPS products so they are continuously monitoring for and able to detect the latest attacks. Signature-based IDSs are good at detecting already known attacks but not as good at detecting new kinds of attacks.

- *Anomaly-based IDSs/IPSs* are better at detecting unknown attacks. Whereas a signature-based IDS/IPS is good at knowing "what bad looks like," an anomaly-based IDS is good at knowing "what good looks like." An anomaly-based IDS/IPS uses specialized methods such as artificial intelligence and machine learning to build a picture of what normal activity looks like on the network or system. Then if the IDS/IPS sees activity that deviates from the norm, it passes an alert to indicate the activity should be investigated. Anomaly-based IDSs are good at detecting previously unknown attacks for which signatures may not exist.

Whereas IDS and IPS products use the same technology and methods to detect potentially malicious activity, the difference lies in what each one does about that activity. An IDS simply reports the activity so the security staff can see the alert and perform an investigation to determine if the alert represents actual malicious activity or a breach and then determine the appropriate course of action. An IPS goes beyond mere detection and reporting by automatically taking action to try to stop the attack or minimize its impact. Some of the actions an IPS may take include blocking traffic from a particular IP address, turning off a port on a firewall, resetting a device such as a router, or even changing data to remove or replace malicious messages or files.

 NOTE A newer name for products that protect endpoints (computers, servers, routers, mobile devices, IoT, etc.) is called endpoint security or endpoint protection software. This family of products is essentially the same thing as HIDS/HIPS. They all monitor what is going on within hosts and detect and report malware or malicious activity and can take action to defend the asset.

Antivirus Software

Antivirus software is exactly as its name implies. It protects the device on which it is installed against attacks from viruses. Most antivirus products detect and remove many types of malware and in addition protect computers against other threats, including spam and phishing attacks.

Most antivirus software works by looking for patterns of behavior that match similar patterns, or signatures, stored in its database of known malware. However, antivirus software also uses machine learning and heuristics to detect variations in known malware behaviors. Since the threat environment is ever-changing antivirus software must be kept up to date, and most are purchased as subscription services, so they are continually updated with the latest malware threat intelligence information to protect the computer against the latest threats.

Zero-Day Vulnerabilities, Exploits, and Attacks

Zero-day is a term that refers to vulnerabilities, exploits, or attacks that were previously unknown to cyber professionals and product vendors. Typically, product vendors discover security vulnerabilities in their products and release patches to fix them in a timely manner, However, during the period in which there is no patch, either because the vendor is not yet aware of the vulnerability or they haven't come up with a fix yet, the product remains vulnerable. The same is true for new exploits such as new malware. It takes time for antivirus vendors to learn about them and figure out how to detect them. Zero-day attacks are particularly troublesome because specific defenses against them are not yet in place. The term zero-day applies to the following:

- **Zero-day vulnerabilities**   A recently discovered security vulnerability in a product, operating system, or application that is unknown to the vendor or for which there is no available fix or patch.

- **Zero-day exploits**   A recently discovered exploit such as malware that is unknown to countermeasure organizations (e.g., malware unknown to antivirus software vendors).

- **Zero-day attacks**   Any attack that takes advantage of zero-day vulnerabilities and/or zero-day exploits.

Since zero-day vulnerabilities, exploits, and attacks are by definition unknown entities, they can be difficult to defend against using methods that require knowledge about them. Organizations defend against zero-day attacks by using a holistic security program applying defense-in-depth to ensure there are multiple layers of defense. Modern antivirus and IDS/IPS systems are getting better at detecting zero-day activity by the use of machine learning and behavior-based approaches that look for malicious-looking activity not specific to just one type of attack.

Wireless Security

Wireless networks present natural security risks for a few reasons. First, you can't physically see what devices are connected to them, so it's harder to distinguish an authorized device from a rogue one. Second, they can extend outside of an organization's physical perimeter, which not only limits visibility of what is connected but also makes it easier for cyber criminals to connect to or listen in on the traffic that is riding on them because the cyber criminal can do these things from outside the facility.

Wireless networks have gone through a few iterations of security improvements since they were first introduced in the late 1990s. The first security protocol for wireless was Wireless Equivalent Privacy (WEP). However, although WEP used encryption, it was implemented very poorly and could easily be defeated. In 2003 the Wi-Fi Protected Access Protocol (WPA) was introduced, which had better encryption. WPA evolved through WPA2, which uses Advanced Encryption Standard (AES) encryption to WPA3, which is now considered the best practice. Most organizations and vendors now use either WPA2 or WPA3 for wireless security.

Wireless protected setup (WPS) is a feature on some wireless access points that provides a shortcut during the setup process when connecting new devices to the access point. The feature allows the user to simply press a button and enter a personal identification number (PIN) for the devices to authenticate to each other. This method, while convenient, is inherently nonsecure and should not be used. WPS should be disabled, and most organizations do so.

Since wireless networking devices are part of the network infrastructure, organizations take the same approaches and precautions when using them as they do for any network device:

- Wireless routers and access points should be patched on a regular basis as part of an organization's patch and vulnerability management program to ensure vulnerabilities discovered by the product vendor are not left unresolved.

- Many wireless devices have default administrator passwords that should be changed by the organization upon installation to a secret, strong password known only to the organization.

- Wireless networks can be segmented from other parts of the network as part of the organization's overall network security design approach using subnetting or VLANs. Likewise, some organizations use firewalls to filter traffic to and from wireless networks to enforce security policies.

Internet of Things Security

The Internet of Things (IoT) is a general term that refers to many different kinds of physical devices that connect to the Internet or IP networks. IoT devices are sometimes called smart devices because they frequently contain processing capability, often in combination with sensors, robotics, and automation technology. IoT devices are used in home automation, manufacturing and associated control systems, medical and health-care, infrastructure and power control systems, environmental monitoring, military communications and weapons systems, and many other applications. Any device that has an IP connection is an IoT device.

IoT devices present unique security issues because security is not typically built into these devices. While IoT devices do have many of the same security issues found in traditional devices, they tend to be more problematic from a security standpoint. Security flaws abound in IoT. Here are a few examples:

- **Security vulnerabilities**   IoT devices can have inherent security vulnerabilities that can allow hackers to make unauthorized connections to them or take control of them. This is because many IoT products were not designed with security in mind.

- **Poor authentication**   Many IoT devices have poorly implemented authentication mechanisms such as hardcoded default passwords, weak passwords, or no authentication at all.

- **Lack of security features on the interface**   Many IoT devices have an IP interface (and some have an API) but lack security features such as encryption and authentication.

- **Physical access**   Due to their nature many IoT devices are deployed in environments where physical security controls may be difficult to implement. Manufacturing floors, power plants, waste treatment facilities, hospitals, warehouses, etc., make for challenging environments for physical security, which can lead to cybersecurity vulnerabilities and exploits.

IoT devices should be part of any organization's information security program, as they are assets connected to the enterprise and bring their own inherent risks. Here are a few things organizations do to ensure IoT devices do not enable cyberattacks and data breaches:

- **Security policies**   An organization's security policies should include IoT devices within their scope. Policies should address IoT usage, configuration, vulnerabilities, security testing, and all aspects of their acceptable use within the organization.

- **Patch management**   IoT devices should be part of an organization's patch management program to ensure IoT devices are kept up-to-date with the vendor's latest security updates.

- **Use appropriate authentication**   For access to and use of IoT devices, use authentication using strong passwords, dual factor, and Privileged Access Management (PAM) where possible.

- **Use compensating controls**   In instances where IoT devices lack their own built-in controls, organization use compensating controls such as firewalls, additional network segmentation, or proxies to implement security controls.

- **Use encryption**   Many organizations encrypt traffic to and from IoT devices as a means of defense.

- **Change defaults**   As with any network device, organizations change defaults such as default settings and default administrator passwords to increase the work factor for attackers.

Security Assessments and Testing

Organizations with good security programs perform security assessments on a regular basis as part of their network defenses. Security assessments give the organization a picture of how effective their security controls are as well as the extent to which they are in compliance with regulatory requirements. Security assessments include automated and manual testing to measure the effectiveness of program components and of the security program as a whole.

Security program assessments and security testing are sometimes performed in-house by persons within the organization. However, testing and assessments are often conducted by independent auditors, third-party firms, or as-a-service vendors. Outside firms can provide advantages by having greater testing/assessment expertise or by being able to perform independent, unbiased assessments that may not be possible with in-house personnel.

These individuals or firms work with the organization to develop criteria for the assessment and perform interviews with organization staff; review documentation; plan, write, and perform testing; and may even observe the security staff in action to perform the assessment. Results are presented to the security or organization management for consideration and improvement.

This section presents some of the ways organizations test and assess the security program.

Security Program Assessment

A security program assessment evaluates the organization's information security program, measuring how well it is organized, operated, staffed, and whether it meets its goals. The assessment includes a review of the organization's policies, procedures, staffing, workforce, and operational infrastructure and may include some or all of the following components:

- Regulatory compliance review

- Security policy, standards, and procedures review

- Security organization and staffing review

- Data security review

- Network security review

- Physical security review

- Security operations review

- Incident handling review

- Business continuity and disaster recovery review

- Security training and awareness review

Security program assessments are conducted by reviewing documentation, performing interviews with organization staff, and reviewing the results of audits. These assessments typically do not include testing. Testing is usually part of vulnerability assessments, described in the next section.

Vulnerability Assessments and Scanning

A vulnerability assessment is a comprehensive version of the same type of scanning a hacker does, which we describe earlier in this chapter in the section "Identifying Targets." Vulnerability assessments seek to enumerate all devices found within a targeted range of IP addresses, revealing open ports, running services, and known vulnerabilities in systems. The main difference between the scans that a hacker runs and a vulnerability assessment run by an organization is the purpose and comprehensiveness. A hacker is looking for targets, whereas an organization is looking to uncover all information and vulnerabilities that are present in the enterprise so they can then start to close all the holes.

Vulnerability assessments look at an organization from an external, or Internet, perspective, running scans and tests from the Internet, wireless access points, and even phone lines that may be used by the organization with older technology modems or fax machines. In addition, vulnerability tests are also run from an internal perspective, to learn what kind of information a hacker could learn about an organization's network if they could get behind a border firewall and run scans from there.

Some vulnerability assessments are limited to just scanning, while others involve additional testing. Vulnerability assessments can include

- **Network and system vulnerability testing**   Comprehensive external and internal scanning to discover all devices on the organization's networks and enumerate all vulnerabilities.

- **Application security assessment**   Testing of software applications using automated and manual means to identify application-level vulnerabilities such as cross-site scripting and other coding errors.

- **Physical security assessment**   Testing of physical security controls, including facility perimeter controls (fences, cameras, etc.), interior controls (doors, locks, etc.), and specialized controls (fire suppression, etc.).

- **Human-based vulnerability assessment**   Testing of people's ability to practice proper security hygiene. May include testing of employees' ability to withstand social engineering attacks such as phishing, knowledge of and compliance with policies, and ability of employees to apply security knowledge to their jobs.

Penetration Testing

Penetration testing and vulnerability assessments are often performed in tandem. While vulnerability assessments provide a comprehensive view of an organization's security vulnerabilities, penetration testing demonstrates how selected vulnerabilities could be exploited. Penetration testing shows how exploits could impact the organization and what damage they could cause. Penetration testers usually try to mimic the steps that an actual hacker would take to compromise an organization. These steps were introduced previously in this book:

1. Conduct research
2. Identify targets
3. Exploit targets
4. Do bad things

By documenting their activities in a report, penetration testers provide the organization's management with a revealing and sometimes eye-opening account of how, and sometimes how easily, cyber criminals could execute a successful cyberattack against the organization's assets. Vulnerability assessments and penetration testing can have great value in helping organizations understand their security posture. When performed on a regular basis, they can help organizations improve their security over time.

Security Compliance Assessments

Some organizations, due to the nature of their business, must comply with legal and regulatory requirements such as HIPAA or the Gramm-Leach-Bliley Act (GLBA), both of which have security requirements that certain businesses must comply with. Or some organizations must comply with business-related security requirements due to their industry, such as the Payment Card Data Security Standard (PCI DSS), which is a set of rules for organizations that store, process, or transmit credit card information. These organizations test their compliance with the requirements they are obligated to comply with.

Network Defenses Summary

Here are the important topics to remember and study about network defenses:

- Organizations using defense-in-depth use architectural elements to help secure the environment, including
  - Network segmentation
  - Demilitarized zones
  - Virtual private networks
  - Network access control
- Firewalls, e-mail, and web application filtering are all technologies that limit the kinds of traffic that can occur on the network.
- Network operations elements, including threat intelligence, IDS/IPS, antivirus software, and security assessments and testing, are detective and preventive security controls.

Network Infrastructure

In the "Network Fundamentals" section of this chapter, we reviewed the key fundamentals of computer networks such as ports, protocols, network models, and various network devices. At the end of the day, these network devices and infrastructure need to exist somewhere. For most organizations, this is a datacenter. In this section we are going to review some key considerations regarding the underlying datacenter infrastructure that supports the organizations. The two main types of datacenter infrastructure models include

- On-premises datacenter infrastructure
- Cloud infrastructure

The main difference between an on-premises datacenter infrastructure and cloud infrastructure lies in how the service is provisioned, managed, and utilized.

On-Premises Datacenter Infrastructure

Having an on-premises datacenter infrastructure means that your organization owns or rents a datacenter that must be appropriately staffed and managed. Datacenters typically hold the crown jewels for an organization centralized in a single space that must be properly secured and maintained. This includes everything from the physical security of the datacenter; the network and computer hardware; power, heating, and cooling; and so on. When leveraging a cloud service these functions are handled by the cloud service provider. However, with an on-premises datacenter model, the organization must decide how these functions are managed. In this section we will review the following key considerations when operating an on-premises datacenter:

- Staffing models
- Datacenter physical security
- Datacenter environmental protection
- Datacenter system redundancy

Staffing Models

Datacenter personnel are either hired directly by the organization as in-house employees (known as insourcing) or the organization may hire a third-party provider (known as outsourcing).

Insourcing   Organizations may elect to hire resources in-house to manage all or some aspects of the on-premises datacenter (e.g., physical security, hardware, facilities management, datacenter operations). This may include roles such as

- Facilities manager to oversee datacenter buildings operations
- Safety officer to oversee personnel safety
- Security guards to manage and monitor physical security
- IT personnel to manage technical components

Outsourcing   Organizations may elect to contract with a third party to manage some or all aspects of the on-premises datacenter. In some cases, the organization may own the datacenter and in other cases it may be rented from a third party. In any outsourcing arrangement, it is critical that the appropriate contracts are in place to govern and manage the relationship such as service level agreements (discussed more later in this chapter).

Datacenter Physical Security

Datacenters often contain highly sensitive information centralized in a single facility or building. This makes them a valuable target to attackers, and the repercussions of a physical security incident could be disastrous. The following are some key physical security aspects of operating a datacenter that must be considered:

- **Physical access control** Physical access controls (covered in Chapter 2) are important for preventing and controlling access (using badge systems, doors, fencing, physical barriers, etc.) as well as monitoring access (using security guards, access logs, cameras, alarms, etc.).

- **Supply systems** Organizations must ensure that supply systems (such as power, wiring, network cabling, temperature systems, etc.) are properly secured and can't be tampered with to prevent interruptions to datacenter operations.

- **Segmentation** Physical segmentation is often used in datacenter design to physically divide and separate areas with different security and risk levels (sometimes referred to as *security zones*). These might include things like wiring closets, power and cooling systems, or systems and servers that store or process more sensitive information.

Datacenter Environmental Protection

When operating a datacenter, it is important to have systems in place to manage and control the environment to manage temperature, humidity, and so on. Due to the nature of computer equipment, the environmental controls needed in a datacenter are unique compared to other facilities. This impacts the design and implementation of systems such as heating, ventilation, and air conditioning and fire detection and suppression systems.

Heating, Ventilation, and Air Conditioning It is important that the datacenter temperature and humidity levels are maintained at proper levels. Servers and other computer equipment generate a lot of heat and are sensitive to heat. If the equipment gets too hot, it can overheat and shut off. Similarly with humidity, high humidity can cause computer components to corrode, and low humidity can introduce static electricity. This is why it is important to have heating, ventilation, and air conditioning (HVAC) systems in place to maintain the datacenter environment.

Fire Detection and Suppression Fires can happen from things like electrical failures, ignition of combustible materials, personnel carelessness, or even arson. Organizations must ensure that proper systems are in place to detect and suppress fires if they occur. Fire detectors typically operate by detecting heat, smoke, or flame. Upon detection, the system deploys suppression agents (such as water or other gas agents). Gaseous systems are typically preferable for datacenters because they are the least destructive to the equipment (servers, network equipment, etc.) but are also generally more expensive. In addition, portable fire extinguishers should be available and leveraged where appropriate.

Datacenter System Redundancy

The redundancy of datacenter supply systems is critical to maintaining the continuity of ongoing operations. This includes having alternate and backup power supply systems as well as the appropriate contracts with vendors and suppliers in place (such as service level agreements) to ensure components can be replaced and services restored within an appropriate timeframe in the event of an outage or disaster. Organizations must consider things like connectivity between systems, hardware replacement, alternate power supply, alternate facilities, and so on. These requirements should be assessed and evaluated as part of the organization's business continuity and disaster recovery program (discussed in Chapter 5).

Business Continuity and Disaster Recovery   Organizations plan for disasters that may impact the datacenter and datacenter operations. This includes having appropriate response plans in place such as a business continuity plan (BCP) and a disaster recovery plan (DRP). In addition, the level of redundancy required varies based on the needs of the organization and the system in question. These requirements are analyzed and documented through a process known as business impact analysis (BIA). These concepts are discussed in Chapter 5.

Hardware and Network Infrastructure   Hardware and network redundancy helps prevent loss of system and service availability due to the failure of hardware or physical network connectivity. Hardware redundancy can be implemented by having backup hardware components or devices on hand (network devices, servers, or other computer hardware components) and through contracts with hardware vendors for replacements and service. Appropriate service level agreements should be established with hardware and other support vendors to ensure timely service in the event of a disaster.

In order for the computers and servers in a datacenter to communicate and operate, they require network connectivity. Network redundancy is used to ensure network connectivity in the event of an issue that impacts the network (such as a bad network cable or outage from the telecommunication service provider). This can be implemented by having multiple network communication paths for network traffic so data can keep flowing in the event of a disaster. For Internet connectivity, that could mean having a contract with an alternate telecommunication service provider (ISP). Within the datacenter network, this means having multiple communication lines between systems where applicable. In some cases, organizations even run devices in a high availability pair (known as an HA pair) where two systems (such as firewalls, storage devices, etc.) are connected and configured in such a way where if one goes down the other can take over. This helps prevent the risk of a *single point of failure* where the failure of a single component or device prevents a system from operating.

Power   Power is essential for all critical systems in a datacenter to operate. Power outages can be caused by a variety of factors including severe weather, equipment failure, physical damage to power systems, or an outage on the side of the electric utility company. This is why organizations plan to have both primary and alternate power supply strategies. Alternate power supply often comes from batteries, electric generators that run on diesel fuel or natural gas, or a contract with another electric utility provider for a redundant power line.

These strategies cover alternate power supplies; however, you don't want your servers to immediately shut down from a power outage (as this can cause data loss and other problems), and you may need time to run over and start the backup generator. To help with this, organizations often use uninterruptible power supplies. An *uninterruptible power supply (UPS)* is a special backup battery connected to systems to ensure they don't immediately shut off during a power outage. UPS systems are generally used to provide a short window of power until the alternate power systems kick in.

Alternate Facilities   Organizations should have strategies in place to recover operations if their datacenter or other facilities are damaged or inoperable. When this happens, operations must be moved to an alternate facility. Organizations may elect to have a dedicated alternate site, lease/rent a facility, or enter into an agreement with another organization. Organizations sometimes establish formal agreements with other organizations to aid each other during a disaster by allowing the use of each other's datacenters or facilities or providing other aid. These are documented in agreements such as reciprocal agreements, memorandums of understanding (MOUs), memorandums of agreement (MOA), mutual aid agreements, or other contracts. In any case, it is important these agreements are formally documented in legal contracts that outline the roles and responsibilities associated with the partnership. The various types of alternate facilities are discussed in more detail in Chapter 5.

Preventative Maintenance

Almost all supporting systems in a datacenter require some sort of ongoing upkeep and preventative maintenance. Candidate systems for maintenance include HVAC systems, fire suppression systems, generators, and so on. These all require ongoing preventative maintenance that is often performed by the equipment vendor or another third-party provider due to the specialization of the equipment. Regular preventative maintenance ensures that these systems are running smoothly and operating effectively and reduces the chance of an outage due to system failure.

Cloud Infrastructure

The National Institute of Standards and Technology (NIST) defines cloud computing as "a model for enabling ubiquitous, convenient, on-demand network access to a shared pool of configurable computing resources (e.g., networks, servers, storage, applications, and services) that can be rapidly provisioned and released with minimal management effort or service provider interaction." An easy example of cloud computing is when you use a web browser to log in to a web-based e-mail service, such as Gmail. You don't have to manage the physical hardware (servers, networking equipment, etc.) that runs the e-mail service. All you have to do is log in and voila! This is an example of a cloud service. In this section, we review the key characteristics of cloud computing, the main cloud service, and cloud deployment models, as well as some methods for evaluating the security of a cloud service provider. These are illustrated in Figure 3-14.

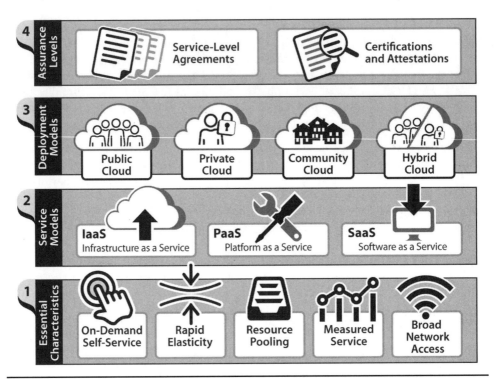

Figure 3-14   Cloud characteristics, service models, deployment models, and assurance levels

NOTE   Cloud computing is enabled by *virtualization,* which is a technology that allows hardware equipment to run many virtual instances (such as virtual operating systems, applications, storage, networking, etc.).

Who Are the Entities Involved?

When discussing cloud services, there are some key terms to think about that describe the entities involved: the cloud service provider and the cloud service customer.

- **Cloud service provider**   The *cloud service provider (CSP)* is the organization that provides the cloud service/resources that are consumed by the cloud service customer.

- **Cloud service customer**   The *cloud service customer (CSC)* is the entity that has a relationship with the cloud service provider to use their cloud service.

In many cases, the CSC and CSP are different entities, such as an organization leveraging a CSP (like Azure or AWS) to host their infrastructure. However, in some cases, the "customer" and "provider" could even be in the same organization.

For example, an organization's IT department may develop a private cloud (discussed later in this section) to allow other teams in the organization (e.g., engineering, development) to create and provision their own virtual computing resources as needed.

Cloud Computing Characteristics

When the term "cloud" began to first gain traction, there was not a standard agreed-upon definition. Organizations like NIST and ISO/IEC defined essential characteristics for cloud computing to help clarify the terminology and define a standard for its usage. The following are the five essential characteristics of cloud computing as defined in NIST Special Publication 800-145, *The NIST Definition of Cloud Computing*:

- **On-demand self-service**   Cloud service customers can configure the computing resources they need (what they need, when they need it), allowing them to tailor resources to their needs. The key component is self-serve, meaning the customers can provision and deprovision the resources themselves (through some web portal or similar interface) without having to ask an administrator of the CSP.

- **Rapid elasticity**   Cloud service customers can rapidly scale resources (in some cases automatically) as needed to acquire more or less capability. This allows customers the ability to only use what they need, as they can scale up or scale down when appropriate.

- **Resource pooling**   Computing resources of the CSP are pooled and shared across multiple consumers (referred to as cloud service customers or tenants) in a manner that abstracts the consumer from the underlying implementation.

- **Measured service**   The amount of resources used by the CSC can be automatically metered and measured. This allows the customer to understand and report on their usage and only pay for what they use. This is similar to how we receive an electricity bill for our usage.

- **Broad network access**   CSC access is enabled over the network and supported by many different client platforms running on a wide variety of endpoint devices (e.g., laptops, desktops, mobile phones).

ISO/IEC 17788, *Information technology — Cloud computing — Overview and vocabulary* provides a definition for cloud computing that consists of six characteristics, including those mentioned previously, with the addition of multitenancy. *Multitenancy* describes the allocation of cloud computing resources in a way that multiple tenants (also known as customers) can utilize a pool of resources while keeping their data and computing isolated from other tenants.

EXAM TIP   CC candidates should have an understanding of the NIST characteristics of cloud computing described earlier.

Cloud Service Models

The *cloud service model* describes the category of service provided by the CSP. The primary cloud service models are infrastructure as a service, platform as a service, and software as a service, described in more detail next:

- **Infrastructure as a service (IaaS)**   In an IaaS model, the CSP gives customers self-service access to a pool of infrastructure resources (such as network, server, storage, etc.) that can be virtually provisioned and deprovisioned on-demand. The CSP manages the underlying physical infrastructure and the physical hosts that support that infrastructure. The customer manages the platforms and software such as OS, development tools, applications, and virtual hosts that they provision.

- **Platform as a service (PaaS)**   In a PaaS model, the CSP gives customers access to platforms where they can develop, test, and run code for applications developed in various programming languages.

- **Software as a service (SaaS)**   The SaaS model is likely the model folks are the most familiar with. This is when a software service or application is hosted by the CSP and provided to customers (typically over the Internet). The cloud provider manages the infrastructure and platform, and the customer only needs to manage specific configurations within the application. Examples of SaaS include web-based e-mail, social media sites, and other web-based applications.

The cloud service models help describe how the responsibility for certain functions shifts from the customer to the provider. This is best illustrated in the shared responsibility model, shown in Figure 3-15. This shows how the cloud provider takes on increasing levels of responsibility when looking at on-premises, IaaS, PaaS, and SaaS.

Figure 3-15
Cloud shared
responsibility
model

Responsibility	On-premises	IaaS	PaaS	SaaS
Data Classification and Accountability	○	○	○	○
Client and end-point protection	○	○	○	◕
Identity and access management	○	○	◕	◕
Application-level controls	○	○	◕	◕
Network controls	○	◕	●	●
Host infrastructure	○	◕	●	●
Physical security	○	●	●	●

○ Cloud Service Customer   ● Cloud Service Provider

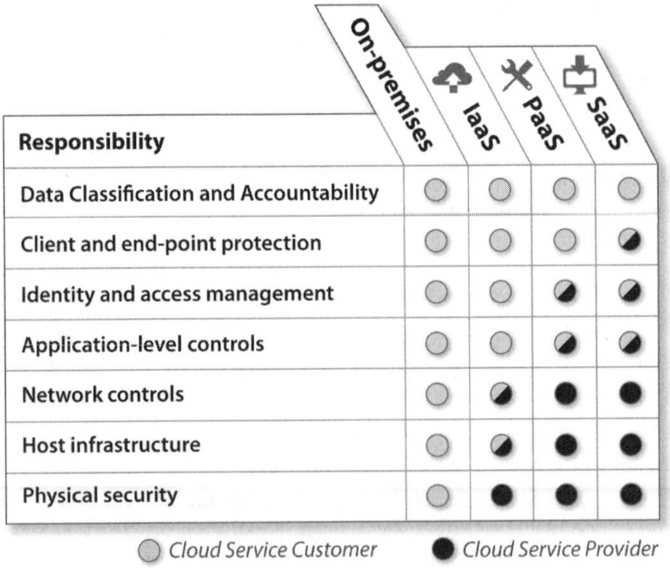

NOTE At the end of the day, every organization is accountable for ensuring it is protecting its data and the data of its customers. Even if the organization is outsourcing some responsibilities to a third party (such as a cloud service provider), the organization remains liable and accountable for ensuring that service providers they are contracting with are implementing good security practices.

As a Service Models

The term "as a service" is often used to describe other cloud-based service offerings. One example is identity as a service (IDaaS), which may be used by some service providers to describe a cloud-based offering that provides identity and access management capability. This may include things like the ability to provision and revoke identities, directory synchronization, single sign-on, and federated identity (discussed in Chapter 2). Although "as a service" terminology is used to describe other services, like IDaaS, IDaaS really falls under a SaaS service model, as it is a software service used to manage identities. IaaS, PaaS, and SaaS are the industry-standard service models.

Cloud Deployment Models

The *cloud deployment model* describes how the cloud service is deployed, managed, and consumed. The primary cloud deployment models include public, private, community, and hybrid. These are each described in the sections to follow.

Public Cloud   A public cloud consists of cloud computing resources operated by a third party that are deployed for use by the general public for purchase and consumption (typically a subscription or on-demand pricing model). Examples of public CSPs include Amazon Web Services (AWS), Microsoft Azure, Google Cloud Platform (GCP), and Oracle Cloud Infrastructure (OCI).

Private Cloud   A private cloud consists of dedicated cloud computing resources used by a single organization. The key here is the exclusivity of use, as the resources aren't shared among other entities like they are in a public cloud model. The cloud resources may be owned and operated by the organization, a third party, or a combination of both. The example provided earlier was that an organization's IT department might run a private cloud to allow other teams in the organization (engineering, development, etc.) to provision their own resources.

Community Cloud   A community cloud is a slight variation of a private cloud where cloud resources are shared between multiple communities, organizations, or businesses typically for a specific purpose or mission (such as collaboration, security or compliance requirements, or some other reasons). Like a private cloud, a community cloud is only available to members of the community, not the general public. The cloud resources may be owned and operated by one or multiple organizations in the community, a third party, or a combination of both.

Hybrid Cloud A hybrid cloud is a combination (hybrid) of two or more of the other models (public, private, or community). For example, an organization might operate a private cloud in their own on-premises datacenter but leverage a public cloud provider (such as AWS, Azure, Google, or OCI) to help load-balance traffic if there is a spike in demand.

Cloud Security Assurance

One of the greatest concerns organizations often have when utilizing a cloud service is ensuring that the CSP is implementing good security practices. When an organization elects to use a third-party CSP, they are outsourcing certain functions that become the responsibility of the service provider (such as management of the datacenter, hardware, etc.). These responsibilities will vary based on the cloud service model. However, even if the organization outsources some of these functions, the organization is still accountable for the security of its own data (and the data of its customers) and must ensure that the CSP is implementing appropriate security practices.

The challenge becomes that CSPs (such as Google, AWS, Azure, and so on) are typically not going to let customers come in and audit their security practices. Instead, these providers have legal contracts in place with their customers that outline the provider's responsibilities and practices. In addition, CSPs often hire third-party auditors to perform an audit of their practices and provide the audit reports to their customers. In this section we review some common elements used to assist organizations in evaluating CSPs to determine if they meet their security and business requirements:

- Service level agreement
- SOC reports
- ISO/IEC certification
- FedRAMP authorization
- CSA STAR program

Service Level Agreement A *service level agreement (SLA)* is a legal contractual agreement between a service provider or supplier and a customer that defines the level of service the customer can expect. These include provisions around things like performance, availability, security, response times, and accountability, as well as metrics by which the service can be measured to ensure the provider is adhering to stated requirements. SLAs (and other similar contracts) are very important when it comes to a customer's ability to govern the relationship with the provider, as they serve as the primary legal and contractual guarantee of the level of service and responsibility the provider takes on. Organizations must thoroughly review and understand the SLA with their providers to ensure that the providers meet the requirements for the organization around things like security, availability, compliance, and so on.

 NOTE While SLAs are being discussed under the context of cloud service providers, these contractual elements are applicable to any vendor or provider.

SOC Audits A *service organization controls (SOC)* audit is an audit performed on a service organization (such as a CSP) by a third-party audit firm that assesses the internal controls of the provider. When the audit is concluded, the audit firm issues a report (SOC report) attesting to the controls implemented by the service provider. There are three types of SOC audits and reports:

- **SOC 1** Audit of financial controls, results in the issuance of a SOC 1 report
- **SOC 2** Audit of security and privacy controls, results in the issuance of a SOC 2 report
- **SOC 3** Public version of a SOC 2 report with less detail, often used for marketing

SOC reports provide a way for a CSP to demonstrate to customers that strong internal controls are in place that have been evaluated by a third-party audit firm.

ISO/IEC Certification The *International Organization for Standardization (ISO)* and the *International Electrotechnical Commission (IEC)* work together to develop joint international standards. The ISO/IEC 27000 series is a family of standards focused on best security practices. One of the more well-known standards is ISO/IEC 27001, *Information technology – Security techniques – Information security management systems – Requirements*. The ISO/IEC 27001 standard is focused on the establishment of a holistic information security program. As is the case with many ISO/IEC standards, organizations may seek to become certified against one of the standards by being audited by an accredited third party. ISO/IEC 27001 certification provides another means by which a customer can evaluate prospective CSPs to ensure they are implementing appropriate security controls.

NOTE More information on ISO standards may be found at https://www .iso.org.

FedRAMP Authorization The *Federal Risk and Authorization Management Program (FedRAMP)* is a U.S. federal government program that provides a standard for assessing, authorizing, and continuous monitoring of cloud-based products and services. CSPs generally must be FedRAMP authorized in order to sell their cloud service to the U.S. government. A CSP becomes FedRAMP authorized by having their security controls assessed by an accredited third-party assessment organization (3PAO). While FedRAMP is primarily for the U.S. government, other organizations may elect to choose FedRAMP-authorized providers as part of their due diligence to ensure that the provider is implementing best security practices.

NOTE Cloud service products that have been authorized are listed on the FedRAMP website at https://www.fedramp.gov.

CSA STAR Program The *Cloud Security Alliance (CSA) Security Trust Assurance and Risk (STAR)* program is an assurance program managed by the Cloud Security Alliance that enables CSPs to document the security controls provided with various cloud services they offer. The program has different assurance levels ranging from self-assessment to certifications issued after an audit by an approved third-party assessment firm. CSCs can use the STAR registry (https://cloudsecurityalliance.org/star/registry/) to find CSPs that have been submitted into the registry as well as their corresponding assurance level.

> **NOTE** More information on the Cloud Security Alliance and the STAR program may be found here: https://cloudsecurityalliance.org/star/

Network Infrastructure Review

The two main ways that an organization can manage and provision computer infrastructure is to build or lease an on-premises datacenter or leverage a cloud service.

- On-premises datacenter considerations
  - Staffing the datacenter
  - Physical security measures
  - Environmental controls (HVAC, fire detection and suppression, and so on)
  - Redundancy (hardware, power, alternate facilities, and so on)
- Cloud computing
  - Essential characteristics of cloud computing include on-demand self-service, rapid elasticity, resource pooling, measured service, and broad network access.
  - Cloud service models include infrastructure as a service (IaaS), platform as a service (PaaS), and software as a service (SaaS).
  - Cloud deployment models include public, private, community, and hybrid.
  - Organizations often evaluate and manage the security of cloud providers through service level agreements (SLAs) as well as the review of third-party audit and attestation reports (e.g., SOC 2, ISO, FedRAMP).

Chapter Review

Computer networks consist of a variety of hardware, software, and other technologies used to allow various devices to communicate and link the network together. Modern computer networking occurs over local and wide area networks. Networks can be wired (connected via physical cables) or wireless (leveraging wireless technologies).

Computers and other network devices have special addresses (MAC address and IP address) used to identify them on the network and the Internet. There are two versions of IP: IPv4 and IPv6. IPv4 is still the more widely used protocol. In order for devices to talk to one another, they use ports and protocols. Protocols are rules and standards for network communication. A logical port is a number that is mapped to a particular service running on a computer (e.g., port 443 for a web server using HTTPS). A physical port is a slot on a computer or device that another device or cable can be plugged into. Network models are used to help describe the various layers and functions that make up a computer network. The two most common are the OSI and TCP/IP models. The Open Systems Interconnection (OSI) model is a conceptual framework that describes the functionality at each layer of the network stack. The OSI model is made up of seven layers: Application Layer (Layer 7), Presentation Layer (Layer 6), Session Layer (Layer 5), Transport Layer (Layer 4), Network Layer (Layer 3), Data Link Layer (Layer 2), and Physical Layer (Layer 1). The Transmission Control Protocol/Internet Protocol (TCP/IP) model is an older model developed by the DoD. TCP/IP is designed around a suite of protocols that also fit into various layers of the OSI model. The TCP/IP model consists of four layers: Application Layer (Layer 4), Host-to-Host Layer (Layer 3), Internet Layer (Layer 2), and Network Access Layer (Layer 1).

Cyberattackers don't necessarily follow a disciplined process to carry out their attacks; however, by observing what they do, we can describe a typical cyberattack in steps: step 1, in which the cyber criminal conducts research to learn about potential targets; step 2, where the cyberattacker identifies targets by conducting scans to enumerate systems and vulnerabilities; step 3, where the attacker exploits targets such as conducting physical, password, social engineering, or phishing attacks or deploying malware; and step 4, where the attacker does bad things like stealing data, demanding and collecting ransom, conducting DoS attacks, or executing an advanced persistent threat.

Organizations defend against cyberattacks using multiple layers of defense. They build networks resilient to attacks using network segmentation, DMZs, and VPNs, which allows them to set up security zones to limit who can access which portions of the network and for what purpose. Organizations use network devices, including firewalls and web and e-mail filters, to screen and control traffic to only that which is allowed. Security organizations use antivirus, IDS, and IPS systems to detect and prevent malicious activity on their endpoint devices and networks. These systems use threat intelligence feeds from private and public sources to inform them about what to look for. Wireless networks provide great convenience but present some security risks. Organizations use WPA2 or WPA3 for the best security. IoT devices present security challenges because they typically are not built with security in mind and they have security flaws. Organizations use a variety of types of security assessments and testing to measure their security posture and compliance with security requirements. Common security testing includes vulnerability scanning and assessments, penetration testing, and security program assessments.

The two main ways that an organization can manage and provision their computer infrastructure is to build or lease an on-premises datacenter or leverage a cloud service. For on-premises datacenters, organizations must consider how they will staff the datacenter, implement physical security measures, manage environmental controls (HVAC, fire detection and suppression, and so on), and have redundancy in place (hardware, power, alternate facilities, and so on). With a cloud service, these are managed by the CSP.

Cloud computing is defined using the NIST characteristics of cloud computing, which include on-demand self-service, rapid elasticity, resource pooling, measured service, and broad network access. Depending on the organization's needs, there are various cloud service models to choose from (IaaS, PaaS, and SaaS) as well as cloud deployment models (public, private, community, and hybrid). Although certain functions may be outsourced to the provider (e.g., physical security), organizations are still accountable for the security of their data and the data of their customers and must ensure that the CSP is implementing appropriate security practices. This is typically managed through SLAs as well as the review of third-party audit and attestation reports (e.g., SOC 2, ISO, FedRAMP).

Quick Review

Network Fundamentals

- Modern computer networking occurs over two fundamental types of computer networks: local and wide area networks.
- Computer networks can be wired (devices are connected via physical cables) or wireless (leveraging wireless technologies).
- Computers and other network-connected systems and devices have special addresses in order to identify them on the network and the Internet. These include MAC addresses (also known as the physical address) and IP addresses (also known as the logical address).
- Networks are made up of various devices with different functions and purposes used to link the network together to enable communication.
- Protocols are rules and standards for network communication (e.g., HTTPS)
- A logical port is a numerical identifier that is mapped to a particular protocol to tell a receiving computer what service is trying to be used.
- A physical port is a slot on a computer or device that another device or cable can be plugged into.
- Network models are used to help describe the various layers and functions that make up a computer network. The two most common are the OSI and TCP/IP models.
- The OSI model consists of the following layers:
  - Application Layer (Layer 7)
  - Presentation Layer (Layer 6)
  - Session Layer (Layer 5)
  - Transport Layer (Layer 4)
  - Network Layer (Layer 3)
  - Data Link Later (Layer 2)
  - Physical Layer (Layer 1)

- The TCP/IP model consists of the following layers:
  - Application Layer
  - Host-to-Host Layer
  - Internet Layer
  - Network Access Layer

Network Threats and Attacks

- The general steps of a cyberattack are
  - Conduct research
  - Identify targets
  - Exploit targets
  - Do bad things
- Malware is software designed to infiltrate and gain unauthorized access to computer systems for the purpose of causing damage or disruption.
- A virus is a type of malware that infects a legitimate program with a payload and causes the program to perform a function it was not designed to do.
- A trojan is a malicious program that tricks the user into running it because it appears to be a legitimate program.
- A worm is similar to a virus but is able to replicate itself.
- A botnet is a group of infected systems that are remotely controlled by cyber criminals.
- Ransomware is a type of malware that forces its victim to either pay a ransom or lose valuable assets.
- Rootkits are tools that enable and maintain privileged access to an operating system.
- Buffer overflows are a type of attack where input is provided to a program that is greater in size than the program is designed to handle. Buffer overflows can be used to cause a system to execute commands without the correct authorization.
- Cross-site scripting (XSS) is a type of attack whereby the attacker injects a malicious script into a website that is trusted by the intended victim(s) of the attack.
- HTTP response splitting is a type of attack where an attacker sends a malicious script to a website and can be used to launch cross-site scripting attacks, or "poison" the web cache with false data.
- SQL injection is a type of attack whereby the attacker puts SQL commands into a form or web page, which are then executed by the SQL database without proper authorization.
- A timing attack, also called a race condition attack, is an entire family of attacks in which the attacker takes advantage of the time between a sequence of events.

- Backdoor is a broad term used to describe any method whereby an unauthorized user can bypass security controls to gain access to a system or program.
- Social engineering refers to the use of deception to trick someone into doing something that may not be in their best interest.
- Phishing is a term that refers to e-mail–based attacks in which the cyber criminal crafts and sends e-mails that look like legitimate e-mails from a real business but the e-mail is really fraudulent.
- Spear phishing attacks are phishing e-mails sent to specific individuals or employees of organizations.
- Cyber criminals attempt to get passwords using attacks including social engineering, phishing, spear phishing, brute force, dictionary, and rainbow tables.
- Man-in-the-middle (MITM) are a class of attacks in which a cyberattacker intercepts communication between two entities.
- Cyber criminals are motivated by many things, but cyber criminal activity usually comes down to three possible motivators: monetary, personal, or political.
- Exfiltration is essentially the unauthorized transfer of data from a computer or network.
- Cyber extortion attacks involve the cyber criminal forcing people or organizations to pay money or release data to the cyber criminal.
- Denial of service (DoS) is any attack that causes a legitimate user to be unable to access an information system or network.
- Distributed denial of service (DDoS) attacks refer to DoS attacks launched from many computers, usually in the form of a botnet.
- An advanced persistent threat (APT) is an attack in which the attacker's goal is to maintain a long-term presence within the victim's system or network, stealthily doing malicious activity over a period of time.

Network Defenses

- Defense-in-depth means that rather than rely on just one control, a better strategy is to use multiple layers of security controls.
- Network segmentation is a network design approach that allows organizations to group portions of the network into segments, each acting like a small network.
- With micro-segmentation, anything on the network, any device or any application, can be its own segment.
- A DMZ is a network segment that is positioned in between the organization's connection to the Internet and their internal networks.
- A virtual private network (VPN) is a secure connection into a private network through a public network such as the Internet.

- Network access control (NAC) is a technology that allows organizations to implement controls that limit what devices can connect to their network.

- A firewall is a network device used to control access between two networks or two segments of a network. Firewall types include packet filters, proxies, and stateful/dynamic packet filters.

- E-mail filters examine an organization's inbound and outbound e-mail traffic looking for evidence of phishing, spam, malware, suspicious links, disallowed attachments, and other threats.

- Web filters act as web firewalls.

- Organizations use threat intelligence to help them perform risk management and choose the right approaches to defending against threats.

- Organizations use IDSs and IPSs on their networks to detect if and when they are under attack.

- Antivirus software protects the device on which it is installed against attacks from viruses.

- Zero-day refers to a recently discovered vulnerability, exploit, or attack.

- Most organizations and vendors now use either WPA2 or WPA3 for wireless security.

- IoT is a general term that refers to many different kinds of physical devices that connect to the Internet or IP networks. IoT devices should be part of any organization's information security program, as they are assets connected to the enterprise and bring their own inherent risks.

Network Security Infrastructure

- Organizations manage computer networks leveraging either an on-premises datacenter or a cloud service.

- When using an on-premises datacenter, organizations must consider
  - Staffing the datacenter
  - Physical security measures
  - Environmental controls (HVAC, fire detection and suppression, and so on)
  - Redundancy (hardware, power, alternate facilities, and so on)
- Essential characteristics of cloud computing include
  - On-demand self-service
  - Rapid elasticity
  - Resource pooling
  - Measured service
  - Broad network access

- Cloud service models include
  - Infrastructure as a service (IaaS)
  - Platform as a service (PaaS)
  - Software as a service (SaaS)
- Cloud deployment models include
  - Public
  - Private
  - Community
  - Hybrid
- Organizations evaluate and manage the security of cloud providers through service level agreements (SLAs) as well as the review of third-party audit and attestation reports (e.g., SOC 2, ISO, FedRAMP).

Questions

1. Which of the following is referred to as a physical address in computer networking?

   A. IPv4 address

   B. IPv6 address

   C. MAC address

   D. Loopback address

2. How many layers are there in the OSI model?

   A. 8

   B. 7

   C. 6

   D. 5

3. Which of the following terms best describes a computer that provides content to other computers such as a website or an application?

   A. Client

   B. Server

   C. Endpoint

   D. Router

4. What is the name of the seventh layer of the OSI model?

   A. Application

   B. Session

   C. Presentation

   D. Network

5. Which of the following attacks are most likely to be carried out by a botnet?

    A. Advanced persistent threat attack

    B. DDoS attack

    C. Trojan horse attack

    D. Backdoor attack

6. What is the best description of the difference between a phishing e-mail and a spear phishing e-mail?

    A. A phishing e-mail is sent to a specific person; a spear phishing e-mail is sent to an entire company.

    B. A phishing e-mail is sent to random recipients; a spear phishing e-mail is sent to specific recipients.

    C. A phishing e-mail is sent to an entire company; a spear phishing e-mail is sent to a specific person.

    D. A spear phishing e-mail is sent to random recipients; a phishing e-mail is sent to specific recipients.

7. Which of the following is not a true statement about a worm?

    A. It can replicate itself.

    B. It is a type of malware.

    C. It is a type of botnet.

    D. It does not require a host program to infect and deliver it to the victim system.

8. A rainbow table attack seeks to mitigate the limitations of dictionary or brute force attacks by precomputing the hash of passwords and storing them for later comparison.

    A. True

    B. False

9. What is the primary difference between an IDS and an IPS?

    A. They both do the same thing.

    B. An IDS detects malicious activity, whereas an IPS prevents the activity from happening in the first place.

    C. An IDS detects malicious activity, whereas an IPS monitors system performance.

    D. An IDS detects malicious activity, whereas an IPS detects malicious activity and takes action on it.

10. Joe is a cyber criminal who has targeted a web server for a potential cyberattack. Joe wants to know if the server has any unpatched vulnerabilities he might be able to exploit. Which of the following actions is Joe most likely to take?

    A. Launch a smurf attack against the target server.

    B. Run a vulnerability scan against the target server.

    C. Send a phishing e-mail to the target server.

    D. Send a spear phishing e-mail to the target server.

11. _____ is a method of attack where a hacker enters SQL commands into fields on a vulnerable web page. The commands are executed without proper authorization.

    A. Buffer overflow

    B. SQL injection

    C. HTTP response splitting

    D. Backdoor

12. Most cyber criminals would agree that _____ are the weakest link in cybersecurity.

    A. Passwords

    B. Backdoors

    C. Laws

    D. People

13. A hacker uses a phishing attack to obtain a user's credentials, access their company's database, and steal proprietary information. This is an example of _____.

    A. Denial of service

    B. Advanced persistent threat

    C. Extortion

    D. Data exfiltration

14. A sophisticated cyber criminal gains access to a financial institution's e-mail server, installs malware, and then over a period of weeks, moves to other servers and systems on the company's network, installing other malware and tools, finding other credentials, stealing data, and scrubbing logs to cover her tracks. Which term best describes this type of activity?

    A. Denial of service attack

    B. Advanced persistent threat attack

    C. Extortion attack

    D. Website defacement attack

15. Mary is a network engineer who wants to install a firewall in front of a database server to hide its IP address. What type of firewall should Mary choose?

A. Proxy

B. Packet filter

C. Stateful/dynamic packet filter

D. Database filter

16. Antivirus software vendors use _____ to keep up with the latest information about viruses and threats.

A. Google

B. National Vulnerability Database

C. Threat intelligence

D. National Security Agency

17. When leveraging a third-party cloud service provider, which of the following is always the responsibility of the provider?

A. Data security

B. Physical security of the datacenter

C. Identity and access management controls

D. Endpoint protection

18. An organization is utilizing a public cloud from a cloud service whose service offering allows the organization to use a framework to build and deploy custom applications. Which of the following cloud service models is being utilized?

A. IaaS

B. PaaS

C. SaaS

D. On-premises

19. An organization is using a cloud service provider to host their infrastructure. The cloud service provider manages the underlying infrastructure, and the organization manages the platforms and software (such as the OS, development tools, and applications). Which of the following cloud service models is being utilized?

A. IaaS

B. PaaS

C. SaaS

D. On-premises

20. An organization has built out a cloud environment in their own datacenter for exclusive use by their employees to allow other teams to provision and manage virtual resources. Which of the following cloud deployment models is this an example of?

   A. Public

   B. Private

   C. Community

   D. Hybrid

21. An organization is hosting applications in a private cloud environment and also making use of Amazon Web Services (AWS) to load-balance the traffic for applications if there is a spike in demand. Which of the following cloud deployment models is this an example of?

   A. Public

   B. Private

   C. Community

   D. Hybrid

22. An organization is utilizing Google Mail (Gmail) as their e-mail service provider. Which of the following types of cloud service models is being utilized?

   A. SaaS

   B. PaaS

   C. IaaS

   D. On-premises

Questions and Answers

1. Which of the following is referred to as a physical address in computer networking?

   A. IPv4 address

   B. IPv6 address

   C. MAC address

   D. Loopback address

   C. Media access control (MAC) addresses are often referred to as a physical address or hardware address since they are assigned to the device's physical hardware. Internet Protocol (IP) addresses are known as logical addresses. A loopback address is a special type of IP address.

2. How many layers are there in the OSI model?

  A. 8

  B. 7

  C. 6

  D. 5

B. There are seven layers in the OSI model. These Include Application, Presentation, Session, Transport, Network, Data, and Physical.

3. Which of the following terms best describes a computer that provides content to other computers such as a website or an application?

  A. Client

  B. Server

  C. Endpoint

  D. Router

B. Server is a term that describes a computer that serves content or provides a service to another computer on a network. A client is a computer that accesses or uses the content or service provided by the server. An endpoint is a computing device on a network, which could include a server but is not the best answer. A router is a network device that routes traffic on a network.

4. What is the name of the seventh layer of the OSI model?

  A. Application

  B. Session

  C. Presentation

  D. Network

A. The Application Layer is Layer 7 (the uppermost layer) of the OSI model. The order of the layers from top (Layer 7) to bottom (Layer 1) are Application, Presentation, Session, Transport, Network, Data Link, and Physical.

5. Which of the following attacks are most likely to be carried out by a botnet?

  A. Advanced persistent threat attack

  B. DDoS attack

  C. Trojan horse attack

  D. Backdoor attack

B. A botnet is a group of computers under the control of an attacker, most often for a coordinated attacker such as a DDoS attack. Advanced persistent threat and backdoors are not specific types of attacks, but rather features of attacks. A trojan horse is a type of attack but unlikely to be carried out by a botnet.

6. What is the best description of the difference between a phishing e-mail and a spear phishing e-mail?

   A. A phishing e-mail is sent to a specific person; a spear phishing e-mail is sent to an entire company.

   B. A phishing e-mail is sent to random recipients; a spear phishing e-mail is sent to specific recipients.

   C. A phishing e-mail is sent to an entire company; a spear phishing e-mail is sent to a specific person.

   D. A spear phishing e-mail is sent to random recipients; a phishing e-mail is sent to specific recipients.

   B. A phishing e-mail is sent to random recipients; a spear phishing e-mail is sent to specific recipients. A phishing e-mail is literally like going fishing—you cast a wide net randomly and you see what you get. Conversely spear phishing is literally like spearfishing—you have a specific target in mind, and you shoot the spear directly at it. A spear phishing e-mail is sent to a specific person or specific people or an organization.

7. Which of the following is not a true statement about a worm?

   A. It can replicate itself.

   B. It is a type of malware.

   C. It is a type of botnet.

   D. It does not require a host program to infect and deliver it to the victim system.

   C. A worm is not a type of botnet. A worm can replicate itself and is a type of malware, but since it isn't a virus, it does not require a host program to infect and serve as the delivery mechanism.

8. A rainbow table attack seeks to mitigate the limitations of dictionary or brute force attacks by precomputing the hash of passwords and storing them for later comparison.

   A. True

   B. False

   A. The answer is true. Dictionary and brute force attacks take a lot of processing time and resources, whereas rainbow table attacks do the processing ahead of time and store the hashes in a table or database.

9. What is the primary difference between an IDS and an IPS?

   A. They both do the same thing.

   B. An IDS detects malicious activity, whereas an IPS prevents the activity from happening in the first place.

C. An IDS detects malicious activity, whereas an IPS monitors system performance.

D. An IDS detects malicious activity, whereas an IPS detects malicious activity and takes action on it.

> **D.** An IDS, which stands for intrusion detection system, detects malicious activity, whereas an IPS, which stands for intrusion prevention system, detects malicious activity and takes action on it.

10. Joe is a cyber criminal who has targeted a web server for a potential cyberattack. Joe wants to know if the server has any unpatched vulnerabilities he might be able to exploit. Which of the following actions is Joe most likely to take?

A. Launch a smurf attack against the target server.

B. Run a vulnerability scan against the target server.

C. Send a phishing e-mail to the target server.

D. Send a spear phishing e-mail to the target server.

> **B.** The answer is to run a vulnerability scan, as that is the only one of the choices that will reveal vulnerabilities on the server.

11. _____ is a method of attack where a hacker enters SQL commands into fields on a vulnerable web page. The commands are executed without proper authorization.

A. Buffer overflow

B. SQL injection

C. HTTP response splitting

D. Backdoor

> **B.** If a web server software does not properly check the data input by the user, it could allow an attacker to put SQL commands in the field, which are then executed by the SQL database without proper authorization. This is called a SQL injection attack.

12. Most cyber criminals would agree that _____ are the weakest link in cybersecurity.

A. Passwords

B. Backdoors

C. Laws

D. People

> **D.** It is widely acknowledged that people are the weakest link in cybersecurity. Despite extensive progress in technical tools and controls, deliberate or accidental acts by people lead to the largest number of and most damaging security breaches.

13. A hacker uses a phishing attack to obtain a user's credentials, access their company's database, and steal proprietary information. This is an example of _____.

   A. Denial of service

   B. Advanced persistent threat

   C. Extortion

   D. Data exfiltration

   D. The correct answer is data exfiltration, which is the unauthorized transfer of data from a computer or network.

14. A sophisticated cyber criminal gains access to a financial institution's e-mail server, installs malware, and then over a period of weeks, moves to other servers and systems on the company's network, installing other malware and tools, finding other credentials, stealing data, and scrubbing logs to cover her tracks. Which term best describes this type of activity?

   A. Denial of service attack

   B. Advanced persistent threat attack

   C. Extortion attack

   D. Website defacement attack

   B. During an advanced persistent threat attack, there is a sophisticated cyber criminal seeking to expand the attack over time, probing the network, finding more systems with vulnerabilities, exploiting them, and gaining unauthorized access to more and more systems and data, all the while doing things to cover their tracks.

15. Mary is a network engineer who wants to install a firewall in front of a database server to hide its IP address. What type of firewall should Mary choose?

   A. Proxy

   B. Packet filter

   C. Stateful/dynamic packet filter

   D. Database filter

   A. A proxy firewall impersonates the system at the other end of the connection and hides the IP address of the devices within the network it is protecting.

16. Antivirus software vendors use _____ to keep up with the latest information about viruses and threats.

   A. Google

   B. National Vulnerability Database

C. Threat intelligence

D. National Security Agency

C. Organizations and product vendors use threat intelligence from a variety of sources. By collecting and studying data about threats, vendors can prepare for and defend against them.

17. When leveraging a third-party cloud service provider, which of the following is always the responsibility of the provider?

   A. Data security

   B. Physical security of the datacenter

   C. Identity and access management controls

   D. Endpoint protection

   B. Physical security of the datacenter is always the responsibility of the cloud service provider.

18. An organization is utilizing a public cloud from a cloud service whose service offering allows the organization to use a framework to build and deploy custom applications. Which of the following cloud service models is being utilized?

   A. IaaS

   B. PaaS

   C. SaaS

   D. On-premises

   B. Platform as a service (PaaS) provides cloud service customers with development or application platforms to build and deploy applications.

19. An organization is using a cloud service provider to host their infrastructure. The cloud service provider manages the underlying infrastructure, and the organization manages the platforms and software (such as the OS, development tools, and applications). Which of the following cloud service models is being utilized?

   A. IaaS

   B. PaaS

   C. SaaS

   D. On-premises

   A. Infrastructure as a service (IaaS) provides customers with access to a pool of infrastructure resources such as network, server, and storage resources that can be virtually provisioned. The cloud service provider manages the underlying physical infrastructure, and the cloud service customer manages the platforms and software (such as OS, development tools, and applications) that run on the infrastructure.

20. An organization has built out a cloud environment in their own datacenter for exclusive use by their employees to allow other teams to provision and manage virtual resources. Which of the following cloud deployment models is this an example of?

   A. Public

   B. Private

   C. Community

   D. Hybrid

   B. A private cloud deployment model consists of computing infrastructure and resources that are dedicated for use by a single organization.

21. An organization is hosting applications in a private cloud environment and also making use of Amazon Web Services (AWS) to load-balance the traffic for applications if there is a spike in demand. Which of the following cloud deployment models is this an example of?

   A. Public

   B. Private

   C. Community

   D. Hybrid

   D. A hybrid cloud deployment model is a mix of the other models (such as a public and private model).

22. An organization is utilizing Google Mail (Gmail) as their e-mail service provider. Which of the following types of cloud service models is being utilized?

   A. SaaS

   B. PaaS

   C. IaaS

   D. On-premises

   A. Software as a service (SaaS) provides customers with access to an application hosted by the cloud service provider (such as an e-mail service).

Security Operations

This chapter discusses the following topics:
- Data security
- System hardening
- Best practice security policies
- Security awareness training

This chapter covers the Certified in Cybersecurity Domain 5. Like Chapter 3, this chapter covers security controls—in this case, controls that (ISC)² has put into a category they call security operations. We start with a discussion of data security controls, including coverage of cryptography and how it is used for different kinds of data protection. Data handling is covered next with a description of the data lifecycle in a typical organization, followed by a discussion of how organizations typically use logging and monitoring as security controls.

The next section describes the use of system hardening methods to protect the enterprise, including patching, secure configuration baselines, and configuration management. We follow with coverage of industry best practices in security policy usage, including descriptions of (ISC)²'s suggested security policies for CC candidates to know. The chapter ends with a discussion of security awareness training, which is an important security control that seeks to combat what many people feel is the weakest link in cybersecurity, which is human errors causing security breaches.

Data Security

Data security is a set of practices aimed at protecting information important to the organization. Information requiring protection may include employee records, sensitive customer data, or confidential company information such as intellectual property. This information must be appropriately secured to protect against unauthorized access, modification, and disclosure. Data security controls are technical measures implemented in computer hardware and software to protect sensitive information. There are three key data security practices that (ISC)² wants CC candidates to be aware of. These are listed here and are discussed in the sections that follow:

- Data lifecycle
- Cryptography
- Logging and monitoring

Data Lifecycle

Much as a living organism goes through a series of changes during its lifetime, data also goes through a series of changes during its existence within an organization. The term *data lifecycle* refers to the series of changes data goes through in an organization and how the organization handles the data during each phase of its life. Data typically passes through stages starting from when data comes to be (acquisition/creation) and progressing through how it is stored, used, shared, and eventually destroyed when it no longer serves a purpose. The data lifecycle includes the following phases, illustrated in Figure 4-1:

- Create
- Store
- Use
- Share
- Archive
- Destroy

Figure 4-1
Data lifecycle

Create

The first phase of the data lifecycle is when the data comes to exist within the organization. The data could be acquired from another organization (such as a vendor, customer, or another party) or created from scratch within the organization itself. When data comes to exist, the organization must decide how to appropriately protect the data (e.g., encryption, access controls, monitoring). In addition, the organization must consider various privacy requirements around how data may be used and shared.

Data Classification

Some organizations, especially government, military, and intelligence organizations, use *data classification* as a way to categorize, label, and control different kinds of data within the organization. Data classification is the process of assigning classification levels to data types based on risk. For instance, an organization's most sensitive data might be classified as "Top Secret" or "Company Proprietary," whereas the least sensitive data may be classified as "Public" or "Unrestricted." The classification of the data dictates the controls that are utilized to protect it appropriately. Each classification level has specific requirements to ensure the data is appropriately protected (e.g., encryption) and only accessible by those with proper authorization (e.g., access control and monitoring). Once data is classified, it is marked and labeled so that others in the organization know what it is and how to handle it properly (as defined by policy). Labeling may be done at various levels such as labeling the physical media (hard drive, universal serial bus [USB], etc.), labeling the document (print or electronic), or labeling specific data elements in a database using tags.

Store, Use, and Share

Data that is created and classified is placed into production, where it is stored, used, and shared based on the organization's security policies and procedures and the appropriate security controls. Security controls may vary based on the classification of the data.

Archive

When data is no longer needed in the production environment but needs to be kept for future use (or due to legal requirements), it may need to be archived. There are many state and federal laws that require organizations to retain data for certain periods of time. As a result, when data is no longer needed by an organization, it may still need to be stored for a period of time. This type of storage is called *data retention,* and it is accomplished using data archival media such as tape, disk, or optical media, any of which can be on-premises or cloud implementations.

Destroy

When data is no longer needed, the primary requirement is ensuring that sensitive data cannot be recovered from the media it was stored on. For example, when you delete data by pressing the DELETE key on a computer or emptying the recycle bin on your desktop (also known as *erasure*), the data is not actually removed from the hard drive. Instead, this action merely tells the operating system that the location on the hard drive is available for future use. But until then the data is still there and anyone can easily download free tools to be able to access it. To properly remove data from media, *sanitization* methods must be used. Sanitization methods include overwriting, degaussing, and physical destruction, as explained next:

- **Overwriting/zeroization/clearing**   Data is overwritten with other data such as binary 1's and 0's using other data, patterns, or random data. The more times the data is overwritten (referred to as a pass), the harder the original data is to recover.

- **Degaussing**   Magnetic media is demagnetized by exposing the media to an extremely powerful magnetic field. This sanitizes the magnetic media. The media itself can then be reused; however, degaussing will make most modern hard drives inoperable.

- **Physical destruction**   Physical media (hard drives, disks, etc.) can be destroyed so that it cannot be reused and the data cannot be accessed. Physical destruction includes shredding, crushing, burning, disintegration, or dissolving using chemical compounds.

Cryptography

Cryptography is one of the oldest and most fundamental means of protecting information. It is the practice of using mathematical formulas to protect information by transforming the information into another format to ensure the information cannot be read or accessed by unauthorized parties. To protect data, it is important to consider how it is protected *at rest* (stored on computers, servers, physical media, etc.) and *in transit* (data moving between computers on a network) as part of the data lifecycle and in line with the organization's data classification. Data at rest can be protected by implementing disk encryption on a computer or server drive, database encryption, or encryption at the data level such as file, folder, or field-level encryption. Data in transit (also known as *data in motion*) is protected by utilizing encrypted network connection protocols such as Secure Sockets Layer/Transport Layer Security (SSL/TLS) and virtual private network (VPN) encryption. In this section we dive into some of the specific cryptographic techniques used to protect data, including encryption and hashing.

Encryption

Encryption is the process of transforming *plaintext* (information that is in a readable format) into *ciphertext* (information that is in an encrypted, unreadable format). *Decryption* is the process of transforming ciphertext back to plaintext. This process is illustrated in Figure 4-2.

Figure 4-2
Encryption and decryption

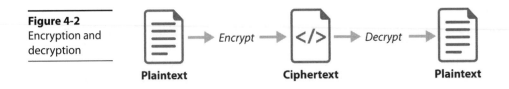

Plaintext → Encrypt → Ciphertext → Decrypt → Plaintext

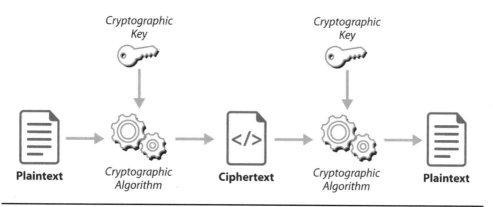

Figure 4-3   Cryptographic keys and algorithms

The encryption and decryption processes are implemented by utilizing cryptographic algorithms and cryptographic keys, as illustrated in Figure 4-3. A *cryptographic algorithm* is a mathematical equation that is used to perform a cryptographic function (such as encryption/decryption). A *cryptographic key* is a value that is used as input into a cryptographic algorithm that enables it to perform its cryptographic function. Together, keys and algorithms allow for encryption and decryption operations to take place to transform plaintext to ciphertext and vice versa.

In this section, we review the main types of encryption, which include symmetric encryption and asymmetric encryption.

Symmetric Encryption   *Symmetric encryption* uses the same key for encryption and decryption. The sender and receiver of a message need to both have a copy of the same key in order to encrypt/decrypt the message. This process is illustrated in Figure 4-4. As a result, the security of this key is critical, and it must be kept private, since anyone with access to this key can decrypt the messages. This is why it is referred to as a private key. Presently, the Advanced Encryption Standard (AES) algorithm is the most commonly used symmetric encryption algorithm due to its maturity, security, and international recognition.

Let's look at how this works in Figure 4-4. Suppose Alice and Bob want to exchange sensitive information but don't want anyone to be able to intercept and read their messages. To communicate with Bob, Alice encrypts messages with the private key to convert plaintext to ciphertext, and Bob decrypts the messages from ciphertext to plaintext using the same private key. Likewise, if Bob wants to send a message to Alice, he encrypts the message with the shared private key, and Alice decrypts the message with the same private key. In order for this to work, Alice and Bob must both have a copy of the same private key. Symmetric encryption provides confidentiality through encryption as long as the private key is only shared with authorized parties.

Asymmetric Encryption   Whereas symmetric encryption uses one key for both encryption and decryption, asymmetric encryption uses two keys that are mathematically related: a *public key* and a *private key*. Asymmetric encryption is sometimes called

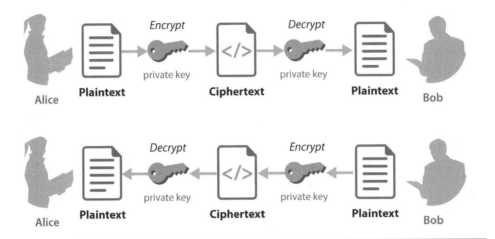

Figure 4-4 Symmetric encryption

public key cryptography due to there being a *public key* that can be freely shared with anyone the sender wants to communicate with securely. The *private key* must remain private and only be known to the owner. Common asymmetric algorithms include Diffie-Hellman, Rivest-Shamir-Adleman (RSA), and Elliptic Curve Cryptography (ECC).

Let's look at how asymmetric encryption works in Figure 4-5. Suppose Alice and Bob want to exchange sensitive information but don't want anyone to be able to intercept and read their messages. To communicate with Bob, Alice encrypts messages with Bob's public key (which has been shared with her) to convert the plaintext message to ciphertext. When Bob receives the message, he decrypts it with his private key (only known to him). Similarly, if Bob wants to send a message to Alice, he encrypts the message with Alice's public key, and Alice decrypts the message with her private key.

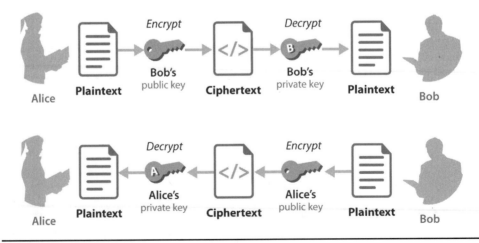

Figure 4-5 Asymmetric encryption

Public Key Infrastructure

One challenge with asymmetric encryption is ensuring that the public key you receive actually came from the person you think it came from. For example, what if Alice and Bob are communicating but an attacker (Laura) intercepts (e.g., man-in-the-middle attack from Chapter 3) Bob's public key as he was sending it to Alice and instead substitutes her own public key. In this case, Alice would send messages back to Bob encrypted with Laura's public key, allowing the attacker to decrypt the messages intended for Bob. Alice needs some way of verifying who the actual owner of that public key is. This is where PKI comes in.

Public key infrastructure (PKI) is a framework and technology that allows for the management of public key encryption. This is accomplished through the creation, distribution, management, and revocation of digital certificates. A *digital certificate* (sometimes referred to as a *public key certificate*) is an electronic certificate that links a public key to its owner. Digital certificates are issued by trusted third-party organizations (the *certificate authority*) that have verified the identity of the public key owner. Once the identity is verified, the certificate authority issues a certificate containing the name of the owner and digitally signs the certificate. PKI and digital certificates are similar to the state department of motor vehicles and driver's licenses. There is a trusted third party that verifies the identity of an individual and issues a license (or certificate). You have most commonly seen a digital certificate when interacting with a website. Figure 4-6 is a screenshot of a digital

General   Details

Issued To

Common Name (CN)	*.mhprofessional.com
Organization (O)	<Not Part Of Certificate>
Organizational Unit (OU)	<Not Part Of Certificate>

Issued By

Common Name (CN)	Amazon RSA 2048 M01
Organization (O)	Amazon
Organizational Unit (OU)	<Not Part Of Certificate>

Validity Period

Issued On	Monday, February 13, 2023 at 6:00:00 PM
Expires On	Thursday, July 13, 2023 at 6:59:59 PM

Fingerprints

SHA-256 Fingerprint	8C 85 E7 04 8A 48 9C 60 61 C0 EC 56 57 10 F9 D1 3D FA 0B 86 26 C7 4A A1 26 17 89 EE 63 2B 45 37
SHA-1 Fingerprint	FA 26 8C 35 53 ED C0 69 F3 E5 8B B2 F8 AE C8 14 37 52 6B E8

Figure 4-6 Digital certificate example

certificate issued for McGraw Hill for their website, which was issued by Amazon (the trusted third party). PKI provides confidentiality through encryption as well as integrity, nonrepudiation, and authentication through digital signatures and digital certificates.

 NOTE At the time of this writing, public key infrastructure is not included in the CC Exam Outline and may not be on the exam. However, it is a core cryptographic technique that is important for cybersecurity practitioners to be aware of.

Hashing

Hashing is another type of cryptography that uses special algorithms known as hash algorithms that transform information into fixed-length output known as a message digest (MD). An MD output is also commonly referred to as a hash, hash value, or fingerprint. Unlike encryption, which can be reversed via decryption, hashing is a one-way process, meaning the original information or message cannot be reproduced from the hash value output. In addition, there is no key involved when using a hash algorithm. Common hash algorithms include MD5, SHA-1, SHA-2, and SHA-3.

Since hashing is a one-way function, it is not used for encryption/decryption like symmetric or asymmetric cryptography. Instead, hashes are most often used to provide integrity checking to ensure that a message or file has not been modified. If one single bit of a message or file changes, the corresponding hash value changes. Figure 4-7 shows an example of an MD5 hash value for the text "secret" and the text "Secret." The hash value for "secret" is "dd02c7c2232759874e1c205587017bed," while the hash value for "Secret" is "6657d705191a76297fe693296075b400." As you can see, simply changing the one letter drastically changed the hash value.

 EXAM TIP CC candidates should be familiar with the purpose of hashes and how they are used.

Password Salting

As discussed in Chapter 3, passwords are often hashed when they are stored so that if a hacker were able to breach the system and access the password database, they only have access to the hashed password value (versus the plaintext password). However, attackers will still try to determine the password by performing dictionary and rainbow table attacks to create a list of hashes to compare to the password database hash values.

Figure 4-7
Hash example

```
[bash-3.2$ echo secret | md5
dd02c7c2232759874e1c205587017bed


[bash-3.2$ echo Secret | md5
6657d705191a76297fe693296075b400
```

Figure 4-8
Example of
password salting

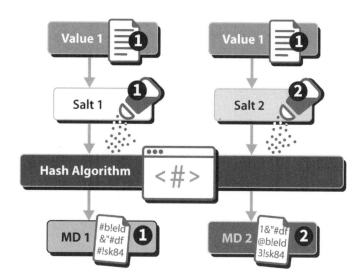

To add further resiliency against these types of attacks, salting is often used. A *salt* is a random value that is added to a message (or password) during the hashing process. Often a different salt value is used for each hash operation, ensuring that the same message (e.g., two users with the same password) will result in a different hash/MD value in the password database. This is illustrated in Figure 4-8. Remember that changing one bit of a message drastically changes the hash output.

NOTE In Chapter 3 we discussed how passwords are often hashed and stored in a database. The system takes the password, hashes the password, and stores the message digest instead of the actual password. When salting is used, the system also must store the salt values in order to be able to validate the user input (password value) against the salted message digest value.

Digital Signature

A *digital signature* is a mathematical technique used to protect messages transmitted electronically such as with e-mail. It performs several functions: it proves the message has not been altered since it was created (providing integrity) and proves the message came from a certain person (providing authenticity and nonrepudiation). It does these things using a stamp (or signature) created using a combination of asymmetric cryptography and hashing.

Algorithm Summary

Symmetric cryptography uses fast algorithms but has limited use because the two users at each end need to have the same key. This makes key management difficult and causes the organizations to have to manage large numbers of keys. Asymmetric cryptography, especially public key infrastructure (PKI), makes key management much easier;

Attribute	Symmetric	Asymmetric	Hash
Keys	One key shared between entities	Each entity has a public and private key	None
Key Exchange	Out of band	Public key is safely distributed	N/A
Algorithm Speed	Fast	Slow	Fast
Number of Keys	Grows as number of users grows	Grows but not uncontrollably	N/A
Use	Bulk encryption, large files	Key encryption and key exchange	File and message integrity
Services Provided	Confidentiality	Confidentiality, authentication, nonrepudiation	Integrity

Table 4-1 Algorithm Summary

however, the algorithms are more complex and therefore run much slower, consuming more resources. In practice, symmetric cryptography is mostly used for encrypting large amounts of data such as encrypting files and communication paths. Asymmetric cryptography is used for encrypting small amounts of data such as keys. The two technologies can be combined to leverage the best features of both (sometimes called *hybrid cryptography*) by using asymmetric cryptography to protect symmetric keys while using symmetric cryptography to protect the actual message. Table 4-1 provides a quick summary of cryptographic methods:

 EXAM TIP CC candidates should be familiar with the differences between symmetric and asymmetric encryption, in particular that symmetric encryption uses the same key for encryption/decryption and asymmetric encryption uses different keys (public and private).

Cryptography in Action

So far, we have discussed various types of cryptography (symmetric encryption, asymmetric encryption, hashing, and salts) as well as the components that make up a cryptosystem (algorithms, keys, etc.). In practice, these cryptographic methods and techniques are used together to build security solutions. In fact, many modern security protocols such as Secure Shell (SSH) and SSL/TLS (which is used for Hypertext Transfer Protocol Secure [HTTPS]) leverage symmetric encryption, asymmetric encryption, and hashes in combination.

Logging and Monitoring

Organizations must have processes in place to be able to track events and actions that occur throughout their environment. This is achieved by having proper logging (the recording of events) and monitoring (the examination of events) capabilities in place to be able to go back and see what happened at certain points in time while investigating a security incident or system error.

Logging is the capturing and storing of events that occur for later analysis. An *event* is an occurrence of an activity on any endpoint system or device. Logging is used to support auditing, troubleshooting, system analysis, and security incident response. *Monitoring* is the examination of events and other activities. This can be done manually or using automated leveraging tooling that ingests and analyzes events and alerts on those that require review. In the following sections, we review various types of logs, log sources, and common monitoring techniques.

Logging

Logs are files that store information about various events that occur on a system. Systems and applications have the capability to generate these logs based on configuration settings. Examples of events that may be logged include

- Authentication information (e.g., successful and failed authentication attempts)
- Account changes (e.g., account creation and deletion, changing privileges)
- Application events (e.g., application startup, shutdown, errors)
- Transaction information (e.g., size of transaction, transaction status)
- Use of privileged commands

Logs can come from a variety of sources which include but aren't limited to the following:

- Endpoints and servers
- Applications
- Databases
- Security appliances (e.g., intrusion detection system [IDS], intrusion prevention system [IPS], firewall)
- Network devices (e.g., routers, switches)

One important consideration with regard to logging is ensuring that systems are configured to log relevant events. Many operating systems, devices, and applications allow administrators to configure which events to log and only log a certain subset of events by default. If organizations do not review these configurations, they may realize they weren't logging security-relevant events that may be beneficial during future investigations. Organizations such as the Center for Internet Security, Open Web Application Security Project, and SANS Institute provide hardening standards and checklists that can aid organizations in determining which events are important to log.

Log Management

Log management refers to all activities undertaken to capture, store, and maintain logs so that they are useful to the organization. Logs are not only highly valuable to the organization but also highly sensitive and should be protected from modification/deletion and should be accessible only by authorized users. Logs must be considered during storage capacity planning to ensure that logs do not fill up the available storage and run out of room, resulting in the failure to log important data. Logging and monitoring result in the capture and reporting of large amounts of data. This information is beneficial; however, there is a price to pay in storage and processing of the data. Every organization must consider how much information it can practically log and monitor based on the risk and capacity of the organization.

Monitoring Techniques

It is critical that organizations are capturing the appropriate events in order to be able to perform troubleshooting and investigation of security incidents. In order to reap the benefits of logging events, organizations implement processes to regularly review and monitor the logs using manual or automated methods, described next:

- **Manual** Manual log review is when an authorized person logs into a system and manually reviews the log files. This is typically done when investigating the cause of a system error or security incident. Manual log review is very tedious and does not scale well when you have many (e.g., hundreds or thousands) of systems. For that, more automated monitoring techniques are critical.

- **Automated** Automated review is accomplished by leveraging tools that aggregate, correlate, and alert on log data ingested from many different sources (such as operating system [OS] logs, application logs, network logs, IDP/IPS, antivirus, and so on). This is often accomplished by leveraging a *security information and event management (SIEM)* system. A *SIEM* system is a tool that ingests logs from various sources and serves as a central secure log repository. SIEMs also include analysis and correlation capability and often come with built-in rules that look for suspicious events identified in logs (for example, many failed logins that may indicate a brute force password attack) and allow security personnel to write their own custom rules to alert on.

Data Security Summary

Here is a summary of the important topics regarding data security that should be reviewed for the CC exam:

- The data lifecycle includes creation, storage, usage, sharing, archival, and destruction.

- Encryption is the process of transforming plaintext (information that is in a readable format) into ciphertext (information that is in an encrypted, unreadable format). Decryption is the process of transforming ciphertext back to plaintext.

- The main types of encryption include symmetric encryption and asymmetric encryption.

- Hashing uses special algorithms that transform information into fixed-length output known as a hash value, message digest, or fingerprint.

- Logging is the capturing of events, and monitoring is the examination of events and other activity.

System Hardening

Systems—in this case any endpoint such as servers, desktops, laptops, mobile devices, network devices, and databases—are potential targets of attacks. System hardening is the practice of making these devices harder to attack by reducing the entry points an attacker can potentially use to compromise a system.

System hardening usually includes the following activities:

- Mitigating known vulnerabilities in operating systems and applications (via patch management).

- Applying configuration settings to the system that reduce their attack surface (via secure configuration baselines). Such settings include disabling unneeded ports, services, and features; restricting access; implementing security policies; and configuring logging and alerts.

- Using good configuration management processes to ensure all systems in the enterprise are properly managed and changes to them are properly controlled.

Let's examine each of these hardening activities in more detail.

Patch Management

Patch management is the discipline of ensuring that all systems in the enterprise are kept fully patched with the most recent security updates from the respective software product sources. When developers discover bugs or features in their products that indicate a security vulnerability, they will design a fix for it, then release a patch to their customers to install the fix. Installing the patch installs software that corrects the bug and resolves the vulnerability. However, many organizations have hundreds or thousands of systems that can contain large numbers of applications with vulnerabilities. This situation results in vendors publishing patches all the time. It takes considerable effort and coordination for an organization to keep up with the latest patches, install them, test them, and put them into production. To do this effectively, most organizations follow some kind of patch management process or lifecycle. A typical patch management process looks like this:

- **Asset management**   You can't patch what you don't know you have. Patch management starts with asset discovery, which is an understanding of what systems the organization has and what operating systems, software applications, and versions are installed on those systems. The information obtained during asset discovery is stored, sometimes in simple spreadsheets or in a database. Some organizations keep track of their assets using asset inventory software that automatically scans the network looking for devices and then builds and maintains a database of all asset information.

 NOTE   Assets have a lifecycle that is similar to the data lifecycle presented earlier in this chapter. The important similarity is that assets can contain data, and when assets are no longer needed by the organization, the data must be removed from the asset using any of the methods described earlier before the asset is discarded by the organization.

- **Vulnerability discovery and management**   Organizations take steps to actively learn about the vulnerabilities in their environment. One way to do this is by subscribing to the latest intelligence information from product vendors or open source feeds that publish information about known vulnerabilities. Ultimately, the goal is to map which systems have which vulnerabilities so the organization knows which systems to patch. To do this, some organizations periodically run vulnerability scans like the ones described in Chapter 3. Modern scanners not only identify which systems have which vulnerabilities, but many also have up-to-date patching information showing which patches need to be installed from which manufacturers or sources to remediate the vulnerabilities discovered during scanning.

- **Patch acquisition and validation**   Most modern software and operating system vendors have services available whereby they automatically inform customers of security patches. This is how most organizations learn about patches available for installation into their environment. However, some product vendors do not have such a sophisticated service, and if an organization uses open source software, automatic notification of patches may not be available. Organizations must dedicate resources to keep up with the latest vulnerabilities in, and security patches for, all of the products installed in the enterprise.

  Once a patch is obtained, it cannot necessarily be installed in the organization's production environment without first considering the impact it might have. Patches are changes to the software. As such, they can change the operation of the software, sometimes in ways that the manufacturer could not predict or may not have properly tested for. Before deploying any patch, it should first be studied by an engineer or architect to fully understand what impact it may have to the environment. The organization should attempt to predict the impact of the patch on system operation, function, performance, speed, etc.

In addition to predicting the impact of installing a patch, the organization may weigh the risks of either installing or not installing it. What are the risks of installing the patch and potentially losing the functionality of the product altogether? Is it worth the risk? These questions are asked and considered as part of the patch evaluation process.

The industry standard best practice is that prior to deploying a patch in a live production environment, it is first deployed in a separate test environment. This is because the patch may cause unintended issues that could impact operations. Deploying such a patch in a live environment could have disastrous consequences for the organization or its customers. As a result, organizations test patches first when it is practical to do so.

Patch validation testing requires creating a separate test environment that duplicates the real production environment as closely as possible. The purpose of testing is to test the patch in real operational scenarios. During patch testing, organizations compare the operation and performance of applications before and after patch installation to detect any issues. During testing, the organization monitors not just the patched application but also the operating system and other applications to detect issues or impacts. Testing also includes rollback testing, which tests what happens when the patch is removed. For instance, upon removal of the patch, the system should return to a predictable operational state. Rollback testing finds out if this is the case.

- **Deployment and reporting**   After testing and approval, patches can be deployed to live production systems. Upon each installation, asset documentation is updated to maintain current records of the configuration of what is installed on every system.

Many organizations use automated tools to assist with patch management and deployment. Some tools perform both vulnerability scanning and patch management, while others perform these functions exclusively. Some of the better tools assist in the patch deployment process by automating the processing of creating the patch installation packages, which consist of all of the executables and other files necessary to configure and execute the patch installation correctly.

Configuration Baselines

In the same way that security vulnerabilities in software can make it easy for a cyberattacker to compromise a system, *security misconfigurations* can also lead to compromises. Security misconfigurations are settings on an operating system or application that are improperly configured or left nonsecure. They can come about due to poorly managed system administration processes or inexperienced system administration or operations personnel. Examples of misconfigurations are

- Network shares left open
- Leaving default accounts, permissions, or credentials enabled
- Enabling unnecessary features such as unneeded services, accounts, and ports

- Ignoring recommended security settings for applications, frameworks, libraries, databases, etc.
- Using outdated or vulnerable software components
- Using weak or incorrect permissions

The best way to avoid security misconfigurations is to write down the correct settings for every system in its own document called a *security baseline* and establish rules that require everyone to use the baselines whenever systems are configured. As a result, using security baselines has become an important part of many organizations' security programs.

A security baseline is how an organization implements security controls within an operating system or application. Based on the results of the organization's risk assessment and analysis activities, the organization decides what controls to put into place. Security settings are a reflection of decisions stemming from the risk assessment. For guidance on creating security configuration baselines, many organizations turn to product vendors or third-party organizations. Vendors such as operating system and network device producers provide configuration guides, which are baselines for security hardening of their products. Third-party organizations, including the U.S. Defense Information Systems Agency (DISA) and the Center for Internet Security (CIS), publish recommended security baselines for many operating systems, databases, devices, and applications. Many of these recommended baselines not only provide documented recommendations but also include downloadable scripts for easy implementation of the hardening settings.

Many organizations use vendor or third-party hardening guides as a starting point for creating their own security baselines. From the starting point, they tailor the settings to arrive at security controls that reflect their needs based on their own risk assessment and business environment.

Configuration Management

In a modern network there may be hundreds, if not thousands, of endpoints installed, each of which must be properly patched and securely configured with the correct settings to reflect the organization's security policies and controls. If even one device is left unpatched or one configuration setting is incorrect, the entire organization can be at risk. To combat this, the best organizations use solid configuration management (CM) processes.

CM is the process of establishing consistency in engineering, implementation, and operations. CM ensures that every system in the enterprise is configured the way it should be. CM is implemented by following a disciplined process that includes establishing baselines, controlling changes to them, and making sure that all systems on the network are configured using the approved baselines. By following good CM practices, organizations ensure that every system on the network is configured correctly. CM generally has three components:

- **Baselining** A baseline is a reference point for comparison of something. In engineering, a baseline is the set of data that reflects a design. For the purposes of securing an IT environment, the baseline normally consists of all documentation, files, and settings that reflect the as-built systems.

In a normal IT environment, the organization establishes baselines for all of the documentation and data for the enterprise, including network diagrams, manuals, configuration settings, software, libraries, databases, applications, etc. Organizations place these items under baseline control by storing the data in safes, databases, or secure locations and media. Access to baselines is tightly controlled, and changes to baselines are not permitted unless those changes go through a formal change control and approval process.

- **Version control** Every time a baseline is changed, a new version is created. This way, all changes are tracked, and if the organization needs to go back to a previous version of a configuration or operating system, they can easily do so. Every time a change to a baseline is considered, it must go through a formal process before it can be implemented. Changes to baselines are formally requested in writing. The request is reviewed by a committee, sometimes called a change review board, staffed by representatives from security and technical and business stakeholders within the organization. Once the change is approved, the baseline is updated and a new version is published for use.

- **Auditing** On a periodic basis the network can be audited to make sure the systems that are deployed and operating are configured in accordance with the approved baselines. Each system, application, and setting is compared against approved baselines, and any discrepancies are reported and resolved.

System Hardening Summary
The important topics to review about system hardening are

- System hardening includes the following:
  - Patch management using asset management, vulnerability management, patch acquisition, testing, deployment, and reporting
  - Configuration baselines to deploy security controls and avoid misconfigurations
  - Configuration management using baselining, version control, and auditing

---

Best Practice Security Policies

Security policies are the backbone of any security program. They lay out the security-related rules that everyone in the organization must follow. Just as an organization's human resources (HR) policies communicate the personnel practices the organization wants their employees to follow, the security policies communicate the required security practices everyone must follow. By carefully scripting the security policies, the security leadership lays out the foundational requirements of the organization's security program.

Ideally, everything the organization does for security should be traceable back to a security policy. The policy isn't just the requirement—it's the reason why the organization does what it does. As explained in Chapter 1, an organization performs risk analysis to understand the risks it faces, enumerate the assets it must protect, and prioritize its assets and threats. One of the first steps in implementing security based on the risk analysis is to create security policies, which define the security requirements for the organization.

The best security policies have a few things in common. First, they are developed and maintained following a consistent lifecycle. Second, they have a structure that includes, at a minimum, a statement of purpose, requirements statements, and sections describing policy compliance and enforcement.

Although the details of the security policy lifecycle vary from organization to organization, most organizational processes for security policy development have three elements: a creation phase, an implementation phase, and a maintenance phase, each of which are explained as follows:

- **Policy creation** Security policies are usually created by a team or committee under the direction of the security leadership, which may be a chief information security officer (CISO), vice president of security, etc. Security policies are created based on the findings and conclusions of the organization's risk assessment and analysis activities and planning sessions held by the security team. The requirements that are expressed in the policies are the rules that the organization will follow to implement security; therefore, they are best developed as a collaborative effort led by the security organization with buy-in from all parts of the organization.

- **Policy implementation** After a thorough and iterative review process, the policies are rolled out for implementation. Some organizations do this softly or in phases, some do it all at once, while others have a pilot program to test the policy or policies prior to full implementation. Some organizations roll out the policy initially in just a portion of the organization or one department or region as a pilot. And many organizations forgo a soft rollout altogether and jump right in with a full implementation.

- **Policy monitoring and maintenance** After implementation of the policy two things should occur: (1) monitoring to see how well the policy is working and how much people are complying with it and (2) regular updates and revisions to make sure the policy is kept accurate, up to date, and is ever-improving and the security program improves and matures.

In order to clearly convey the organization's plans, rules, and practices, a good and effective security policy should contain the following elements:

- **Title** The title should be clear and consistently conveyed. Organizations cause confusion by calling a policy one name on the title page and another name within the document and yet another name referenced in other policies. We've seen this mistake, and it doesn't help. Consistency in naming is important.

- **Effective date** It is important to establish the date of the policy so it is not confused with prior versions.

- **Purpose** The purpose and objective of the policy should be clearly stated. The purpose should explain why the policy exists and what the objective is for having the policy. If there are external drivers such as a regulation or law that requires the policy, that should be stated.

- **Scope and applicability** This section should clearly identify what the policy covers. What assets, systems, data, departments, regions, staff, and people does the policy apply to and in what manner and to what extent? Sometimes in this section it is important to state what the policy does not apply to as well.

- **References** If the policy relies on other documents, either internal or external, for its understanding or clarity, they should be listed.

- **Policy statements** This section is the meat of the document. It contains the policy statements, which are requirements. Good policy statements use the word "shall" to clearly state the requirement in unambiguous terms, such as, "Passwords shall contain at least 16 characters." Shall statements are sometimes clarified with explanations and can be grouped into sections and subsections.

- **Compliance** This section describes how the organization will measure its own compliance with the policy or check to ensure that people are complying with it. The section may require periodic measures of testing of systems or people to measure compliance. This section may also require reporting on testing or measures of compliance to be sure that information is brought to the attention of the right individuals.

- **Enforcement** This section lays out the ramifications of noncompliance. If there are punishments for noncompliance (fairly common) or rewards for compliance (not so common), they are described in this section.

CC-Recommended Security Policies

(ISC)² has decided there are a few core security policies that all CC candidates should be familiar with and which may be covered on the CC exam. They are

- Data handling policy
- Password policy
- Acceptable use policy (AUP)
- Bring your own device (BYOD) policy
- Change management policy
- Privacy policy

NOTE The CC-recommended security policies are certainly not a comprehensive list of all of the policies a typical organization may have. Similarly, the names used for these policies are not universally applied throughout the industry. However, the topics covered by these policies are frequently included in the security policies of organizations, although they may not be found in their own standalone policy documents. For instance, in the real world, AUP and BYOD are sometimes standalone policies but just as often these topics are covered within other policies. For guidance in helping organizations craft their own security policies, many turn to third-party organizations. The Center for Internet Security (https://www.cisecurity.org) publishes critical security controls with recommended policy templates for each. SANS (https://www.sans.org) publishes a good set of recommended security policy templates. And many firms publish policy templates that map to NIST-recommended security controls.

Data Handling Policy

The data handling policy is sometimes called a data protection policy or data classification and handling policy. It tends to be a broad policy that defines the requirements for how the organization manages and protects data throughout the data lifecycle from inception to destruction. The policy usually covers requirements for data classification, storage, processing, transmission, and destruction as well as data protection requirements (such as use of encryption) for various classification types and phases of the data lifecycle.

Password Policy

The password policy defines the requirements for password size and format, usage, and protection. The policy usually covers requirements for password creation, changes to passwords, practices for protecting passwords such as secure storage and transmission, and use of passwords in applications. Password creation requirements usually include requirements for password length to create passwords of the desired strength.

Acceptable Use Policy (AUP)

Employees and consultants of an organization are users of the organization's IT assets. Misuse of the IT assets can lead to security breaches, compromises of data, and losses to the organization. The purpose of the AUP is to define how IT resources can and should be used by any and all types of users. The policy defines both acceptable and unacceptable usage of IT resources. Typically, the AUP requires that IT resources are only used for official business purposes and not for personal use or for purposes not directly related to the official business of the organization.

Bring Your Own Device (BYOD) Policy

The BYOD policy is used by organizations that want to allow their employees to use their personally owned devices such as laptops or smartphones for official business purposes.

Nowadays many organizations do not have a BYOD policy, as they do not permit using personal devices due to security concerns. If a personal device is to be used for business use, the device must meet certain security requirements and it must be used in a prescribed manner, and that's where the BYOD policy comes in.

The BYOD policy usually requires the employee to install tools onto their device. The tools can be used to allow the employee to remotely access the organization's network and/or to inspect the device for compliance with security configuration standards or to be sure it is free from malware. The BYOD policy may also define requirements for secure storage of organization data on the personal device and for securely sanitizing data from the device when it is no longer needed.

Change Management Policy

This policy defines the requirements necessary to ensure that device configurations and documentation are maintained and modified using a consistent repeatable process. The change management policy ensures IT resources are inventoried, configured, and documented in a consistent and repeatable manner. The policy requires that only authorized, tested, and approved changes are made to computing assets and that they are made in an orderly and controlled manner.

Privacy Policy

There are two kinds of privacy policies. One is published along with the other policies in this section. It addresses the organization's requirements for protecting privacy and privacy data. However, another kind of privacy policy is one that organizations publish on their website that tells visitors how the organization protects their privacy. While similar, each type of privacy policy has its own characteristics.

Privacy policies published as part of an organization's suite of security policies define how the organization protects personal data provided by users. The policy may specifically apply to regulated personal data such as personal health information (PHI), other healthcare data, personally identifying information (PII), and other personal identifying information; credit card information; social security numbers; and the like. The policy defines the requirements for protecting such information during storage and transmission.

The other kind of privacy policy is a legal statement contained on an organization's website that provides details to users regarding how the organization intends to use their data. The statement describes what kind of data it collects and what it will and will not do with each kind of data. The statement is intended to demonstrate compliance with regulations, such as General Data Protection Regulation (GDPR), and to instill trust in their users.

 EXAM TIP CC candidates should be familiar with the purpose and content of each of the CC-recommended policies described herein.

Best Practice Security Policies Summary

Here is a summary of the important topics regarding security policies that should be reviewed for the CC exam:

- The basic elements of a security policy
- The purpose and function of the following security policies:
  - Data handling policy
  - Password policy
  - Acceptable use policy (AUP)
  - Bring your own device (BYOD) policy
  - Change management policy
  - Privacy policy

Security Awareness Training

As evidenced by the previous chapters in this book, organizations go to great lengths to develop, deploy, and maintain technical defenses to reduce their risk against cyber threats. However, it takes people to implement and use these technologies properly. People are the administrators of systems; people are users; and people are responsible for reading, obeying, and implementing security policies. Unfortunately, people make mistakes. The purpose of security awareness training is to try to prevent mistakes that lead to security breaches by teaching people within the organization about their role in security and how to practice good security hygiene.

Security awareness training is required because most people in an organization are not necessarily tuned to practicing good security. For most people at work, job performance is more important than cybersecurity. People are under pressure to do their jobs well, and practicing good security may not be part of how an employer measures employee success. Therefore, being security-aware may not be at the forefront of an employee's attention. In addition, people are not necessarily on alert for cyberattacks. People tend to be trusting of others and may not be on the lookout for potential malicious cyber activity.

To create an environment in which employees are compelled to follow security policies, comply with rules, and use best practice processes for security, organizations use security awareness training solutions. These training programs can be very comprehensive and usually include a combination of commercial off-the-shelf (COTS) training courses purchased from vendors and customized training. The COTS training usually covers general security topics, such as concepts found in this book, while customized training is developed to teach organization-specific topics, such as what the organization's security policies say or how certain types of data should be handled.

Components of Security Awareness Training

A security training and awareness program ideally includes not merely training classes but also a comprehensive program consisting of awareness, training, practice, exercises, and employee testing—all performed on a continuous basis. Let's explore the components of a security awareness training program further.

Awareness

An employee security awareness program uses a variety of methods to create a security-aware workplace culture. In many cases the degree to which security is important to the employee workforce is a reflection of how important security is to the organization's leadership. The security culture starts at the top of the organization. As a result, security-awareness messaging of the organizations with the best security programs tends to originate from the top. In these organizations an employee security newsletter or monthly publication is sent out with an opening message from the CISO or security leadership. The publication is often part of a security awareness internal website where employees can go for the latest information and reminders about security news, policies, practices, breaches, risks, and job-related information to help employees be more security-aware and practice better security hygiene. In fact, some organizations require their employees to visit the security website and read its material on a regular basis as a matter of policy.

In addition to newsletters and websites, organizations use a program of reminders such as posters, e-mails, and announcements to continuously remind employees of the importance of security. Reminders can also take the form of contests, such as who can make the best security awareness poster or which department has the lowest number of security incidents during a given time period.

Training

Training can take many forms, including classroom-style bootcamps, webinars, online videos, or interactive multimedia training. Many organizations use combinations of these delivery methods to provide variety to employees and keep them interested and engaged. Security awareness training courses offered by organizations should have the following features and characteristics:

- **Establishing training goals** As with all training, security training starts with the development of goals. What exactly must the student know for the organization to meet its security threats? Security training is a countermeasure; therefore, there should be a clear understanding of what risks and threats the organization is attempting to combat in its security training and awareness. These goals should be documented and form the basis for all courses, awareness products, and testing activities that are part of the program.

- **Relevance** The training should be relevant to the organization's business environment and to the work the employee does. Some organizations have purchased COTS training products, hoping that they will apply to their business, only to find that such training misses the mark. For instance, most COTS training is general in nature and is focused on office environments. Such training is nice but may not be relevant to workers on a manufacturing floor, in a retail setting, or at a construction site. Relevance brings the training closer to the users and helps them relate to the material better. This aids in learning retention and, more importantly, helps employees apply the learned skills to their jobs.

- **Conformity**   The training must conform to the organization's security policies and practices so that it reinforces them. One of the most common mistakes organizations make in choosing information security training is selecting training courses that do not match, or even conflict with, the organization's security policies. If the training tells employees to take one action but a policy says to take a different action, it creates confusion and increases the likelihood of a security breach.

- **Skills oriented**   Cybersecurity training should not just teach *knowledge;* it should also teach the *skills* that employees need to practice good security. By focusing on skills, the employee can practice what they learn in situations they may face in their job.

- **Modular learning library**   Courses should be available to the students in a well-organized library that makes it easy for the student to know which courses they need to take and how to take them. A large library of short training modules tends to be more effective than a small library of longer courses.

Testing, Practice, and Exercises

Watching videos and attending classes are important parts of training. But what really makes the training stick is *practice,* especially practice using scenarios that are as close to the real world as possible. A program of *practicing and exercises* helps to reinforce what is learned, while *testing* provides the organization, and the student, with metrics that indicate how well the student is learning and how well they are improving over time.

Testing is accomplished using traditional question-and-answer tests administered shortly after the student participates in training events. Practice uses learning modules that present the student with problems they must solve in an individual or group setting. Practice sessions can be tabletop exercises where students discuss problems and solutions around a table or may implement actual software and tools an employee may use at their job.

Tracking

Organizations keep track of each employee's learning progress, recording which courses or learning modules the employee attends or participates in successfully. The results of employee security testing are also recorded. All of this information is recorded in a data store such as a database. In this manner the organization always has a view of which employees have accomplished which security training and what their security test scores are.

Employees can be viewed as if they are like assets. In the same way that assets can have security vulnerabilities in them, so can employees. And in the same way that good vulnerability management dictates keeping track of which systems in the environment are patched and hardened, keeping track of which employees have attended which training and what their scores are is a good way to reduce and manage human vulnerabilities in the environment. One of the goals of security awareness training is to reduce human security vulnerabilities.

Security Awareness Training Topics

Security awareness training programs should, at a minimum, cover the following topics:

- Security best practices
- Organization security program and policies
- Social engineering and job-specific defenses

Security Best Practices

All employees should have a general understanding of cybersecurity threats, risks, and defenses. The purpose of this training is to give the employees a basic understanding of security topics so that they will be able to understand the security policies that they are required to support, follow, and possibly enforce.

Organization Security Program and Policies

Every employee should receive training about the organization's security program and specifically the security policies that define the security requirements that everyone must follow. Security policies aren't effective unless employees know what they say, what they are for, and what the impacts of noncompliance are. Every employee should know where to go to find out about the policies, which policies apply to them, and how they impact the employee's job.

Employees should also be trained about the functions of the organization's security department, including who the players are and what they do. This training should include how an employee can spot a security issue, what they should do if they encounter one, and who they should report issues to.

Social Engineering and Job-Specific Defenses

Employees are often the targets of social engineering attacks. As a result, many organizations now incorporate social engineering defense training into their security training programs. This training, which often includes hands-on practice, teaches employees how to recognize and defend against social engineering methods that they are most likely to encounter in their jobs.

In social engineering training, organizations commonly cover handling physical intruders and visitors, telephone calls and inquiries, phishing e-mails, USB drop attacks, recognizing legitimate and fraudulent websites, etc.

Some organizations develop and present security training to employees that is job-specific. For instance, security-related tasks such as how to handle company-sensitive information or what to do in the event of a security incident may be the topics of job-related training modules organizations require employees to take.

Security Awareness Training Summary

These are the security awareness training topics to study and review for the CC exam:

- Security awareness training purpose
- Components of security awareness training:
  - Awareness newsletters, websites and announcements
  - Training features and characteristics
  - Testing, practice, and exercises
  - Tracking training activities
- Topics frequently covered in security awareness training:
  - Security best practices
  - Security policies
  - Social engineering defenses

Chapter Review

Data security consists of security controls applied to data as part of its lifecycle. The data lifecycle defines how data is handled by an organization throughout its life, which includes creation, storage, usage, sharing, archival, and destruction. Data is protected by leveraging security controls such as cryptography to protect data at rest and in transit. Cryptography includes the use of techniques such as symmetric encryption, asymmetric encryption, and hashing. Systems and data are monitored using logging to track changes and actions that occur and by monitoring those logs using manual and automated techniques.

Organizations make it harder for cybercriminals to attack endpoint devices by hardening them. Hardening involves eliminating known vulnerabilities in the endpoints by making sure they are kept up-to-date with the latest security patches. Hardening also involves configuring the endpoints with secure settings, usually by following established security configuration baselines.

Another security control that organizations use is to create and maintain a set of security policies that define the requirements for all security actions the organization takes. The policies are derived from the risk management and analysis activities the organization performs; therefore, the security policies ensure that the security controls the organization deploys are based on the organization's understanding of their threats, their tolerance for risk, and the specifics of their business environment.

Security awareness training is an important control that addresses a serious weakness in cybersecurity: employee errors that lead to security breaches. The most effective security training programs include more than just training. They also include practice, exercises, and testing to reinforce, measure, and improve employee security performance over time.

Quick Review

- The data lifecycle includes creation, storage, usage, sharing, archival, and destruction.

- Encryption is the process of transforming plaintext (information that is in a readable format) into ciphertext (information that is in an encrypted, unreadable format).

- Decryption is the process of transforming ciphertext back to plaintext.

- The main types of encryption include symmetric encryption and asymmetric encryption.

  - Symmetric encryption is primarily characterized by the use of the same key for encryption and decryption.

  - Asymmetric encryption uses two keys that are mathematically related: a public key (can be shared with anyone) and a private key (must remain private).

- Hashing uses special algorithms that transform information into fixed-length output known as a hash value, message digest, or fingerprint.

- Logging is the capturing of system events for later analysis.

- Monitoring is the examination of events and other activity.

- Monitoring can be done manually or using automated leveraging tools.

- System hardening is the practice of making endpoint devices harder to attack by reducing their attack surface. Hardening includes

  - Eliminating all known vulnerabilities via patch management

  - Applying configuration settings to the system that reduce their attack surface (via secure configuration baselines)

  - Using good configuration management processes

- Patch management is the discipline of ensuring that all systems in the enterprise are kept fully patched with the most recent security patches from the respective software product sources.

- A security baseline is how an organization implements security controls within an operating system or application.

- Configuration management is a disciplined process that includes establishing baselines, controlling changes to them, and making sure that all systems on the network are configured using the approved baselines.

- Security policies lay out the security-related rules that everyone in the organization must follow.

- The data handling policy defines requirements for how the organization manages and protects data.

- The password policy defines the requirements for password creation, usage, and protection.

- The purpose of the acceptable use policy is to define how IT resources can and should be employed by users.

- The BYOD policy is used by organizations that want to allow their employees to use their personally owned devices for official business purposes.

- The change management policy defines the requirements necessary to ensure that device configurations and documentation are maintained and modified using a consistent, repeatable process.

- The privacy policy addresses the organization's requirements for protecting privacy and privacy data. Another kind of privacy policy is one that organizations publish on their website that tells visitors how the organization protects their privacy.

- A security training and awareness program ideally includes not merely training classes but also a comprehensive program consisting of awareness, training, practice, exercises, and employee testing, all performed on a continuous basis.

- An employee security awareness program uses a variety of methods to create a security-aware workplace culture.

- Training can take many forms, including classroom-style bootcamps, webinars, online videos, or interactive multimedia training.

- What really makes the training stick is practice, especially practice using scenarios that are as close to the real world as possible.

- Organizations keep track of each employee's learning progress, recording which courses or learning modules the employee attends or participates in successfully.

- All employees should have a general understanding of cybersecurity threats, risks, and defenses.

- Every employee should receive training about the organization's security program and policies.

- Many organizations now incorporate social engineering defense training into their security training programs.

Questions

1. Alice sends Bob a message encrypted with a private key. Bob decrypts the message with the same private key. Which of the following types of encryption is this an example of?

   A. Asymmetric

   B. Symmetric

   C. Hashing

   D. None of the above

2. Which of the following is not a secure method of data deletion?

   A. Emptying the recycle bin on your computer desktop

   B. Physical destruction of a hard drive

   C. Zeroization

   D. Overwriting

3. Which of the following can be used to create message digests?

   A. Symmetric encryption algorithms

   B. Asymmetric encryption algorithms

   C. Hash functions

   D. All of the above

4. A security administrator is looking for ways to automate the monitoring of logs throughout the environment. Which of the following solutions would help provide automated monitoring capability?

   A. Regularly review the logs

   B. Store the logs on a centralized log server

   C. Implement a SIEM

   D. Implement a firewall

5. Which of the following types of encryption uses two keys: one for encryption and a separate key for decryption?

   A. Asymmetric

   B. Symmetric

   C. Hashing

   D. None of the above

6. As the new CISO of his organization, Joe decided to initiate a comprehensive set of scans. The scans reported that nearly all of his endpoints have known operating system vulnerabilities. What is the most likely root cause of this situation?

   A. The organization is the victim of an advanced persistent threat.

   B. The endpoints do not have up-to-date antimalware software installed.

   C. The endpoints have not been kept up-to-date with the latest security patches.

   D. Brute force attack.

7. A network administrator found that one of the firewalls was no longer configured in accordance with recommended settings from DISA as it once was. What is the most likely reason for this?

   A. The settings from DISA were incorrect.

   B. Configuration management procedures for the device were not followed.

   C. Privilege creep.

   D. Data integrity.

8. Mary isn't sure if she is allowed to use her company-owned laptop to send messages to her friend on Facebook. To find out if she can, which policy should she refer to?

   A. AUP

   B. BYOD policy

   C. Data handling policy

   D. None of the above

9. Of the policies listed, which one is most likely to provide guidance on connecting a home computer to the work network via VPN?

   A. AUP

   B. BYOD

   C. Data handling policy

   D. None of the above

10. An employee notices a poster in the lunchroom reminding her about not writing down her passwords but instead to use the company-provided password vault software. What is this an example of?

    A. Security awareness

    B. Security training

    C. Security policy

    D. Security testing

11. What is the best reason to provide social engineering training to employees?

    A. To show people how to perform a social engineering attack

    B. So employees can report security violations to management

    C. To teach people what to look out for

    D. None of the above

Questions and Answers

1. Alice sends Bob a message encrypted with a private key. Bob decrypts the message with the same private key. Which of the following types of encryption is this an example of?

   A. Asymmetric

   B. Symmetric

   C. Hashing

   D. None of the above

   B. Symmetric encryption uses the same key for encryption and decryption. This means that the sender and receiver of a message need to have a copy of the same key in order to encrypt/decrypt the message.

2. Which of the following is not a secure method of data deletion?

   A. Emptying the recycle bin on your computer desktop

   B. Physical destruction of a hard drive

   C. Zeroization

   D. Overwriting

   A. Pressing the DELETE key on a computer and emptying the recycle bin on your desktop are not secure methods of data destruction, as the data is not actually securely deleted from the hard drive. These actions simply tell the operating system that the location on the hard drive is free for use.

3. Which of the following can be used to create message digests?

   A. Symmetric encryption algorithms

   B. Asymmetric encryption algorithms

   C. Hash functions

   D. All of the above

   C. Hash functions transform information into fixed-length output known as a hash value, message digest, or fingerprint.

4. A security administrator is looking for ways to automate the monitoring of logs throughout the environment. Which of the following solutions would help provide automated monitoring capability?

   A. Regularly review the logs

   B. Store the logs on a centralized log server

   C. Implement a SIEM

   D. Implement a firewall

   C. Implementing a security information and event management (SIEM) system is one example of how an organization can implement automated monitoring. A SIEM system is a tool that ingests logs from various sources, serves as a central secure log repository, and contains rules that alert on suspicious events identified in logs.

5. Which of the following types of encryption uses two keys: one for encryption and a separate key for decryption?

   A. Asymmetric

   B. Symmetric

   C. Hashing

   D. None of the above

   A. Asymmetric encryption uses two keys: a public key (for encryption) and a private key (for decryption).

6. As the new CISO of his organization, Joe decided to initiate a comprehensive set of scans. The scans reported that nearly all of his endpoints have known operating system vulnerabilities. What is the most likely root cause of this situation?

   A. The organization is the victim of an advanced persistent threat.

   B. The endpoints do not have up-to-date antimalware software installed.

   C. The endpoints have not been kept up-to-date with the latest security patches.

   D. Brute force attack.

   C. The most likely reason endpoints have known operating system vulnerabilities is they do not have the latest patches installed from the vendors. Poorly configured antimalware software or a brute force attack would not cause this, and an APT might be the result of this situation but not the cause of it.

7. A network administrator found that one of the firewalls was no longer configured in accordance with recommended settings from DISA as it once was. What is the most likely reason for this?

   A. The settings from DISA were incorrect.

   B. Configuration management procedures for the device were not followed.

   C. Privilege creep.

   D. Data integrity.

   B. The best answer is that it is most likely that someone changed a setting without the proper approval and documentation; therefore, CM procedures were not followed.

8. Mary isn't sure if she is allowed to use her company-owned laptop to send messages to her friend on Facebook. To find out if she can, which policy should she refer to?

   A. AUP

   B. BYOD policy

   C. Data handling policy

   D. None of the above

   A. Of the choices provided, the AUP is the one most likely to provide guidance concerning whether or not Mary can use the company-owned laptop for nonbusiness use.

9. Of the policies listed, which one is most likely to provide guidance on connecting a home computer to the work network via VPN?

    A. AUP

    B. BYOD

    C. Data handling policy

    D. None of the above

    B. Of the choices provided, the BYOD policy is the best choice. The BYOD policy is used by organizations that want to allow their employees to use their personally owned devices to connect to the corporate network.

10. An employee notices a poster in the lunchroom reminding her about not writing down her passwords but instead to use the company-provided password vault software. What is this an example of?

    A. Security awareness

    B. Security training

    C. Security policy

    D. Security testing

    A. The use of posters and reminders in the workplace is an example of security awareness.

11. What is the best reason to provide social engineering training to employees?

    A. To show people how to perform a social engineering attack

    B. So employees can report security violations to management

    C. To teach people what to look out for

    D. None of the above

    C. The correct answer is to show people what kinds of things they should look out for as a way to defend against social engineering attacks.

Business Continuity (BC), Disaster Recovery (DR) & Incident Response Concepts

This chapter discusses the following topics:
- Incident response
- Business continuity
- Disaster recovery

This chapter explores how organizations respond to and recover from security incidents, disasters, and other events that impact an organization's operations. Generally, there are three aspects of handling incidents, and organizations typically define plans and processes for each of these three functions as discussed next.

- *Incident response* involves planning, processes, and tools for how an organization prepares for and responds to security incidents. Typically, organizations try to predict the types of incidents that are most likely to occur and have plans in place for how they monitor for these security incidents, investigate indicators of incidents, and remediate and recover from incidents. Typically, incident response includes when and how incidents are investigated and when and how to involve law enforcement if criminal activity is involved or suspected.

- *Business continuity* involves planning for how the business will continue to operate when a disaster or incident occurs. Business continuity plans usually focus on those essential functions that are most important to the business and what the organization does when an incident occurs to preserve those essential business functions.

- *Disaster recovery* is usually a subset of business continuity that is focused on recovering the IT or information processing aspects of the business that are impacted during a disaster or security incident. Disaster recovery includes the architecture, design, and operational aspects of the information systems that provide for the restoration of data and services after an incident.

Organizations coordinate their incident response, business continuity, and disaster recovery planning and execution activities, and some organizations do this in a prescribed manner. (ISC)² endorses an approach in which organizations write their plans so that if the incident response and business continuity plans fail, the disaster recovery plan takes over. That's one approach but certainly not the only approach to coordinating between business continuity, disaster recovery, and incident response plans. Other organizations use these plans hierarchically, using the business continuity plan as the "master" plan and the incident response and disaster recovery plans as subplans. There is no right or wrong way as long as an organization has a well-planned approach to preparing for, handling, and recovering from incidents.

NOTE In this chapter when discussing business continuity or disaster recovery, we use the terms security incident and disaster somewhat interchangeably, as either type of event can be the triggers for these functions. However, incident response is focused primarily on security incidents.

Business Continuity and Disaster Recovery Plans . . . Who Needs Them?

Organizations that do not have plans in place for what to do, or how to recover, when a security incident or disaster occurs are quite literally playing with fire. Consider the computer virus attack that hit a network of hospitals in the UK in 2016. The hospital system had no business continuity plans in place. As a result, for five days the hospital system was completely disabled. Patients had to be turned away at the door no matter how serious their medical condition. Nearly 3,000 medical procedures were canceled because the hospital system was not prepared and had no way to restore operations during and after the computer virus infection. The human, legal, and financial cost of being unprepared for this event was calamitous for the system's hospitals and the communities they served.

In contrast, in 2013 a datacenter owned by a managed services provider (MSP) in South Carolina caught fire due to a lightning strike. The fire completely destroyed the MSP's infrastructure, including computer hardware, cabling, the building, and telecommunications. Imagine if your organization was the customer of this MSP and all of your data and operational capability were lost. But this MSP was prepared. They had a business continuity plan in place with disaster recovery procedures ready for just this kind of disaster. They had a remote datacenter at the ready and data had been backed up, allowing them to restore data and critical functionality to the remote servers. The MSP's customers did not experience significant disruption in their service and the MSP was able to keep operating, maintain revenue, and avoid legal liabilities because they were properly prepared for this threat.

These contrasting examples show the benefit of sound business continuity and disaster recovery planning. But doing the right preparation takes time and money. Organizations must weigh the balance between investing in planning and preparation versus the cost of dealing with the disaster after the fact.

EXAM TIP CC candidates should understand the purpose of business continuity, incident response, and disaster recovery plans.

Incident Response

The boxer Mike Tyson once famously said, "everyone has a plan until they get punched in the mouth." While this quote was specific to boxing, it is an applicable metaphor to cybersecurity and, in particular, incident response. In boxing it is important to have proper defense and be able to block the incoming punch (think preventive controls from Chapter 1). However, if your training has not conditioned and prepared your body to take a punch and your strategy is based purely on the assumption you will never get hit, your chances of recovering from a punch are not great. The reality of life is that bad things happen, and oftentimes it is how we prepare, respond, and recover from these situations that is most meaningful.

Similarly in cybersecurity, cyberattacks happen to organizations of all shapes and sizes. Organizations that rely purely on preventive controls to defend themselves often suffer greater losses when an attack is successful, as they haven't properly planned for and developed response capabilities to being "punched in the mouth." In other words, they haven't properly trained and conditioned the organization to respond to an attack. In cybersecurity, *incident management* is the collection of processes, tools, technologies, and resources used to respond to an incident. *Security incident response* is the process of preparing, detecting, analyzing, containing, eradicating, and recovering from a security incident (such as virus/malware infections, credential theft, sensitive data exfiltration, etc.). The organization must have processes, technologies, and resources in place to understand what happened and respond appropriately. The goal is to minimize the impact to the organization and ensure the health and safety of personnel. This section discusses the following topics:

- Incident response terminology
- Incident response governance elements
- Incident response process

 EXAM TIP   The number-one priority of any kind of continuity management, including incident response, is to ensure the health and safety of people in the event of an incident.

Incident Response Terminology

As is the case with any information security domain, it is important to have an understanding of the fundamental terminology to facilitate the discussion. Following are some of the key terms that are relevant to incident response:

- **Event**   An occurrence of an activity on an information system.
- **Incident**   One or more events that jeopardize the confidentiality, integrity, or availability of an asset. If the incident results in unauthorized access to data or a system, it may be referred to as a *breach, intrusion,* or *compromise.*
- **Exploit**   An action, program, or tool that takes advantage of a system vulnerability.

- **Threat**   An event with the potential to damage the organization (e.g., cyberattack, social engineering, natural disaster, physical intrusion).

- **Threat actors**   An individual or group that has the potential to damage the organization (e.g., hacker, cyber criminal, insider threat).

- **Vulnerability**   A weakness that has the potential to be exploited by a threat agent. A *zero day* is a specific type of vulnerability that is not widely known.

 NOTE   It is best practice for organizations to define terms, such as the ones listed here, in the appropriate incident response documents. Different organizations often have slightly different definitions for these terms, and it is important that they are codified in the organization's incident response documentation (e.g., policies, plans, internal standards, procedures) so that consistent language and meaning are used.

Incident Response Governance Elements

In Chapter 1, we introduced the concept of security governance elements, which are used to help the security program meet the requirements and objectives of the organization. These governance elements include policies, plans, procedures, and the structure of the teams that make up the security program. Organizations often develop plans, policies, and procedures for each security subprogram, forming a library of documents that define the requirements for the program. This is particularly important for incident response. In this section, we look at the following elements commonly used to govern the incident response program:

- Incident response policy
- Incident response plan
- Incident response procedures
- Incident response team

Incident Response Policy

The *incident response policy* is a collection of high-level management statements focused on governing and setting forth the requirements for the incident response function. Some organizations have a dedicated incident response policy, while others may have a general information security policy with incident response policy statements that reference a corresponding incident response plan. An incident response policy includes information such as

- The purpose statement for the policy
- The scope of the incident response policy
- Definitions of the roles and responsibilities for the incident response function
- Requirements for sharing of sensitive incident information

- Requirements for prioritization and severity ranking thresholds
- References to corresponding incident response plans and procedures

Incident Response Plan

The *incident response plan* is perhaps the most important governance element, as it lays the foundation for the organization's approach to responding to incidents. Whereas the incident response policy contains high-level statements and requirements, the incident response plan provides the roadmap for implementing those requirements. In some cases, this includes the specific procedures for responding to incidents (such as preparation, detection and analysis, containment, eradication, recovery, and post-incident activity). In other cases, the incident response plan may reference separate procedure documents. Regardless of how an organization structures its incident response governance elements, having an incident response plan is important. An incident response plan might typically include

- The objectives, strategy, and mission of the plan
- The definition of the organization's approach to incident response
- Definitions of key incident response terms to ensure consistent language is utilized
- Procedures for responding to incidents or references to separate procedure documents
- Communication plans and templates for communicating both internally and externally
- Lists of entities that require incident notification
- Contact information for the incident response team as well as other relevant contacts
- Definitions of the roles and responsibilities of the incident response personnel
- References to relevant policies, procedures, and other plans (such as a BCP or DRP)
- The process for maintaining and improving the plan
- Lists of relevant laws, regulations, and external standards

Incident Response Procedures

Incident response procedures are documented step-by-step processes on how specific incident response tasks are to be performed based on the requirements set forth in the incident response policy and plan. In some cases, incident response procedures are integrated into the incident response plan. In other cases, they are separate documents. Incident response procedures cover the technical processes, tools, techniques, and checklists used by incident response personnel. This often covers the processes for leveraging the technologies and tools used by the organization for incident response. It is important that incident response procedures are detailed but also clear and can be followed during the "heat of the moment" when an incident is occurring. This is why training, practice, and testing are so critical for success. If the first time an incident responder has ever read the incident response procedures is during an incident, their likelihood of success is low.

Incident Response Team

The incident response program must be appropriately staffed in order to be able to perform incident response duties. The incident response function is implemented by a team that interacts and coordinates with stakeholders both inside and outside the organization. The incident response team usually has formal interactions with people or groups within the organization to establish monitoring and incident handling policies, plans, processes, and procedures. Such interaction may be part of an integrated incident response committee. Roles with which the team interacts may include the chief financial officer (CFO) or finance team, general counsel or legal team, upper management and department heads, human resources, and the chief information officer (CIO) or information technology group. It is important that incident response be a cross-functional effort with support from across the organization to ensure the approach is complete and comprehensive.

Depending on the size, structure, industry, and needs of the organization, the incident response team may be quite large, with people who specialize in specific aspects of the process or have expertise in unique technologies. Following are some of the roles and team structure models that might be used to staff the incident response function:

- **Roles** The incident response team typically consists of a manager or lead who coordinates the activities of the team and manages communication with the rest of the organization, as well as various levels of analysts (level 1, level 2, etc.) who perform various levels of monitoring alerts and logs, incident triage, and investigation. In some cases, these members are dedicated to the incident response function. In other cases, they may be other technical or engineering staff who wear an incident response "hat" depending on the size of the organization. This team is often supported by internal and external specialists in areas including incident investigation, law enforcement, and recovery or in technical areas such as communications, server technology, or specialized applications.

- **Team structure** In some cases the incident response function is a centralized team focused on monitoring alerts and responding to incidents. The organization might establish a dedicated security operations center (SOC) consisting of a team of dedicated incident response staff, as well as tools and technologies for monitoring and responding to incidents. In other cases, it may be decentralized where there are many separate incident response teams focused on a particular system or organizational unit that coordinate together.

- **Staffing model** Some organizations have an in-house incident response team. This is known as *insourcing*. Other organizations may elect to purchase a third-party service that provides a range of offerings from security monitoring and alerting to full-blown incident response and forensic support. This is known as *outsourcing*. Other organizations may choose a hybrid approach where they outsource part of the function (such as forensic investigations) but perform other functions in-house (such as monitoring).

For some incidents, additional individuals or their associated departments may be involved in incident response activities. For instance, the legal counsel or legal department would certainly be involved in the decision to contact law enforcement agencies. Likewise, the human resources group would be contacted if the incident investigation indicates employee misbehavior or violations of policy or when human safety is a factor.

Incident Response Process

Security incident response begins with preparation and ends with incident resolution and closing. There are many steps along the way, and each step must be well planned, guided by policies, and performed following a well-crafted incident response plan and corresponding procedures. As with all aspects of security, the extent to which the organization plans, rehearses, and documents the incident response process is based on the nature of the organization. The incident response process is commonly implemented using a model similar to that depicted in Figure 5-1. This figure shows the current industry standard practice for handling incidents according to NIST Special Publication 800-61, *Computer Security Incident Handling Guide*. Organizations often use this or similar models to structure their incident response plan and procedures.

Although the exact names and number of steps vary from organization to organization (NIST defines a four-step process), the underlying concepts are universal: prepare for incidents ahead of time, investigate and resolve them, restore the organization to normal operations, and then see what can be learned about what happened so incidents like these can be prevented or handled better in the future. Each step from the diagram is discussed in the following sections.

EXAM TIP   CC candidates should be aware of the NIST incident response process and phases and understand the activities performed in each phase.

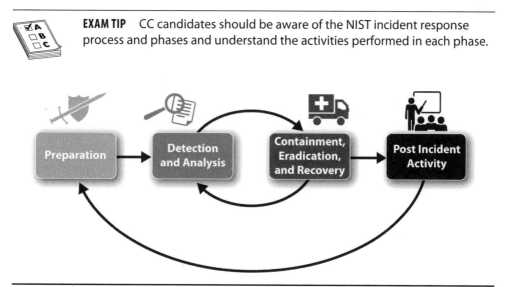

Figure 5-1   Incident response process (Source: NIST SP 800-61)

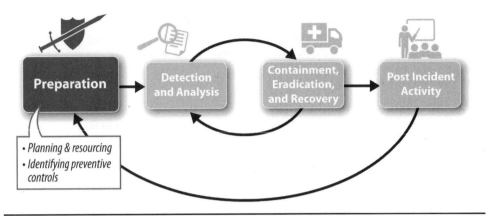

Figure 5-2 Preparation phase (Source: NIST SP 800-61)

Preparation

The first phase in the incident response process is the *preparation* phase, illustrated in Figure 5-2. In security incident response, when the incident response personnel are well prepared to respond to security events and incidents, the chances of minimizing the impact to the organization are increased. Preparation is key in ensuring there are proper resources in place and staff are appropriately trained on the policies, plan, procedures, and tools to use in the event of an incident. In this section we review

- Planning and resourcing
- Identifying preventive controls

Planning and Resourcing   A large part of the preparation phase involves planning to ensure the incident response function is appropriately documented, resourced, and managed. This means developing the governance elements that will be used to manage the incident response function and ensuring resources are in place to execute on the vision. Following are some of the activities that occur in the preparation phase for a healthy incident response program:

- **Documentation**   Develop, publish, and maintain appropriate incident response governance elements that are approved by management. This may include an incident response policy, plan, and corresponding procedures to handle specific types of incidents.
- **Staffing**   The incident response function must be appropriately staffed. All personnel involved should have defined roles and responsibilities to ensure alignment with the incident response plan, policies, and procedures. In addition, contact information should be documented for key staff and stakeholders.

- **Stakeholder coordination**   Consideration must be given to stakeholder coordination and communication. This includes both internal (incident response personnel, senior leadership, etc.) and external stakeholders (customers, regulators, etc.). Plans should be in place outlining which stakeholders are to be contacted and when.

- **Tools and technologies**   In order to facilitate incident response, the organization has to acquire and deploy adequate tools and technology to support incident handling activities. This includes ensuring the appropriate sources are being monitored in order to determine when an incident has occurred.

- **Training**   An appropriate training program is put in place to ensure that personnel are adequately trained in incident handling processes and methods.

Identifying Preventive Controls   While it is not always feasible, it is preferable to stop an incident before it happens. This can be aided through the implementation of preventive controls, which prevent or stop adverse incidents from occurring in order to mitigate risk to the organization. Preventive controls are often more cost-effective than the cost of recovering from an incident; however, this does not negate the need to have monitoring, recovery, and incident response systems and processes in place. Preventive controls simply provide a means to reduce the probability of an incident occurring. Here are some examples to consider:

- **Data security**   Data security controls protect sensitive data from unauthorized access, disclosure, and modification. This includes encryption of data at rest (data stored on systems or external media) and in transit (data moving between systems on a network).

- **Endpoint security**   These types of controls are used to help secure endpoints on a network to reduce the likelihood of an incident. An endpoint can be a computer, server, mobile device, and so on. Securing endpoints consists of ensuring systems are patched, appropriately configured, and leveraging security software such as antivirus/antimalware protection.

- **Network security**   Many different types of network security controls may be implemented to help prevent incidents from occurring. These include boundary protection measures such as firewalls that block certain types of network traffic as well as network design techniques like network segmentation that help prevent access to an organization's network.

- **Security awareness training**   Training is another important preventive control, as many incidents are caused by employees unknowingly clicking on malicious links or installing malicious software on their computer. Security awareness training can help prevent this by educating employees on security best practices and how to identify malicious links or e-mails, as well as how to report suspicious events.

- **Access control**   Having proper access controls in place helps prevent attackers from gaining access to systems. This includes both physical access controls (such as doors and locks to protect against physical threats such as theft) and logical access controls (such as password-protected systems and multifactor authentication protecting against cyber threats).

When thinking about incident prevention, it is often beneficial to think about ways to reduce the entry points for the attacker. In a typical home, the entry points are the different entrances into the home (e.g., front door, back door, windows, garage). For a typical organization, the entry points for an attacker come from systems, software, services, websites, web applications, and so on. By minimizing and reducing these entry points, we limit the organization's exposure to various attacks. This might be accomplished by removing or uninstalling software or services that are not needed or disabling the universal serial bus (USB) ports on a computer to prevent malware from being installed from external media.

Detection and Analysis

The next phase is the detection and analysis phase, which is shown in Figure 5-3. The purpose of the *detection and analysis* phase is to determine when something bad is happening. This is accomplished by having logging and monitoring tools and capabilities in place to identify events occurring throughout the environment, processes in place to determine when an event becomes an incident, and procedures in place to prioritize the incidents. In this section we explore the following topics:

- Common attacks
- Sources of incident information
- Incident documentation and triage
- Incident notification process

Common Attacks   It is important to consider various attacks in the development of incident response policies, plans, and procedures to ensure the organization is prepared to respond to a range of incidents. However, it is often impractical to develop response plans for every possible attack that might occur. Organizations often attempt to predict the most common security incidents they will face and ensure response plans and

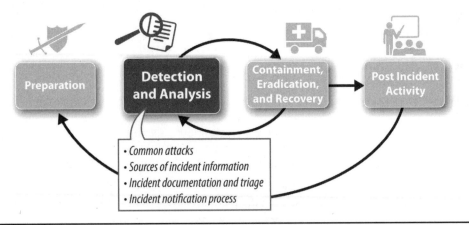

Figure 5-3   Detection and analysis phase (Source: NIST SP 800-61)

procedures are in place for those specific types of incidents. Examples of common attacks are included here:

- **Web application**   Software flaws in web applications may allow an attacker to compromise a web application (e.g., injecting malicious code into a website or extracting data from a database).

- **Network**   Network threats can include attacks that attempt to overload a network resource (such as a denial of service attack) or attacks against vulnerable services running on network devices.

- **Social engineering**   Social engineering is a common attack where an attacker tricks an employee into performing an nonsecure activity such as clicking on a malicious link or attachment in an e-mail or providing them their login credentials.

- **External media**   Attacks can come from external media such as USB or thumb drives that can introduce malicious code into a system when plugged in.

- **Misconfiguration**   Misconfigurations occur when personnel do not appropriately configure a system or device, resulting in unintended exposure (e.g., accidentally exposing an internal resource to the public Internet).

- **Compromised credentials**   User or system credentials might become compromised, resulting in an attacker gaining access to a system or environment.

- **Insider threats**   Insider threats come from trusted personnel who are given heightened access to sensitive systems. The motivation may be intentional (such as being bribed by an external party or disgruntled personnel who want to harm the organization) or unintentional (such as misconfigurations).

- **Theft**   An attacker might steal a system or device that contains sensitive information.

 NOTE   This is not a comprehensive list of possible security attacks. These are simply some of the common attacks that an organization might consider preparing for in the development of incident response plans and procedures.

Sources of Incident Information   When an incident is occurring, the security team must be able to identify what is happening. This starts when a team member sees evidence of a suspicious event occurring. They may begin to see alerts from security detection and monitoring tools in place, indications of anomalous activity in log files, unusual network activity, or receipt of reports from employees. Detection can come from both technical sources (e.g., system logs, security tools) and nontechnical sources (e.g., employee or customer reporting). This begins with having the proper logging (the recording of events) and monitoring (the examination of events) capabilities in place. Having these capabilities in place helps the organization identify incidents. Incident information comes from a variety of sources. Following are some of the common ones:

- **Logs**   Servers, workstations, databases, applications, and network devices have the capability to perform logging to capture events and store them for later retrieval and analysis. These logs are useful to identify suspicious activity or to help reconstruct past security events.

- **IDS/IPS**   Intrusion detection and prevention systems have the ability to analyze events and take automated action. *Intrusion detection systems (IDSs)* merely detect and alert personnel that an attack may be occurring. *Intrusion prevention systems (IPSs)* have the ability to detect events and then actively block or prevent attacks.

- **SIEM**   Many organizations employ some kind of *security information and event management (SIEM)* system that aggregates and correlates event logs from a variety of sources into a central repository. This allows security teams to analyze information on events from sources all across the environment.

- **Endpoint protection**   Endpoint protection tools come in a variety of forms but typically include antivirus/antimalware capability and might include other features such as file integrity monitoring or additional incident response capabilities (such as isolating a system from communicating with other systems on the network). Endpoint security tools are often one of the first tools to detect security events.

- **Threat intelligence**   Many organizations receive information on vulnerabilities and threats from organizations such as the U.S. Computer Readiness Team (US-CERT), National Vulnerability Database (NVD), and Information Sharing and Analysis Centers (ISACs). Some organizations also pay for third-party threat intelligence feeds or subscriptions to leverage as part of their security portfolio.

- **People**   People are often one of the most important incident sources because they can be the first to notice when suspicious activity or events are occurring. This can include people within the organization (such as an employee noticing strange behavior on their computer) as well as outside the organization (such as a customer noticing something strange with your organization's website). This is why it is critical to ensure personnel are appropriately trained on how to report suspicious activity or events that may have cybersecurity implications.

At some point, the evidence (or accumulation of evidence) reveals that a security incident may have occurred (or is in the process of occurring).

Incident Documentation and Triage   For incident documentation, many organizations leverage some kind of centralized ticketing system for documenting and tracking incident investigations. This helps provide a centralized audit trail of the events and timeline and allows the organization to restrict access to incident investigation information. The tracking system should only be accessible to those who have a *need to know,* as incident investigations often cover very sensitive information. Incident documentation includes elements such as

- Date and time of events
- Source of incident reporting
- Status of incident
- Summary of incident
- Actions taken involving the incident
- Contact information for relevant parties
- Evidence gathered
- Notes from the incident response team
- Proposed next steps

The organization must have processes in place to triage events and prioritize incidents. Not every event that is received is an incident, so there must be a process for analysis. In addition, processes need to be in place to analyze and prioritize the incidents to ensure those with the greatest organizational impact are being prioritized. This often includes categorizing the incident based on the data or systems impacted and leveraging some type of incident severity matrix. Table 5-1 provides an example of security incident categorization.

NOTE The incident categorization system used varies from organization to organization. Severity levels are often created based on the importance of the systems impacted, the sensitivity of the data involved, and the magnitude of the impact to the organization. Some organizations build their own categorization process or leverage guidance from best practice standard organizations such as NIST and ISO.

Incident Notification Process The incident notification process is executed following documented processes and procedures around incident notification. The incident notification process starts with notifying the appropriate internal personnel as part of response activities such as the appropriate incident response participants as well as key stakeholders.

Severity Level	Description
Low	Incidents that have a low level of impact and cause a minor disruption to organizational operations
Medium	Incidents that have a medium level of impact and cause a moderate disruption to organizational operations
High	Incidents that have a high level of impact and cause a critical disruption to organizational operations

Table 5-1 Incident Severity

This often includes a range of stakeholders such as legal, public relations and communications, IT, security, human resources, and so on and will often depend on the type of incident in question. Notification plans should also include processes for contacting external parties. It is important that there are clearly defined roles and responsibilities noting specific personnel authorized to make the decisions around when and how external entities are to be contacted. External notifications might include law enforcement if legal action is being pursued, customer notifications, or other entities required under legal or regulatory reporting requirements. Oftentimes organizations develop templates with preapproved messages to be able to quickly leverage these in the event of an incident.

Containment, Eradication, and Recovery

Once an incident has been detected and properly analyzed, the next phase is *containment, eradication, and recovery,* which is shown in Figure 5-4. In an organization's incident response efforts, the response team must have tools, techniques, and procedures in place for incident containment, eradication, and recovery. This means containing the incident so it does not propagate to other systems or environments (e.g., malware spreading to more computers), eradicating the incident from the environment (e.g., quarantining and removing the malware), and ensuring the impacted systems are recovered in order to resume normal operations. This phase could also be called the "fix it" phase, as the focus is to get things back to normal. In this phase we will explore the following topics:

- Evidence handling
- Containment strategies
- Eradication and recovery activities

Evidence Handling   Throughout the incident response process, a variety of evidence is collected to support the resolution of the incident. However, evidence may also be required if the organization intends to pursue legal action against the attacker. This is why it is critical that the organization has processes in place for how evidence is properly collected, handled, and preserved in accordance with applicable laws and regulations.

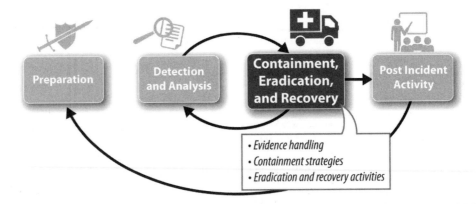

Figure 5-4   Containment, eradication, and recovery phase (Source: NIST SP 800-61)

This is important to consider from the very beginning of the incident response lifecycle to ensure the admissibility of evidence. The admissibility of evidence is determined by the judge when evidence is submitted to the court as part of a criminal or civil trial. To be admissible, the evidence must be relevant (related to the incident in question) and reliable (accurate and obtained/handled to ensure its integrity).

To ensure evidence is reliable and admissible, proper chain of custody must be followed. Chain of custody is a paper trail that shows how evidence was obtained, stored, and handled during its entire lifecycle. The organization must have written procedures for incident responders to follow for how evidence is collected, handled, and stored to ensure there is a documented chain of custody. This includes procedures for capturing, tagging, packaging, storing, transporting, and maintaining evidence integrity while it is being analyzed. For example, if the contents of a laptop are deemed relevant to an investigation, a record should be maintained of how the laptop was stored, transported, and preserved from the moment it was obtained by the investigators right up until it is presented in court. The intent is to be able to prove that the evidence was not altered since it was first obtained. This is particularly important to consider during the containment, eradication, and recovery phase, as steps to remediate the incident can often alter the configuration of the system and could present challenges during the pursuit of legal action. As a result, it may be necessary to take a snapshot of the system in question for evidence collection purposes before remediation activities are taken.

 EXAM TIP   CC candidates are not likely to be tested on specific forensic or investigative techniques as part of incident response but should be familiar with evidence handling concepts such as chain of custody.

Containment Strategies   Once an incident has been identified, it must be contained in order to minimize the damage and "stop the bleeding." The aim is to prevent the incident from spreading to other systems and environments. The response team must contain the incident so that it can be further assessed while preventing it from spreading or causing additional damage. It is important that containment is effective and complete (encompasses all impacted systems). Containment strategies are typically documented and defined in advance so a specific strategy can be utilized for a given type of incident. Examples of containment strategies may include

- **Perimeter**   Perimeter network containment prevents the spread beyond the network perimeter, using methods such as inbound/outbound traffic blocking, updating perimeter firewall policies, and switching to alternate communication links.

- **Internal**   Internal network containment prevents the spread beyond a portion of the network, such as isolating segments or virtual local area networks (VLANs) and updating router, firewall, and switch settings to block specific Internet Protocol (IP) addresses or ports.

- **Endpoint** Endpoint containment prevents the spread beyond a specific system, device, server, workstation or laptop, such as disconnecting network access for specific endpoints, shutting down a system, disabling certain ports or services, or leveraging antimalware software to quarantine an infection. The ability to disconnect a device from the network is sometimes referred to as endpoint isolation.

- **Account** Account containment strategies include disabling, revoking, or changing user or system account credentials or keys if an account is suspected to be compromised to remove the attacker's access.

The containment strategy that is imposed and implemented varies depending on the type and source of the attack.

Eradication and Recovery Activities Once an incident has been contained, the response team prioritizes eradication and recovery activities for the impacted systems. *Eradication* is focused on removing the attacker's foothold in the environment by removing things the attacker may have done to the organization's network. This may include removing malware from affected systems, updating configuration settings, or disabling user or system accounts that may have been compromised.

Recovery is focused on bringing systems impacted by the incident back to a normal operational state after the source of the incident has been eradicated. In some cases, eradication is combined with recovery, as recovery processes may include steps that eradicate the incident. For example, restoring a system using a clean set of backup data wipes out the bad content and replaces it with good content all in one step. Recovery may include reimaging systems, installing new operating systems and applications, changing passwords, updating firewall rules, hardening system configurations, and installing patches to remediate any vulnerabilities to prevent future incidents from occurring. Recovery brings the system to a new, clean, and fully functional operating state. This is often accompanied by heightened monitoring to help determine if the eradication and recovery strategies were successful.

Post-Incident Activity

The final phase in the process is the *post-incident activity* phase, illustrated in Figure 5-5. Once everything is "back to normal" (e.g., the incident has been contained and eradicated and the organization has recovered), the response team can review everything that happened. The team works to provide a record of what happened, identify any evidence that may need to be retained, and look for opportunities to improve the response process going forward. This includes ensuring the incident events, actions, timeline, and handling activities are properly documented. In the incident response process, the team captures and stores logs, alerts, e-mail messages, and other relevant data and develops and publishes an incident report for management. Management reviews the report and identifies lessons that could lead to changes in architectures, policies, systems, and procedures or whatever is required to improve the organization's security posture as a result of the incident. Post-incident activities include

- Retention of evidence
- Conducting a lessons-learned assessment
- Continuous improvement considerations

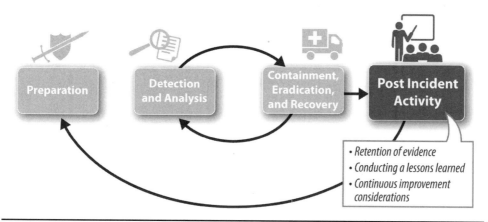

Figure 5-5 Post-incident activity phase (Source: NIST SP 800-61)

Retention of Evidence   During the course of the incident response process, a variety of incident evidence is captured such as logs, alerts, e-mails, and other relevant data. *Retention* is the process of saving data (both physical documents and digital/electronic records and media) for future use or reference. This is influenced by the organization's internal requirements (such as the potential need to access or restore the data in the future) as well as external requirements (such as laws, regulations, or other compliance drivers related to retention). In the case of evidence retention, organizations consider the possibility that the evidence may need to be used in court to prosecute the attacker. To facilitate this, the evidence is appropriately retained according to the organization's policies and procedures, secured, and tracked through proper chain-of-custody documents.

Conducting a Lessons-Learned Assessment   Documenting the lessons learned is a critical part of the post-incident activity phase. A *lessons-learned* assessment is a formal meeting where all involved responders get together and retroactively review what happened during the incident, with a focus on documenting what happened as well as identifying deficiencies and opportunities for improvement. These are sometimes referred to as *postmortems* or *post-incident analysis*. The goal is to answer questions such as

- What happened? What did we learn?
- How was the incident handled?
- Were processes followed?
- How can we do it better next time?

Every incident provides an opportunity to learn, improve, and evolve the incident response process. This may be understanding new threats; determining new tools, technologies, or resources that may be needed; or realizing the process requires some updates to be more effective (such as updating the incident response policy, plan, or corresponding procedures). These opportunities for improvement are documented, aid in process improvement, and serve as a valuable reference for the handling of future similar incidents.

Continuous Improvement Considerations   An important part of the post-incident activity is to take time to look for opportunities for process improvement. This is often accomplished by the development and measurement of metrics such as the number of incidents over a period of time, average time spent per incident, and so on. This is often measured with common metrics such as mean time to detect (MTTD), mean time to respond (MTTR), and so on.

Business Continuity Management

Business continuity management (BCM) encompasses planning for and executing how an organization continues to operate in the event of an incident. Properly implemented BCM usually includes the following attributes:

- Ensures the organization is able to tolerate the impact of an incident
- Identifies the functions that are essential for the business to continue to operate in the event of an incident
- Identifies the controls that must be in place in order to ensure timely resumption of essential business functions
- Ensures personnel and resources are in place in order to recover from an incident
- Ensures personnel are properly trained in business continuity plans and processes
- Ensures business continuity plans are periodically tested and updated

When considering how an organization can recover from an incident, many organizations focus on backing up and restoring data and providing resilient networks and servers. While these functions are important, they are considered part of *disaster recovery*. BCM focuses on the larger picture of how people and processes can continue to communicate and work together to operate the organization in a lesser or minimized state until full operations are restored.

Business Continuity Program Purpose and Governance

Most organizations perform BCM due to direction from the top. If the chief executive officer (CEO) or the board of directors think it's important to perform BCM, they will direct the appropriate managers to do it. This usually starts with the creation of a business continuity policy or similar document, which lays out the goals, standards, and guidelines the organization follows and enforces for BCM. The policy identifies who in the organization is responsible for which aspects of business continuity. The business continuity policy may also include guidance for disaster recovery and incident response, or those topics may be covered in their own policies. The business continuity policy can sometimes include detailed contact information such as call trees and who should be contacted to carry out certain tasks in the event of an incident. A business continuity policy typically contains the following topics:

- Scope of the policy
- Roles and responsibilities

- Requirements for developing and maintaining the business continuity plan
- Requirements for testing the business continuity plan
- Requirements for training staff to implement business continuity processes and perform related activities
- Identification of resources required to implement business continuity
- Requirements for ensuring the business continuity plan is current

Although organizations may create their own processes for BCM, there are industry standards that some organizations follow to avoid reinventing the wheel and take advantage of proven practices. Two common ones are the ISO 22301 Standard for Business Continuity Management and the NIST SP 800-34 *Contingency Planning Guide for Federal Information Systems.*

- The ISO 22301 Standard for Business Continuity Management is used by organizations as a system and method to ensure their resources are safeguarded when business disruptions occur. It has two parts: standards and processes to develop the organization's business continuity management system (BCMS) and guidance for implementing and operating the BCMS. Organizations can even become certified in their implementation of ISO 22301 using independent registrars to audit their business continuity program.
- NIST SP 800-34 lays out a seven-step process that defines the entire BCM lifecycle, from BCM policy creation through implementation of the business continuity program and maintaining the business continuity plan throughout its life. The BCM process described in this chapter is based on NIST SP 800-34.

EXAM TIP While CC candidates should be familiar with business continuity management in general, it is not necessary to memorize the exact steps or features of specific business continuity standards such as those published by NIST or ISO.

Business Continuity Plan

Organizations frequently define their business continuity program in a document called the business continuity plan, which is authored by a business continuity coordinator, sometimes under the auspices of the organization's security program or risk management program. The general process for performing BCM and developing and maintaining a business continuity plan is shown in Figure 5-6.

The business continuity plan and all of its associated procedures comprise a library of documentation that should be carefully tracked and placed under configuration control. This is because when a disaster occurs, it is the documentation that everyone will rely on to put Humpty Dumpty back together again. Procedures are documented because they will be needed during what may be very chaotic and stressful times for the operations personnel. And since environments evolve over time, the documentation should be

Figure 5-6   Business continuity management

reviewed and maintained so it is up to date and reflects the latest procedures for the correct versions of hardware and software that may need to be restored.

The following sections describe each step in the organization's documented business continuity plan.

Continuity Planning Initiation

Business continuity planning is performed by a business continuity coordinator. This individual (or team) is usually someone with a good understanding of the organization and therefore someone who understands how incidents or disasters could negatively impact the organization. The business continuity coordinator oversees the business impact analysis, development of the plan, implementation of the plan, testing, and plan maintenance activities.

The coordinator ensures that all organizational issues are properly addressed. To do this the business continuity coordinator must have the authority not just to lead the business continuity team but also to work with all of the departments to obtain information, resources, and participation. It's important that the coordinator has direct access to the necessary levels of management within the organization to ensure business continuity planning success.

The business continuity plan is managed just like any other project: following sound project management practices. The project should have a project plan with the following components:

- Project goals and requirements
- Project budget and resources
- List of task and resource-to-task mapping
- Project schedule with milestones

- List of deliverables and work products
- Success factors and methods of measuring success

One aspect of business continuity plan initiation is to determine the project scope. Will the plan address the entire organization or just a portion of it? Addressing the entire organization is the ultimate goal, but trying to do it all at the outset may be biting off more that the business continuity team can chew. Instead, some organizations choose to create a plan for just a portion of the organization, such as one department or business/geographical unit, and then expand it from there. This allows the team to go through all of the activities needed to build an entire end-to-end solution for a limited target, which may be much more manageable that trying to address the entire organization at once. If the business continuity team chooses this approach, they usually define the project in phases, first doing business continuity planning for one portion of the organization in one phase and then addressing other portions of the organization in later phases.

Obtaining Management Buy-In

Before proceeding with the business continuity plan project, management approval is first obtained. This is important not just for the usual reasons (management should approve all projects with regard to scope, budget, goals, etc.) but also because it is important to get BCM buy-in from the highest levels of the organization. This is because BCM, by its nature, defines the organization's levels of service during or after a disaster in a compromised state, which could impact customer experience, branding, finances, stock value, and other business factors that require awareness of, and participation from, upper management and the organization's leadership.

The business continuity plan coordinator leads a team, usually a business continuity plan committee. These individuals are responsible for developing the plan and for ensuring the business continuity activities in the event of a security incident or disaster meet the requirements of their respective area of the organization. The team should be made up of representatives from at least the following departments:

- Business unit leaders
- Senior management
- IT department
- Security department
- Facilities department
- Public relations or communications department
- Human resources department
- Legal department

NOTE Ideally, the people who develop the business continuity plan should also be the people who are responsible for executing it.

Business Impact Analysis

After continuity plan initiation, the next step is to perform a *business impact analysis (BIA)*. The purpose of the BIA is to fully understand the organization's business functions, processes, and interdependencies and use this information to determine the most critical business functions and how they can best be restored in the event of a disaster. Here are the steps required to perform a BIA:

1. Identify the organization's critical business functions.

2. Identify the resources the critical functions depend on.

3. Determine how long the functions can be without the resources.

4. Identify the vulnerabilities and threats to these functions.

5. Calculate the risk for each business function.

6. Identify recovery priorities.

Each step is explained in the following sections.

1. Identify the Organization's Critical Business Functions

To identify the organization's critical business functions, the business continuity team first conducts data gathering, commonly in the form of interviews and questionnaires much like an auditor. The purpose is to gather information from department managers, go-to employees, and operations personnel who understand the working of the enterprise. Data gathering is performed using interviews, surveys, and workshops. Data is captured for later use during the analysis steps, so a database can be useful for data collection and retrieval. Functions are documented identifying relevant workflows, processes, transactions, and/or services using process flow diagrams and other tools, which are used throughout the BIA stages.

Once all data is gathered, the team performs *functional analysis* of the data. Usually this involves creating a classification scheme, hierarchy, or scoring system to develop a picture of the relative criticality of the business functions.

How to Identify the Most Critical Business Functions

To determine criticality of a business function, evaluators formulate "what-if" questions, such as: "If Function A is not up and running . . ."

- How will this affect revenue?
- How will it impact manufacturing?

- How will it impact the production environment?
- How much will it increase operating expenses?
- What are the impacts to the organization's reputation?
- What are the impacts to the organization's compliance with laws and regulations?
- What are the hidden or long-term costs?

2. Identify the Resources the Critical Functions Depend On Every business function requires resources. Manufacturing gadgets requires resources such as gadget-making machines, computer systems and networks, gadget-packaging systems, gadget expert staff, etc. For each business function, the business continuity team identifies and records which resources are required to support the business function, including logistical details such as how many are needed and where. Resources may include hardware, software, communications, electrical power, facilities, safety equipment, supplies, people, and anything required to support the critical function. The resources required for each function are recorded in a business continuity database or similar record-keeping system.

3. Determine How Long the Functions Can Be Without the Resources The maximum tolerable downtime (MTD) is a calculation of how long any function or resource can be unavailable. Knowing the MTD of all functions and resources allows the team to understand which items must be brought back online and in what order. It also indicates which items must have fast-restoration capabilities such as hot-swappable devices.

4. Identify the Vulnerabilities and Threats to These Functions For each critical function, the business continuity team tries to think of all of the possible events that might occur that would be a threat to that function. It is impossible to consider every possible threat, so the team tries to identify the most likely threats or simply major categories of threats. Ranges of threats to consider include

- Human: cyberattack, vandalism, burglary, theft
- Natural disasters: storms, earthquakes, floods
- Technical: system, network, or communication system problems
- Supply: power; heating, ventilation, air conditioning (HVAC) outages

5. Calculate the Risk for Each Business Function In Chapter 1 we discussed two forms of risk analysis: qualitative and quantitative. Each method provides a means to understand the relative risk of different threats using either quantitative or qualitative means. These two methods can also be used to evaluate the risk of different business functions. The business continuity team can use quantitative analysis to understand and rank the risk of different business functions and threat scenarios based purely on cost factors.

Likewise, using qualitative analysis, the business continuity team can create a priority ranking of different business functions and threats. Another method commonly used by business continuity teams is to create a risk score for each business function and threat, rating the consequence of the occurrence and the probability of its occurrence. Regardless of which method is used, the goal is for the business continuity team to produce a measure of the business impact of categories of threats against each major business function, taking into account the following:

- Allowable business interruption
- Operational impacts (financial, productivity)
- Regulatory compliance
- Organizational reputation

6. Identify Recovery Priorities   The final step in the BIA is to pull together everything that was learned in the previous steps and develop a list of recovery priorities. This list tells the organization which business functions and resources must be restored and in what order. Recovery priorities are established by examining the following items learned from the previous steps:

- Business process importance and operational impact
- Allowable interruption
- Regulatory compliance requirements
- Financial impact
- Organizational reputation impact

The recovery priorities are used to formulate recovery and backup solutions for each business function.

 EXAM TIP   CC candidates should understand the purpose and importance of the BIA but not necessarily the individual steps that comprise it.

Identify Preventive Controls

At this point in the process, the business continuity team has garnered management support, defined the scope of the business continuity effort, identified the business continuity team members, and completed the BIA activities, which includes identifying critical business functions and supporting resources, analyzing the threats to these resources, characterizing the risks, and identifying recovery priorities. All of this information is used to develop strategies for recovering the business functions in the event of a disaster. But what about prevention? What if the threat can be prevented from bringing down the business function in the first place? What can the organization do to maintain the *availability* of the resources and therefore keep the business function operating?

In some cases, the impacts identified in the BIA can be reduced or eliminated by identifying, designing, and implementing preventive controls. Here is a list of example preventive controls that organizations commonly use. In contrast to the preventive controls listed in the section about incident response, these preventive controls are oriented toward threats due to natural disasters and physical incidents:

- Fortification of facilities (use of construction methods aimed at specific threats, e.g., floods, earthquakes)
- Deployment of uninterruptible power supplies (UPSs)
- Backup power generators
- Communication link redundancy
- Server and computer resource redundancy
- Duplicate physical facilities
- Redundant vendor support
- Additional inventories of critical equipment
- Fire detection and suppression systems

Preventive controls provide a means to reduce the likelihood of an outage occurring in the first place and are used in conjunction with recovery strategies to provide a holistic approach to business continuity.

 EXAM TIP CC candidates should be familiar with preventive controls used to reduce the risk of cyberattacks, natural disasters, and physical incidents.

Develop Recovery Strategies and Solutions

In this phase of BCM the business continuity team determines what the organization has to do to recover from the incident to restore critical business functions. The BIA provides the blueprint for this because it identifies the priorities, resources, minimum downtimes, and recovery times. Using this information, the business continuity team defines recovery strategies to meet the recovery time targets. Recovery strategies are usually addressed in categories such as

- Business process recovery
- Facility recovery
- Data processing recovery
- Communications recovery
- Data recovery
- User environment recovery
- Supply chain recovery

The business continuity team uses metrics to help them model and design what has to happen to restore normal operations.

- **Recovery time objective (RTO)**   This is the time target for restoring a business process or service after a disruption caused by a disaster or security event. This may be expressed in hours, days, or even weeks depending on the business function.
- **Recovery point objective (RPO)**   This is the amount of data that is acceptable to be lost in the event of a disaster.
- **Work recovery time (WRT)**   This is the amount of time to restore the data and perform testing to ensure the capability is fully operational.

To decide on the right recovery strategy, the business continuity team must balance the cost of recovery against the cost of disruption. It may not make sense to spend $1 million to recover a function that is only costing the organization $100 per day due to a disruption. However, if the organization demands a short RTO for that function, the expense may be warranted. The practice is for the business continuity team to define recovery strategies and present them to management for discussion and approval.

Develop the Plan

All of the results of the BIA and the data that contributed to the BIA are consolidated into a business continuity plan. Having all the data in one place allows the plan to be put into action. Once the plan is developed, supporting procedures can be developed along with other documentation that aids the plan such as calling trees, emergency contact lists, etc. No two business continuity plans look the same, but a typical plan might contain the following sections:

- Objective and scope
- BIA results
- Preventive controls
- Employee safety
- Response plans
- Activation criteria
- Communications plans
- Public relations
- Plan testing requirements
- Plan maintenance schedule

It is important that the business continuity plan be available to all personnel who need it. The business continuity team should take care to publish the plan so electronic and paper versions are available at the locations in which they are needed and are used.

However, some aspects of the plan may be highly sensitive or proprietary in nature and should not be disclosed to the public. The business continuity plan may contain descriptions of internal operations, names and contact information of employees and executives, and sensitive financial information, all of which could be very useful to a cyber criminal. Some organizations publish two versions or two portions of the plan: one that is public and one that contains sensitive information that is restricted in its publication.

 EXAM TIP   It's important to know the purpose and importance of the business continuity, disaster recovery, and incident response plans but not specific outlines of them or names of sections within them.

Test the Plan

Key to the success of the business continuity plan are testing activities called out in the plan. This is an area in which organizations frequently fail: They spend large amounts of time and effort in business continuity planning but fail to test the plans. Then, when a real disaster occurs, they find they cannot execute portions of their plan and *then it really is a disaster!* Proper business continuity planning includes testing, testing, and more testing. The time to find out how well your business continuity and disaster recovery planning was developed isn't when a disaster occurs because then it's too late. Business continuity planning requires testing using a variety of methods:

- **Checklist testing**   This type of test is sometimes called a read-though or a desk check. In it, copies of the activation or restoration procedures are distributed to employees who are to implement them. The employees review them and provide comments indicating if steps or details need to be added or anything was omitted. The comments are provided to the business continuity team for review, and the procedures and the business continuity plan are updated accordingly.

- **Structured walk-through testing**   This testing is similar to checklist testing except the review is conducted by a group of representatives from each department involved. By addressing the plan and procedures as a group, the scenarios are considered for their effectiveness, efficiency, accuracy, and completeness. Any discrepancies are conveyed to the business continuity team for updating and improvement.

- **Simulation testing**   In simulation testing, the activation or restoration scenario is rehearsed in a real-world but simulated environment. Sometimes this includes building a test facility using computing and communications equipment and software using real staff to simulate operational conditions. This testing is a good indicator of the staff's ability to react to real-world situations. To be effective, simulation testing must be well-planned, and care must be taken to capture all aspects of what is happening. After the simulation events, analysis takes place to understand how procedures are being carried out, their effectiveness, and how procedures can and should be improved.

- **Parallel testing**   For situations in which operations are to be moved to an alternate offsite facility during an interruption, it's a good idea to run a parallel test. In this test operations take place at both the primary and the offsite facilities simultaneously, and the results are compared to ensure there is no degradation of service at the offsite facility.

- **Full-interruption testing**   This might sound scary, but in full-interruption testing, the operational site is actually shut down to simulate an actual disaster. Obviously, this type of testing is highly intrusive and requires good planning and approvals at the highest levels of the organization. But it is also very revealing and is a great indicator of the organization's preparedness for a disaster or security incident.

 NOTE   Checklist testing and structured walk-through testing are sometimes conducted as *tabletop exercises* in which the review is performed as a live exercise by groups of reviewers in which discussion and collaboration are encouraged.

Regardless of the type of test, all tests must be well-planned with written test procedures and predefined success criteria. Part of the success criteria for testing would have been defined in the continuity planning initiation phase when the "success factors and methods of measuring success" were defined. Those target success factors are tested and measured during the testing phase to see if they were met. Tests should try to mimic real-world situations as closely as possible and should try to point out issues that the business continuity team may not have thought of during initial plan development. The goal is for testing to help to provide robust business continuity plans and procedures.

Testing should be performed extensively during initial business continuity plan development and then on a periodic basis for the life of the plan. Over time the plans and procedures change as the operational environment changes and the organizational business processes change. As a result, the plans and procedures are retested as well. Most organizations perform testing on an annual basis.

 EXAM TIP   CC candidates should be familiar with the purpose and importance of testing the plan but it isn't necessary to memorize the various types of test methods.

Maintain the Plan

Technology changes, as does the nature of business operations of most organizations. As a result, the BCP will quickly become out of date and inaccurate without frequent updates. The BCP should not be treated as a one-time project but as an ongoing process that exists for the life of the organization. Regular updates to the plan are required, usually on an annual basis or as a result of major changes to the organization or the enterprise.

Over the life of the plan recovery personnel are trained on all elements of the business continuity plan, especially those areas that they are responsible for. Also, all employees should be trained in first aid and cardiopulmonary resuscitation (CPR), which may be required during a disaster. Training for personnel with contingency plan responsibilities should be performed on an annual basis.

Business Continuity Activation

Once the business continuity plan is approved by management and put into place, the activation phase begins. Activation is the process of responding when an incident occurs by notifying personnel so they can perform a damage assessment to determine whether activation of the plan is necessary. If the assessment determines activation is necessary, the plan and its procedures are followed and response and recovery activities begin.

Some incidents occur with prior notice, while others do not. A hurricane usually gives pretty good advance warning it is approaching, but a cyberattack is stealthy and sudden. The business continuity plan should have procedures defined for various types of incidents describing how to notify personnel to perform a damage assessment. When an incident occurs, the following activities take place:

1. Determine the cause.

2. Determine the likelihood of further damage.

3. Identify affected business functions and resources.

4. Create an initial time to restore estimate.

5. Compare assessment results to predefined business continuity plan activation criteria.

If the assessment team determines the event and resultant damage meet the criteria for activation, the business continuity plan is activated, and the response personnel are notified and response activities take place following response procedures.

Disaster Recovery

While organizations can use preventive controls to reduce the possibility of a disruption to business operations in the event of an incident, disasters can and do happen. When they do, organizations follow activation procedures according to their business continuity plans. For certain incidents, the activation procedures invoke specific disaster recovery processes, which are documented in their own *disaster recovery plans (DRPs)*. DRPs are used to rescue the organization by putting specific business functions back into place after an incident. This is accomplished through predicting the types of incidents that may occur and creating plans to prepare for and respond to those incidents. DRPs are usually focused on IT and communications functions but they can be developed for any business function. In this section we explore several types of disaster recovery scenarios organizations typically cover in their DRPs and the types of recovery processes they follow.

IT Facility Recovery

During many kinds of incidents, in particular natural disasters such as storms, floods, and fires, IT facilities are damaged and are unavailable to support operations. When this happens, operations must be moved to an alternate facility. Of course, the time to procure the alternate facility is not when the incident occurs, but beforehand, so preparation is key. When preparing, there are several options to choose, from including hot site, warm site, cold site, and multiple processing centers, and things to consider, including site locations and, of course, security considerations. Each of these topics is discussed in its own section.

Hot Site

A hot site is one that is ready to go in a moment's notice—usually *within a few hours*. A hot site is fully equipped and configured with up-to-date software that is fully patched and tested. The only thing needed to make the hot site fully operational is data, which is restored from backup storage at the time it is needed.

A hot site is an expensive option both in terms of the initial cost and ongoing costs to keep the hot site updated, configured, and tested. In addition, most hot sites are rented or leased, which is an additional expense. However, the benefit is that operations can be restored quickly and recovery can be the most reliable option.

Warm Site

A warm site is a facility that is configured with equipment suitable for supporting IT operations but without the computing equipment itself. The warm site has power, HVAC, physical infrastructure, and possibly telecommunications and peripheral equipment. But the computers, network devices, software, people, and data backups must be installed, configured, tested, and brought to a fully operational state before normal operations can resume. Warm site DRPs are usually planned to recover operations in *a day or longer*.

Warm sites are a good choice for organizations that have proprietary or specialized hardware that may not be suitable or cost-effective for a hot site. Warm sites are a lower-cost option from a hot site and are probably the most widely used option. However, warm sites have some risks. Since the equipment is not in place prior to the incident, there is no guarantee the equipment can be obtained, installed, configured, and tested within the timeframe called for in the DRP, so normal operations may not be restored in time to meet an organization's RTO/RPO objectives.

Cold Site

A cold site is essentially an empty building without any equipment or infrastructure. It may have basic electrical wiring, plumbing, or flooring, but some construction is required before equipment can be brought in. It is the least expensive option but requires the most amount of time and effort to achieve normal operations. It usually takes several weeks or longer to get a cold site up and running.

Other Site Options

What if an organization goes through all the time and effort to set up a hot, warm, or cold site and the disaster knocks out the backup site as well? It may sound unlikely, but an earthquake, hurricane, or power grid outage can impact a large geographic area, which may include both the primary and the backup facility. Some organizations prepare for this using a *tertiary site,* which is a secondary backup site that is used in case the primary backup site is unavailable. Tertiary sites can be hot, warm, or cold sites.

Another site option organizations use is called *multiple processing centers*. In this model an organization may have many datacenters around the world, all interconnected and able to share resources and data. If a resource or resources go down in one location, the functions are automatically taken over at another location with little or no loss of data or service.

Yet another option is for two or more organizations to share their resources by executing *reciprocal agreements*. In this arrangement the agreement states that if an incident brings one organization's datacenter down, they can use the datacenter of the other organization. This arrangement works best if the organizations use similar hardware and software and can therefore more easily share resources.

Some organizations use *redundant sites* in which two sites are configured with the exact same equipment and software. This is also called *mirroring*. Data is routed to either or both sites, which means in the event of an incident or disaster impacting one site, the other can take over. This is an expensive but not uncommon disaster recovery option.

Site Locations

When choosing the location of a backup site, it's a good idea for it to be far enough away from the primary site that the likelihood that a single disaster or incident will impact both sites is reduced. Some organizations have regional datacenters to ensure that they can continue to operate nationally if there is a disaster in one region of the country.

Security and Other Considerations

Proper security must be maintained prior to, during, and after activation of DRPs. In fact, the period during and after a disaster or incident may be when an organization is most vulnerable to a cyberattack because the organization may be distracted by the incident and could be caught off guard. Organizational focus on three areas can ensure security is maintained during disaster recovery activation:

- *Security must be designed into the alternate site architecture and operations just like the primary site.* For instance, if whole disk encryption is used as a security control on the primary systems, the same security controls must be in place on the alternate systems as well. Business continuity and disaster recovery should be part of an organization's overall security program. Involvement of the security team in the business continuity plan and DRP helps to ensure confidentiality, availability, and integrity of resources are maintained during all aspects of business continuity and disaster recovery planning and execution.

- *Security must be maintained during activation.* Activation may involve moving data from one location to another, and it is important to maintain security of the data during this transition. Organizations use encryption, access controls, or other technologies to ensure that only those who have need to know can access the data during transition. It is especially important to use integrity checking to ensure data moved from backup storage to operational sites has not been altered. In addition, during recovery, the site may be in a compromised state, and it is important to maintain security during this period. Additional physical security (guards, cameras, etc.) and/or logical security (logging, monitoring, etc.) may be needed during activation.

- *Security responsibility cannot be outsourced.* Alternate sites may be owned by the organization, may be leased, or may be owned by a service provider and procured using an "as-a-service" model in which an organization pays for computing platforms or infrastructure provided by a third-party provider. However, while the service provider may perform some security tasks, the ultimate responsibility for security still lies with the organization. For example, if a healthcare organization that stores patient information uses a cloud service provider to provide a hot site and there is a subsequent data breach, it is the healthcare organization that is on the hook for a potential Health Insurance Portability and Accountability Act (HIPAA) violation. When using a service provider for alternate sites, the organization must be able to maintain control of the security of the environment using testing, monitoring, auditing, and contractual agreements.

Critical to any facility recovery planning is testing. Testing must be performed to ensure all components work together, especially since the equipment at the alternate facility may not be exactly the same as the original equipment. Testing includes functional testing to ensure all hardware and software operates as it is intended, as well as activation testing to ensure the transition process from the primary facility to the backup facility is rehearsed, meets expectations, and is resilient to anomalies. Frequency of testing varies by organization but should be done periodically, usually annually.

User Environment Recovery

When a disaster or disabling incident occurs, the workers of the organization need to be notified as soon as possible. The DRP contains call trees that define who calls whom for each type of incident. Calling is set up in hierarchical trees so that each person only has to call one or two people in order for everyone (or almost everyone) to be notified in a timely manner. Critical users are contacted in order to keep the most critical business functions up and running. In some cases, systems are down so automated tasks are not available and must be carried out manually. Such tasks should have been identified during the BIA and manual procedures developed and documented in the DRP.

If the primary office is no longer available, workers may have to work from home or may be diverted to an alternate work site. For an alternate work site, transportation may be required. This should also have been scoped as part of the BIA and alternate transportation plans made and documented in the DRP.

The loss of a senior executive can be as catastrophic to the organization as the loss of a facility or a datacenter. If a senior executive suddenly resigns, retires, dies, or is killed, it could create a leadership vacuum if the organization is not prepared. The DRP should define key leadership positions and their associated succession plans so the organization is able to handle such an event. The succession plan includes a definition of who takes over which responsibilities (sometimes called a line of succession) and for what period of time. The plan also defines a schedule of events that includes a transition period for the organization to resume normal operations in the senior executive's absence and plans for replacement of the executive long-term.

Data Recovery

The most common approach to being able to recover data in the event of a disaster or incident is to use a data backup solution. Using this approach, data is backed up to a central storage device or system (disk or tape), where it can be retrieved at a later time if and when it is needed. There are three main types of data backup methods, as follows:

- **Full**   A full backup stores a backup of all of the files on the system each time the backup process is run.

- **Differential**   A differential backup backs up all files that have changed *since the last full backup*. To restore the data, the last full backup is restored and then the most recent differential backup is restored.

- **Incremental**   An incremental backup backs up all files that have changed *since the last backup of any type*. Using incremental backups, the restoration process takes longer because first you have to restore the last full backup and then you have to restore each incremental backup since the last full backup.

Backups are good, but there is always a chance a disaster or incident could occur in between backups. In this case the data after the last backup may be lost. One method to prevent this is called *disk mirroring*. In disk mirroring, data is written to two disks at the same time. If one disk is lost due to an incident, the other one is available for operation. Of course, for this to be effective, the two disks should not be located in the same physical location. Also, it is possible that the same event that caused the site to go down produces write errors, which could corrupt data on both disks. As a result, organizations that use disk mirroring typically use some type of backup solution in conjunction with it.

Data can be stored or backed up using a variety of mediums, typically disks or tapes (yes, tapes are still used!). *Redundant array of independent disks* (RAID) or *redundant array of independent tapes* (RAIT) allow data to be written across multiple media for faster read/write operations and redundancy.

Many organizations back up their data to tapes or other read/write media such as optical disks and store the media at a remote location. This is sometimes called *vaulting*. In this manner, an incident impacting the primary site or location will not impact the vault where the data is stored. Basic vaulting involves sending backup tapes or disks to an offsite location. Electronic vaulting transmits data over a network to a remote location where the tape or disk recording devices are operating. Electronic vaulting can be faster for both storage and retrieval of data.

Chapter Review

Cyberattacks happen to organizations on a regular basis, causing great harm to business operations. Organizations most apt to handle cyberattacks are those that have properly planned by developing a security incident response plan. The incident response plan lays the groundwork for the organization's approach to responding to security incidents. Organizations often structure their incident response plan leveraging a framework such as NIST Special Publication 800-61, *Computer Security Incident Handling Guide*.

Regardless of the framework used, security incident response is focused on the process of preparing for an incident, detecting and analyzing incidents, containing and eradicating incidents and recovering impacted systems, and post-incident activity focused on lessons learned and continuous improvement.

Business continuity planning focuses on how the organization will continue to operate when an incident occurs. Disaster recovery planning focuses on restoration of specific business functions, usually IT operations. Both activities involve predicting threats to the organization, assessing their impact to operations, and creating specific plans and procedures to restore operations if those threats are realized. Key to the success of business continuity and disaster recovery planning is testing the plans and restoration procedures and ensuring the safety of people during any disaster or incident.

Quick Review

- Incident management is the collection of processes, tools, technologies, and resources used to respond to an incident.
- Security incident response is the process of preparing, detecting, analyzing, containing, eradicating, and recovering from a security incident.
- Incident response governance elements include the incident response policy, incident response plan, and incident response procedures.
- In some cases, incident response procedures are integrated into the incident response plan. In other cases, they are separate documents.
- The incident response policy is a collection of high-level statements setting forth requirements for the incident response function.
- The incident response plan provides the roadmap for implementing the requirements set forth by the policy.
- Incident response procedures are step-by-step processes covering how specific technical tasks are performed (e.g., tools, techniques, and checklists) as part of the incident response process.
- The incident response process consists of the following phases:
  - Preparation
  - Detection and analysis
  - Containment, eradication, and recovery
  - Post-incident activity
- Business continuity plans focus on those essential functions that are most important to the organization and what the organization does when an incident occurs to preserve those essential business functions.

- The purpose of the BIA is to determine which business functions must be restored after an incident.

- The MTD is a calculation of how long any function or resource can be unavailable.

- Some portions of the business continuity plan may be highly sensitive and should not be released to the public.

- Business continuity plans should be updated on a periodic basis.

- Staff should be trained and tested on business continuity and disaster recovery plans and procedures.

- DRPs are plans used to rescue the organization by putting specific business functions back into place after an incident.

- During many kinds of incidents, in particular natural disasters such as storms, floods, and fires, IT facilities are damaged and are unavailable to support operations, so operations must be moved to an alternate facility such as a hot site, warm site, cold site, or other location.

- Security must be designed into alternate site architecture and operations just like the primary site.

- Security must be maintained during business continuity plan and disaster recovery plan activation.

- While security tasks can be outsourced, security responsibility cannot.

- The most common approach to being able to recover data in the event of a disaster or incident is to use a data backup solution.

Questions

1. During which phase of the incident response process is the incident response plan developed and documented?

   A. Preparation

   B. Containment, eradication, and recovery

   C. Detection and analysis

   D. Post-incident activity

2. During which phase of the incident response process does the lessons-learned assessment take place?

   A. Detection and analysis

   B. Containment, eradication, and recovery

   C. Preparation

   D. Post-incident activity

3. A security analyst is reviewing log files from a system to determine if a security incident has occurred. This is an example of an activity that takes place in which of the following incident response process phases?

   A. Containment, eradication, and recovery

   B. Detection and analysis

   C. Preparation

   D. Post-incident activity

4. In which phase of the incident response process would a security analyst recover a system from a backup?

   A. Preparation

   B. Detection and analysis

   C. Post-incident activity

   D. Containment, eradication, and recovery

5. What phase comes after the detection and analysis phase in the incident response process?

   A. Containment, eradication, and recovery.

   B. Preparation.

   C. Post-incident activity.

   D. Detection and analysis is the last phase of the process.

6. Carol is tasked with creating a business continuity plan for her organization. What should she do to determine which of her organization's business functions should be restored in the event of an incident?

   A. Conduct a risk assessment.

   B. Interview key stakeholders throughout the organization.

   C. Calculate the MTD for each business function.

   D. Conduct a business impact analysis.

7. Of the following which is the most likely reason(s) a business continuity program might fail?

   A. Failure to test the plan and procedures

   B. Failure to document activation procedures

   C. Failure to address the threats the organization is most likely to face

   D. All of the above

8. Alice is responsible for designing her organization's datacenter to provide resiliency in the event of a disaster. If a disaster occurs, she wants to have the new datacenter up and running within a few days, but she does not want to incur the cost of building a full datacenter with all equipment fully installed and configured. Which of the following options is the best choice for her situation?

A. Hot site

B. Warm site

C. Cold site

D. Tertiary site

Questions and Answers

1. During which phase of the incident response process is the incident response plan developed and documented?

A. Preparation

B. Containment, eradication, and recovery

C. Detection and analysis

D. Post-incident activity

A. The incident response plan is developed and documented during the preparation phase of the incident response process.

2. During which phase of the incident response process does the lessons-learned assessment take place?

A. Detection and analysis

B. Containment, eradication, and recovery

C. Preparation

D. Post-incident activity

D. The lessons-learned assessment occurs during the post-incident activity phase of the incident response process.

3. A security analyst is reviewing log files from a system to determine if a security incident has occurred. This is an example of an activity that takes place in which of the following incident response process phases?

A. Containment, eradication, and recovery

B. Detection and analysis

C. Preparation

D. Post-incident activity

B. Reviewing logs to determine if a security incident has occurred is an example of an activity that takes place in the detection and analysis phase of the incident response process.

4. In which phase of the incident response process would a security analyst recover a system from a backup?

A. Preparation

B. Detection and analysis

C. Post-incident activity

D. Containment, eradication, and recovery

D. Recovering a system from backup would take place during the containment, eradication, and recovery phase of the incident response process.

5. What phase comes after the detection and analysis phase in the incident response process?

A. Containment, eradication, and recovery.

B. Preparation.

C. Post-incident activity.

D. Detection and analysis is the last phase of the process.

A. The containment, eradication, and recovery phase comes after the detection and analysis phase of the incident response process. The process steps are Preparation -> Detection and Analysis -> Containment, Eradication, and Recovery -> Post-Incident Activity.

6. Carol is tasked with creating a business continuity plan for her organization. What should she do to determine which of her organization's business functions should be restored in the event of an incident?

A. Conduct a risk assessment.

B. Interview key stakeholders throughout the organization.

C. Calculate the MTD for each business function.

D. Conduct a business impact analysis.

D. The purpose of a business impact analysis is to determine which business functions should be restored after an incident.

7. Of the following which is the most likely reason(s) a business continuity program might fail?

A. Failure to test the plan and procedures

B. Failure to document activation procedures

C. Failure to address the threats the organization is most likely to face

D. All of the above

D. Failure to test the plan and procedures, document activation procedures, and address likely threats are all reasons the business continuity program may fail.

8. Alice is responsible for designing her organization's datacenter to provide resiliency in the event of a disaster. If a disaster occurs, she wants to have the new datacenter up and running within a few days, but she does not want to incur the cost of building a full datacenter with all equipment fully installed and configured. Which of the following options is the best choice for her situation?

A. Hot site

B. Warm site

C. Cold site

D. Tertiary site

B. A warm site is a facility that is configured with equipment suitable for supporting IT operations but without the computing equipment itself. The warm site has power, HVAC, physical infrastructure, and possibly telecommunications and peripheral equipment.

About the Online Content

This book comes complete with TotalTester Online customizable practice exam software with 200 practice exam questions.

System Requirements

The current and previous major versions of the following desktop browsers are recommended and supported: Chrome, Microsoft Edge, Firefox, and Safari. These browsers update frequently, and sometimes an update may cause compatibility issues with the TotalTester Online or other content hosted on the Training Hub. If you run into a problem using one of these browsers, please try using another until the problem is resolved.

Your Total Seminars Training Hub Account

To get access to the online content, you will need to create an account on the Total Seminars Training Hub. Registration is free, and you will be able to track all your online content using your account. You may also opt in if you wish to receive marketing information from McGraw Hill or Total Seminars, but this is not required for you to gain access to the online content.

Privacy Notice

McGraw Hill values your privacy. Please be sure to read the Privacy Notice available during registration to see how the information you have provided will be used. You may view our Corporate Customer Privacy Policy by visiting the McGraw Hill Privacy Center. Visit the **mheducation.com** site and click **Privacy** at the bottom of the page.

Single User License Terms and Conditions

Online access to the digital content included with this book is governed by the McGraw Hill License Agreement outlined next. By using this digital content, you agree to the terms of that license.

Access   To register and activate your Total Seminars Training Hub account, simply follow these easy steps.

1. Go to this URL: **hub.totalsem.com/mheclaim**

2. To register and create a new Training Hub account, enter your e-mail address, name, and password on the **Register** tab. No further personal information (such as credit card number) is required to create an account.

   If you already have a Total Seminars Training Hub account, enter your e-mail address and password on the **Log in** tab.

3. Enter your Product Key: **kb5t-r6tb-hmc3**

4. Click to accept the user license terms.

5. For new users, click the **Register and Claim** button to create your account. For existing users, click the **Log in and Claim** button.

   You will be taken to the Training Hub and have access to the content for this book.

Duration of License   Access to your online content through the Total Seminars Training Hub will expire one year from the date the publisher declares the book out of print.

Your purchase of this McGraw Hill product, including its access code, through a retail store is subject to the refund policy of that store.

The Content is a copyrighted work of McGraw Hill, and McGraw Hill reserves all rights in and to the Content. The Work is © 2023 by McGraw Hill.

Restrictions on Transfer   The user is receiving only a limited right to use the Content for the user's own internal and personal use, dependent on purchase and continued ownership of this book. The user may not reproduce, forward, modify, create derivative works based upon, transmit, distribute, disseminate, sell, publish, or sublicense the Content or in any way commingle the Content with other third-party content without McGraw Hill's consent.

Limited Warranty   The McGraw Hill Content is provided on an "as is" basis. Neither McGraw Hill nor its licensors make any guarantees or warranties of any kind, either express or implied, including, but not limited to, implied warranties of merchantability or fitness for a particular purpose or use as to any McGraw Hill Content or the information therein or any warranties as to the accuracy, completeness, correctness, or results to be obtained from, accessing or using the McGraw Hill Content, or any material referenced in such Content or any information entered into licensee's product by users or other persons and/or any material available on or that can be accessed through the licensee's product (including via any hyperlink or otherwise) or as to non-infringement of third-party rights. Any warranties of any kind, whether express or implied, are disclaimed. Any material or data obtained through use of the McGraw Hill Content is at your own discretion and risk and user understands that it will be solely responsible for any resulting damage to its computer system or loss of data.

Neither McGraw Hill nor its licensors shall be liable to any subscriber or to any user or anyone else for any inaccuracy, delay, interruption in service, error or omission, regardless of cause, or for any damage resulting therefrom.

In no event will McGraw Hill or its licensors be liable for any indirect, special or consequential damages, including but not limited to, lost time, lost money, lost profits or good will, whether in contract, tort, strict liability or otherwise, and whether or not such damages are foreseen or unforeseen with respect to any use of the McGraw Hill Content.

TotalTester Online

TotalTester Online provides you with a simulation of the Certified in Cybersecurity exam. Exams can be taken in Practice Mode or Exam Mode. Practice Mode provides an assistance window with hints, references to the book, explanations of the correct and incorrect answers, and the option to check your answer as you take the test. Exam Mode provides a simulation of the actual exam. The number of questions, the types of questions, and the time allowed are intended to be an accurate representation of the exam environment. The option to customize your quiz allows you to create custom exams from selected domains or chapters, and you can further customize the number of questions and time allowed.

To take a test, follow the instructions provided in the previous section to register and activate your Total Seminars Training Hub account. When you register, you will be taken to the Total Seminars Training Hub. From the Training Hub Home page, select your certification from the Study drop-down menu at the top of the page to drill down to the TotalTester for your book. You can also scroll to it from the list on the Your Topics tab of the Home page, and then click on the TotalTester link to launch the TotalTester. Once you've launched your TotalTester, you can select the option to customize your quiz and begin testing yourself in Practice Mode or Exam Mode. All exams provide an overall grade and a grade broken down by domain.

Technical Support

For questions regarding the TotalTester or operation of the Training Hub, visit **www.totalsem.com** or e-mail **support@totalsem.com**.

For questions regarding book content, visit **www.mheducation.com/customerservice**.

access The permission or ability to enter or communicate with a person or thing. In cybersecurity it is the right that is granted to a subject to perform a function with an object.

access control list (ACL) A list that shows an object and all of the subjects that can access that object as well as their corresponding permissions (e.g., read, write, no access, full control, and so on).

access control matrix A table containing a set of subjects, objects, and permissions. These are used by computer systems to implement rules, define access control permissions, and enforce discretionary access control. An access control matrix is made up of access control lists and capabilities lists.

access control models Conceptual models that illustrate the different methods and techniques employed to control the level of access and permission that subjects (e.g., users or system processes) have over objects (e.g., computers, systems). These models are implemented using a combination of features in tools and technologies such as operating systems and applications.

accountability Subject to the obligation to report, explain, or justify something. In cybersecurity accountability is accomplished through logging and reporting user actions and system events.

activation The action of making something operational. In cybersecurity activation refers to the action of making a plan, such as a business continuity plan, disaster recovery plan, or incident response plan, operational, usually after a disaster or incident has occurred.

administrative controls Management-oriented controls that provide directives and instruction aimed at people within the organization. Administrative controls are also referred to as *soft controls* or *managerial controls*.

advanced persistent threat (APT) A potential cyberattack in which the attacker uses sophisticated methods and/or tools, expands the attack to more and more systems within the target organization over time, and covers up their tracks to avoid detection.

annualized loss expectancy The potential value of a loss on an annual basis.

annualized rate of occurrence An estimate of how many times an event may occur on an annual basis.

antivirus software   A software product designed to be installed on endpoint devices to protect them from malware by searching for, detecting, and removing malware from the device.

archive   A place in which old materials or data is stored so it can be accessed in the future. Also, the act of storing old material or data for future use.

asset management   The process of ensuring an organization's assets are tracked and monitored throughout the asset's lifecycle within the organization.

asset value   The cost of an asset or assets.

asymmetric encryption   A type of encryption that uses two keys that are mathematically related: a *public key* and a *private key*.

ATT&CK   Adversarial Tactics, Techniques and Common Knowledge is a framework developed by MITRE Corporation used to assist in the understanding of cyber threats and attacks.

authentication   The method by which information systems verify that a user who is requesting access to a resource really is who they claim to be.

authenticity   The quality of being genuine, trustworthy, or real supported by evidence.

authorization   The act of granting or receiving official permission for something to happen.

authorized   Having formal permission or sanction to do something.

availability   The state of being present and ready to be used.

backdoor   Any method whereby an unauthorized user can bypass security controls to gain access.

bollards   Pillars or spheres made from concrete, metal, or other hard materials that are typically found outside of buildings between the parking lot and the entrance of the building, intended to serve as a physical barrier to block vehicular access.

botnet   A network of compromised computers used to carry out malicious activity under the control of a hacker.

breach   The act of failing to observe a barrier, law, agreement, or practice.

brute force   A method of achieving something by the application of raw effort or power as opposed to the use of efficiency, skill, or sophisticated techniques.

buffer overflow   A type of cyberattack where the data exceeds the capacity of the memory buffer, causing an erroneous operation.

business continuity   The act of developing plans and procedures for maintaining business operations in the event of a disaster or security incident.

business impact analysis   A process to evaluate the potential effects of threats that interrupt critical business functions for the purpose of determining recovery plans.

capabilities list   A row in an access control matrix showing all of the objects a specific subject can access and their corresponding permissions over each object.

ciphertext   Information that is in an encrypted, unreadable format.

client   Computers that interact with a server by initiating a connection.

client-server model   An architectural model for how computers serve up resources. The computer requesting the service or resource is known as the client, and the computer serving up the resource is referred to as the server.

cloud deployment model   Describes how a cloud service is deployed, managed, and consumed. The primary cloud deployment models include public, private, community, and hybrid.

Cloud Security Alliance (CSA)   An organization that creates standards and best practices for cloud security for service providers as well as customers.

cloud service customer   The entity that has a relationship with the cloud service provider to use their cloud service.

cloud service model   Describes the category of service provided by a cloud service provider. The primary cloud service models are infrastructure as a service, platform as a service, and software as a service.

cloud service provider   The organization that provides the cloud service/resources that are consumed by the cloud service customer.

cold site   An alternate facility that is an empty building with supporting power, plumbing, etc., but without any supporting IT infrastructure. It usually takes several weeks or longer for a cold site to be ready to support normal operations.

community cloud   A cloud deployment model that is a variation of a private cloud where cloud resources are shared between multiple communities, organizations, or businesses typically for a specific purpose or mission.

compensating control   Also called an alternative control, a security control that is used when compliance requirements or other security objectives cannot be met with existing controls. Compensating controls are sometimes used when normal mitigating controls are unavailable or impractical to implement.

compliance   The process of ensuring alignment with applicable laws, regulations, external standards, ethical conduct, and other organizational goals and objectives.

compromise   To reveal or expose something to an unauthorized person or entity. Also, to cause the impairment or degradation of something.

computer   A device, machine, or system that can be programmed to carry out a sequence of operations. A computer normally consists of hardware, software in the form of an operating system, peripheral devices such as storage media, and programs that carry out operations.

computer networks   The infrastructure that allows computers to talk to one another. They consist of hardware, software, and technologies used to allow devices and systems to communicate.

confidentiality   The state of keeping something secret.

configuration baseline   An agreed-to description of the configuration attributes of a product, device, or software that serves as the basis for defining future changes.

configuration management   The process of maintaining a system's attributes, including hardware, software, settings, and documentation, in a desired state.

containment   Actions taken to prevent an incident, breach, or malware from spreading to other parts of the network.

control   A countermeasure or safeguard used to counteract or reduce the security risk relating to an organization's or a person's assets.

corrective controls   Controls that fix a system, process, or activity after an adverse event has occurred.

countermeasure   *See* control.

crime prevention through environmental design (CPTED)   A design technique focused on preventing crime by leveraging environmental design elements that discourage criminal activity by changing human behavior.

critical infrastructure   Resources and assets that are so vital to the communities they support that their continued operation is considered essential. Critical infrastructure includes power generation and distribution systems, transportation systems (road, air, rail, etc.), communication networks, water and other utilities, and buildings necessary to maintain normalcy.

cross-site scripting   A type of cyberattack in which the attacker injects a malicious script into the field of a website or application.

cryptographic algorithm   A mathematical equation that is used to perform a cryptographic function (such as encryption/decryption).

cryptographic key   A value that is used as input into a cryptographic algorithm that enables it to perform its cryptographic function.

cryptography   The practice of using mathematical formulas to protect information by transforming the information into another format to ensure the information cannot be read or accessed by unauthorized parties.

cyberattack   An attempt to gain unauthorized access to a computer or information system for the purpose of causing harm, stealing, disrupting, or degrading normal operation.

cybersecurity   The practice of protecting information resources from unauthorized use. Also known as information security or IT security. Also refers to the various technologies, frameworks, practices, and measures used for protecting information resources.

cyberterrorism   Cyber-criminal activity that is politically motivated.

data classification   The process of assigning classification levels to data types based on risk that determines how the data may be handled as well as the level of protection required.

data lifecycle   A series of changes data goes through during its existence within an organization.

data security   A set of practices aimed at protecting information important to an organization.

decryption   The process of transforming ciphertext to plaintext.

default   A preselected setting or condition that is used when no other is specified. Many information system devices and endpoints have default settings that are used if settings are lost, such as after a power failure.

defense-in-depth   The concept of coordinating and leveraging multiple layers of controls to increase the effort required for a potential attacker to succeed in their nefarious activity.

degaussing   The process of destroying data from magnetic storage media by removing or neutralizing its magnetism.

demilitarized zone (DMZ)   A portion of an organization's network that separates the organization's internal resources from other untrusted resources, usually the Internet, by providing an additional layer of protection.

denial of service   A class of cyberattacks in which the goal is to render the victim system, network, or organization disabled, shut down, inaccessible, or otherwise unable to perform its intended function. A denial of service attack is an attack against availability.

detective controls   Controls that help discover, detect, or identify when something bad might have occurred, such as an adverse activity, event, intruder, or incident.

deterrent controls   Controls that deter or discourage a potential adversary from performing an attack or engaging in unwanted behavior.

dictionary attack   A variant of a brute force password attack in which the brute force processing is performed using a list of common words and phrases to try as passwords.

differential backup   A backup of a system's data in which only the files that have changed since the last full backup was made are backed up each time the backup process is run.

digital certificate   An electronic certificate that links a public key to its owner. Digital certificates are issued by trusted third-party organizations (the certificate authority) that have verified the identity of the public key owner.

directive controls   Controls that serve to communicate expected behavior, such as a "stop" or "yield" sign or an organization's security policy.

disaster recovery   The act of developing plans and procedures for recovering and restoring critical functions of the business, usually focused on IT operations.

discretionary access control (DAC)   An access control model where the owner of the resource, typically the creator, has full control to configure which subjects (e.g., users, groups) can access the object (e.g., file, folder). This allows the user (object owner) the ability ("discretion") to make decisions such as what permissions other users or groups of users have over the object.

disk mirroring   A form of data redundancy in which data is written to two disks at the same time. If one drive fails, data can be retrieved from the other mirrored drive.

distributed denial of service   A class of denial of service attacks in which multiple compromised systems attack the target system to cause the denial of service.

domain   An area over which control is exercised. In IT, a domain is any group of resources (such as users, endpoints, databases, etc.) controlled as an entity.

domain name   An easy-to-remember name used to access a website; for example: mheducation.com.

dual-factor authentication   Authentication that uses two factors or methods of authentication to verify the user's identity.

electronically   By means of electronic equipment, systems, or devices such as computers or information systems.

e-mail   A system for transmitting messages electronically. The term e-mail also refers to the messages exchanged via an e-mail system. Can also be used as a verb to refer to the action of sending an e-mail message.

encryption   The process of transforming plaintext (information that is in a readable format) into ciphertext (information that is in an encrypted, unreadable format).

endpoint   Any computer, appliance, or device that connects to a modern enterprise network, including workstations, servers, printers and peripherals, network devices and access points, mobile devices, and storage devices.

ethics   Moral standards or principles that govern behavior with a focus on acting responsibly with integrity and accountability.

event   An occurrence of an activity on an information system.

evidence   Any information or data that is of value to an investigation of an incident.

exfiltration   In cybersecurity, the unauthorized removal of data from a system.

exploit   An action that takes advantage of a flaw in a computer system or software, usually to perform a malicious act or to achieve unauthorized access.

exposure   The potential that a security breach could occur.

exposure factor   The percentage of loss that would likely occur for a given event.

external standards   Documents developed and published by external standards organizations containing best practices that may be used for the development of security program elements.

extortion   The act of obtaining money through the use of coercion, force, or threats.

Federal Information Security Modernization Act of 2014 (FISMA)   A U.S. federal law that defines how U.S. government agencies and their contractors implement information security.

federated identity management   A variant of single sign-on that allows organizations to establish arrangements to share identity information and authenticate users across multiple different organizations. This allows a user to authenticate with one organization and access resources in another without having to perform a separate login.

firewall   A network security device used to block certain communications while permitting other communications based on a set of criteria.

first responder   A person trained to respond immediately and provide assistance in the event of an accident or incident. Includes firefighters, law enforcement officers, emergency medical technicians, paramedics, and other rescue personnel.

For Official Use Only (FOUO)   A document designation used by U.S. government agencies to indicate information that may not be suitable for public release.

full backup   A backup of a system's data in which all of the data on the system is saved each time the backup processes is run.

General Data Protection Regulation (GDPR)   European Union (EU) privacy law that regulates the processing of the personal data of EU citizens.

GitHub   An Internet-based platform used by software development teams for collaboration and version control of developing applications.

governance   The system or process of overseeing the control or direction of something. It refers to the set of rules, practices, and processes by which an organization operates.

Gramm-Leach-Bliley Act (GLBA)   Also known as the Financial Modernization Act of 1999, it is a U.S. federal law that establishes rules for how financial institutions handle the personal information of individuals.

hacker   Someone who engages in criminal activity to gain unauthorized access to information systems to steal data or disrupt operations. An alternate, older definition of hacker is anyone who enjoys programming; therefore, any programmer can be a hacker, but the more widely used definition is that a hacker is a cyberattacker.

hashing   A type of cryptography that uses special algorithms known as hash algorithms that transform information into fixed-length output known as a hash value, message digest, or fingerprint. Unlike encryption, which can be reversed via decryption, hashing is a one-way process, meaning the original information or message cannot feasibly be reproduced from the hash value output.

Health Insurance Portability and Accountability Act of 1996 (HIPAA)   A U.S. federal law that required the creation of national standards to protect sensitive patient health information from being disclosed without the patient's consent or knowledge.

hot site   An alternate datacenter or business facility that is fully equipped and ready to be operational at a moment's notice.

hub   A network device that is used to physically connect many systems and devices to the network using a wired connection. Hubs have physical ports whereby devices connect to the hub using network cables. Hubs do not have any intelligence in them to make decisions about how the traffic is routed or forwarded.

hybrid cloud   A cloud deployment model that is a combination (hybrid) of two or more of the other cloud deployment models (public, private, or community).

identification   The action of providing identifying information. In cybersecurity it is the act of the subject providing identifying information to a system.

identity management   The process of identifying, authenticating, and authorizing users for access to resources.

impersonate   To pretend to be someone or something else, usually for the purpose of deception.

incident   One or more events that violate an organization's security policies or that may indicate an organization's system has been subject to unauthorized access or data has been compromised. Also, one or more events that jeopardize the confidentiality, integrity, or availability of an asset.

incident response The process of preparing, detecting, analyzing, containing, eradicating, and recovering from a security incident (such as virus/malware infections, credential theft, sensitive data exfiltration, etc.).

incremental backup A backup of a system's data in which only the files that have changed since the last backup of any type was made are backed up each time the backup process is run.

information assurance The measure of information security or the extent to which information security is achieved or implemented.

infrastructure as a service (IaaS) A cloud service model where a cloud service provider (CSP) gives customers self-service access to a pool of infrastructure resources (such as network, server, storage, etc.) that can be virtually provisioned and deprovisioned on demand. The CSP manages the underlying physical infrastructure and the physical hosts that support that infrastructure. The customer manages the platforms and software such as operating system (OS), development tools, applications, and virtual hosts that they provision.

insider An employee, consultant, or other individual who has some level of authorized access to an organization's assets.

insider threat The potential threat presented by an insider who can exploit their access and knowledge of an organization to steal data or disrupt operations.

Institute of Electrical and Electronics Engineers (IEEE) A professional organization that develops and maintains a portfolio of standards for information technology, telecommunications, and computer networking.

integrity The state or condition of being whole or free from damage or defects.

intellectual property (IP) A category of property that refers to the creations of the human mind that are protected by law from unauthorized use. IP includes inventions, literary works, art, designs, images, trade names, and the like.

internal standard Documents used to establish methods for complying with internal policies by defining specific technologies, protocols, methods, or controls to be used. For example, configuration standards are used to establish specific configuration settings for hardware or software used within an organization to ensure a consistent protection level.

International Organization for Standardization (ISO) ISO is an independent international standard development organization that develops and publishes best practice standards on a variety of subjects including information technology, information security, and other technical topics.

Internet Engineering Task Force (IETF) An organization that develops technical standards related to Internet protocols, network management, and other technical specifications.

Internet of Things (IoT)   The collective network of devices and things that connect to the Internet. Usually, the term IoT refers to the nontypical devices that connect to the Internet other than computers such as mechanical and digital machines, sensors, and associated software.

Internet Protocol (IP) addresses   Logical addresses used for identifying devices for the purpose of routing traffic on a local area network (LAN) or over wide area networks (WANs) such as the Internet.

intrusion detection and prevention systems (IDS/IPS)   An IDS is a computer system or appliance that monitors, analyzes, and reports on network events to detect malicious activity. An IPS is an IDS that automatically takes actions based on the activity it detects.

laws and regulations   Rules established by a governmental body or similar agency that specify requirements that are legally enforceable that shape an organization's behavior.

least privilege   *See* principle of least privilege.

local area network (LAN)   A computer network that covers a limited geographic area such as a home, office building, or an organization's datacenter. A LAN enables network communication of computing devices within those facilities. LANs are typically owned and operated by a single entity such as an individual home office network or an organization's enterprise network. LANs can be wired or wireless. Wireless LANs are referred to as WLANs.

log management   Activities undertaken to capture, store, and maintain logs so that they are useful to the organization.

logging   The capturing and storing of events for later analysis.

logical port   Numerical identifiers used to identify which applications or services are running on a computer. Logical ports allow multiple applications and services to share the same connection to a network.

logs   Files that store information about various events that occur on a system.

malicious   The intent to cause harm.

malware   Software that is intentionally harmful or malicious.

management   The processes to execute, operate, and monitor the activities that implement governance strategies.

mandatory access control (MAC)   Access control model that leverages a central authority that regulates access based on security labels, such as the clearance level that a subject (user) has been approved for, as well the classification of the object (file, database, etc.). A clearance level indicates the level of access a subject (user) has been approved for.

man-in-the-middle attack   A cyberattack in which the attacker places themselves in between two communicating parties, systems, or devices to intercept, interfere with, or eavesdrop on the communication.

mantrap   An area that has two locked doors built in such a way that the first door must be closed before the second door can be opened and access to a secure area can be granted.

media access control (MAC) address   Unique serial numbers assigned to the network interface of computing devices.

memorized secrets   Authentication methods that are "something you know" such as passwords, personal identification numbers (PINs), or lock combinations used to authenticate a user to a system or a physical device.

micro-segmentation   A method of creating zones or containers within a network in which access, data, functions, and applications can be finely controlled in accordance with security policy.

monitoring   The review and examination of logs, events, or other activities.

multifactor authentication   Authentication that uses more than one factor or method of authentication to verify the user's identity.

National Institute of Standards and Technology (NIST)   A U.S. government agency responsible for measurement science, standards, and technology. NIST creates and publishes standards and guidelines for cybersecurity and risk management used by government and industry.

nation-state   Government-sponsored or government-owned organization that performs cyber-criminal activities to achieve their goals, which may be political, military, financial, or cultural.

natural disaster   An earthquake; flood; fire; or inclement weather, including storms, hurricanes, tornadoes, etc., for which the negative impact causes significant damage or harm.

need to know   A access control concept whereby access to the subject information or resource is necessary for one to conduct one's official duties.

network access control (NAC)   A set of security controls that seeks to keep unauthorized users and endpoints from connecting to and accessing a private network. For example, when a system checks to make sure a virtual private network (VPN) client has the correct antivirus updates installed before allowing the VPN client to connect to the network, that is an example of NAC.

network interface   A physical piece of hardware integrated into computing devices to allow them to connect to a computer network (typically a LAN).

nonrepudiation   The property that someone cannot deny the validity of something. In messaging it is the assurance that someone cannot deny a message came from them.

nonsecure protocols   Protocols that send data across the network in plaintext (which means anyone can read it).

object A person or thing that something happens to. In cybersecurity it is an entity or resource that is accessed by a subject.

Open Systems Interconnection (OSI) model A conceptual framework consisting of seven layers that describes the functionality at each layer of a computer network.

Open Web Application Security Project (OWASP) An international organization that develops tools, standards, and best practice documents focused on application security.

packet filter A type of firewall that inspects incoming and outgoing packets and controls access based on attributes and a set of criteria.

password A secret that enables someone to gain access or admission to something.

patch management The practice of identifying, obtaining, validating, and deploying patches to operating systems and applications.

patching A software patch is a set of changes to a computer program to repair a bug or make an improvement. Patching is the act of deploying and installing a patch.

Payment Card Industry Security Standards Council (PCI SSC) A global organization that develops and manages standards for payment security, such as the Payment Card Industry Data Security Standard (PCI DSS), which defines security requirements for companies that handle or process credit card data or transactions.

phishing Sending fraudulent e-mails or other electronic communication for the purpose of deceiving the recipient into falling for a scam or social engineering trick.

physical controls Tangible controls put in place to protect physical resources against physical threats, including but not limited to break-ins, fires, theft, physical harm, and so on.

physical port A physical interface on a computer or network device that another device or cable can be plugged into.

ping attack A type of denial of service cyberattack in which the attacker overwhelms the target system with Internet Control Message Protocol (ICMP) ping or echo request messages.

plaintext Information that is in a readable format,

platform as a service (PaaS) A cloud service model that provides a complete platform (hardware, software, infrastructure) for developing and running applications.

policy A set of requirements and rules that dictate how an organization operates.

preventive controls Controls that prevent or stop an adverse event or incident.

principle of least privilege The concept that a user should only have access to the resources that they need in order to do their job but no more than that.

privacy   The ability of an individual or entity to hide information about themselves from others.

private cloud   A cloud deployment model that consists of dedicated cloud computing resources used by a single organization. The cloud resources may be owned and operated by the organization, a third party, or a combination of both.

privilege   A right, benefit, or permission that is granted or available to a person, subject, or group but not granted to others.

procedure   A step-by-step workflow or set of instructions that define how a task should be accomplished.

protocols   Rules and standards for network communication.

provisioning   The creation and maintenance of user accounts and access rights.

proxy filter   A type of firewall that acts as a middleman between the two network segments it is installed between. In client/server applications it hides the client's IP address to the server and its proxy function, allowing the client to connect and operate anonymously.

public cloud   A cloud deployment model that consists of cloud computing resources operated by a third party that are deployed for use by the general public for purchase and consumption (typically a subscription or on-demand pricing model).

public key infrastructure (PKI)   A framework and technology that allow for the management of public key encryption. This is accomplished through the creation, distribution, management, and revocation of digital certificates.

qualitative risk assessment   Seeks to understand risk in non-numerical terms using ratings and priorities.

quantitative risk assessment   Seeks to understand risk by assigning numerical or financial values to assets along with factors with numerical weights such as threat probability, impact of loss, etc.

rainbow tables   A method of password hacking that uses precomputed tables of password hashes to compare against actual password hashes in a password database.

ransomware   Malicious software that threatens to cause damage to an organization's data or computer system unless a ransom is paid to the attacker.

recovery point objective (RPO)   The point in time to which data must be recovered after an outage; it also indicates how much data is acceptable to be lost during an outage.

recovery time objective (RTO)   The acceptable amount of time a system outage can last after a disaster or incident.

redundant array of independent disks or tapes (RAID or RAIT) A method of storage in which data is written across multiple physical disks (or tapes) for increased reliability and performance.

revocation The withdrawal or cancellation of something. In cybersecurity it is the removal of a user's access rights to a resource.

risk The likelihood that a vulnerability could be exploited and the corresponding impact of such an event.

risk transference A method of risk treatment that transfers responsibility for risk, or for mitigating losses, to another party.

risk treatment Possible approaches for handling risk.

role-based access control (RBAC) An access control model that enforces access based on roles that define permissions and the level of access provided to subjects assigned to that role. Roles are typically developed for similar users with the same access needs (e.g., human resources, sales, IT, security).

rootkit Software used by cyber criminals designed to gain unauthorized privileged access to a computer while concealing its presence.

router An intelligent network device that controls and routes data between network segments using Internet Protocol (IP) addresses and in accordance with communication protocols.

salt A random value that is added to a message (or password) during the hashing process.

Sarbanes-Oxley Act of 2002 (SOX) A U.S. federal law that established auditing and financial requirements and regulations for publicly traded companies.

scans and scanning The process of discovering endpoints, characteristics, and identifying security weaknesses in networks.

script kiddie A type of computer hacker who is unskilled and uses programs developed by others to carry out attacks but who may not fully understand how the program works or the damage it can cause.

secure protocols Protocols that encrypt data in transit to prevent unauthorized eavesdropping on communications.

security The state of being free from danger or a threat. Security is the protection from threats posed by others.

security breach An event or occurrence in which an individual is able to gain access to something they are not allowed to access.

security control A countermeasure or safeguard used to counteract or reduce the security risk relating to an organization's or person's assets.

security governance A subset of organizational governance focused on developing strategies to oversee the security program to facilitate alignment with the goals and objectives of the organization.

security information and event management (SIEM) system A security solution that collects and analyzes data from a variety of tools, logs, and system components to help the organization learn about threats and prevent security incidents.

segmentation A network design approach to separate the network into segments or small networks for control, security, and performance management.

segregation of duties The assignment of duties such that more than one person is required to complete a task and one person should not have enough privilege on their own to cause misuse or fraud.

separation of duties *See* segregation of duties.

server A term that describes a computer that serves content or provides a service to another computer on the network.

service level agreement (SLA) A legal contractual agreement between a service provider or supplier and a customer that defines the level of service the customer can expect.

service set identifier (SSID) The name of a wireless network that allows devices to connect to and be part of the same wireless network.

shoulder surfing A type of cyberattack in which someone looks over the shoulder of a computer user to covertly observe what they are doing and steal credentials or other sensitive information.

side channel attack An attack that reads information from a system not from normal communication channels but by examining other characteristics of a system that can reveal information. For example, a system's power supply noise can be representative of the data it is transmitting or processing, and measuring power supply electromagnetic waves can be used for eavesdropping.

single-factor authentication Authentication that uses one factor or method of authentication, such as a password, to verify the user's identity.

single sign-on (SSO) A technology that allows users to seamlessly access a range of resources after authenticating just one time.

smurf attack A type of cyberattack using "ICMP Redirect" messages in which the reply Internet Protocol (IP) address is substituted with the IP address of the system that is the target of the attack.

social media Websites and supporting applications that enable users to create online communities through which they can share ideas, information, and media with other users.

software as a service (SaaS)   A cloud service model that consists of a software service or application that is hosted by the cloud service provider and provided to customers (typically over the Internet). The cloud provider manages the infrastructure and platform, and the customer only needs to manage specific configurations within the application. Examples of SaaS include web-based e-mail, social media sites, and other web-based applications.

software-defined networking (SDN)   A network management approach that allows for granular control of access to data, applications, and functions within containers or micro-segments with the aid of specialized software and application programming interfaces on endpoint devices.

spear phishing   A type of phishing attack in which the target is a particular person, group, organization, company, agency, etc., as opposed to a regular phishing attack, which does not have a specific victim in mind.

spyware   Any software that covertly monitors a user's activity on a computer without their knowledge or permission for the purpose of forwarding it to a third party.

SQL injection   A type of cyberattack in which the attacker uses malicious SQL code to manipulate a backend database to cause unauthorized or harmful operation.

stateful/dynamic firewall   A type of firewall that intercepts and reads packets to understand the state of the communication taking place and makes contextual decisions regarding what traffic to allow and deny.

subject   An entity that is capable of accessing an object, usually by first requesting such access.

supply chain   The set or sequence of processes, suppliers, manufacturers, distributors, etc., by which products or goods are produced and brought to their ultimate destination.

supply chain management   The set of activities to plan, define, handle, control, and execute supply chain operations.

switch   A device that is used to physically segment parts of the network using physical ports to connect to other devices and parts of the network.

symmetric encryption   A type of encryption that uses the same key for encryption and decryption.

SYN flood attack   A type of cyberattack in which the attacker violates the normal Transmission Control Protocol/Internet Protocol (TCP/IP) message sequence and/or content, creating a denial of service against a target system or systems.

technical controls   Hardware or software components that protect computing and network resources such as computers, servers, mobile devices, computer networks, or data stored within a system. Technical controls are also referred to as *logical controls*.

threat (*n.*) Something that is likely to cause damage or danger. (*v.*) A statement or expression of intent to inflict pain, injury, or damage.

threat actor A person who carries out a cyberattack or exploits a vulnerability.

threat intelligence Information collected about potential threats that has been processed, analyzed, and put into a form such that it can be used to support cyber-defense decisions.

timing condition attack A type of cyberattack in which a normally operating program waits for an event to occur, or two tasks must occur in a sequence. In such an instance the attacker could interfere with the sequence, such as by substituting a file in between the time it is checked and the time it is read.

Transmission Control Protocol/Internet Protocol (TCP/IP) model A network model developed by the Department of Defense (DoD) that consists of four layers. It is both a network model and an implementation with a suite of protocols that are the foundational protocols of most networks, including the Internet.

triage Initial investigation of an incident in which an assessment is made and a level of urgency determined, which provide guidance for future investigation and prioritization with other incidents.

trojan A virus that is disguised as something that is useful.

USB drive A portable device that contains flash memory and uses a universal serial bus (USB) interface to provide external data storage for computers and other devices. Also known as a USB flash drive.

virtual local area network (VLAN) A logical group of endpoints that appear to be on the same local area network.

virtual private network (VPN) A secure connection to a private trusted network through a public untrusted network such as the Internet.

vulnerability A flaw or weakness in a computer device, software, or system that could allow harm to occur.

vulnerability assessment A planned test and review of an organization's information system or systems to uncover security vulnerabilities or weaknesses.

vulnerability management A continuous process to keep all endpoints in the network free from vulnerabilities and up-to-date with the latest security patches.

vulnerability scanning The process of using automated tools to uncover security weaknesses in systems, devices, or software.

warm site An alternate facility that is configured with supporting equipment and infrastructure but does not have the actual information-processing equipment installed. Warm sites usually can be ready to fully support operations in several days.

website defacement   A type of cyberattack in which the attacker changes the appearance or content of a website without proper authorization.

wide area network (WAN)   A WAN enables communication between remote local area networks (LANs) and covers a wide geographic area. WANs are networks linked together by infrastructure managed and owned by third-party telecommunication service providers.

Wi-Fi   A family of wireless network protocols used for wireless communication.

Wi-Fi Protected Access Protocol (WPA)   A security technology used to provide authentication and encryption. The current versions in use are WPA2 and WPA3.

wireless access point (AP)   A device that allows wireless-capable devices to wirelessly connect to a network. These are often used in enterprise networks for connecting wireless devices to the organization's local area network (LAN).

Wireless Equivalency Privacy (WEP)   A standard developed for wireless security that contained significant security flaws and is no longer in use. It was replaced by Wi-Fi Protected Access Protocol (WPA).

wireless protected setup (WPS)   A feature provided by some routers and network devices that simplifies the process of connecting wireless devices to a wireless network.

work factor   An estimate of the effort and/or time required for a threat actor to defeat protective security controls.

work recovery time (WRT)   The amount of time it takes to test systems and data once they are restored after a disaster or incident.

worm   A computer malware program that can automatically replicate itself and propagate from one computer to another.

zero day   A previously unknown or recently discovered security vulnerability for which there is not a current patch available.

zero trust   A security concept that requires all users, whether inside or outside of an organization's network, to be specifically authenticated and authorized before being granted access to a network resource such as a device, application, or data.

INDEX

A

ABAC (attribute-based access control), 68
accept approach to risk, 21
acceptable use policies (AUPs), 194
access control
    authentication, 6, 59–61
    authorization, 59
    authorized vs. unauthorized personnel, 55
    concepts, 54–55
    confidentiality, 4
    fundamentals, 53–54
    identification in, 58–59
    identity and access management, 61–62
    incident response, 217
    Internet of Things, 144
    logical, 65–72
    memorized secrets, 57–58
    need to know premise, 56
    physical, 72–78
    principle of least privilege, 56
    privileged accounts, 63–65
    questions, 81–87
    review, 79–81
    segregation of duties, 56–57
    summary, 65
    technical, 33–34
    two-person rule, 57
access control lists (ACLs), 66–67
access control matrices, 66–67
access logs, physical, 77–78
access points (APs), 93
accountability in access control, 59, 63
accounts
    audits, 70
    containment strategy, 224
    privileged, 63–65
ACK (acknowledgment) messages in TCP, 106
ACLs (access control lists), 66–67
actors, threat
    description, 6
    examples, 15–16
    incident response, 212

Address Resolution Protocol (ARP), 107
addresses
    IP. *See* Internet Protocol (IP) addresses
    MAC, 91–92, 101, 107
    system, 91
administration, 28
administrative controls, 31–33, 37–38
Advanced Encryption Standard (AES)
  encryption, 143, 179
advanced persistent threats (APTs), 131–132
agents in SNMP, 105
alarm systems, 78
algorithms in cryptography, 183–184
alternate datacenter facilities, 151
annualized loss expectancy (ALE)
  in risk assessment, 20
annualized rate of occurrence (ARO)
  in risk assessment, 20
anomaly-based IDSs/IPSs, 141
antivirus software, 141–142
applicability element in security policies, 193
Application Layer
    OSI model, 100–101
    TCP/IP model, 103–105
applications
    security assessments and testing, 146
    vulnerabilities, 14
    web, 219
APs (access points), 93
APTs (advanced persistent threats), 131–132
architecture elements in network defenses,
  136–138
archive phase in data lifecycles, 177
ARO (annualized rate of occurrence)
  in risk assessment, 20
ARP (Address Resolution Protocol), 107
assessment step in risk management, 19–21
asset management, 188
asset value (AV) in risk assessment, 19–20
asymmetric encryption, 179–180
attacks. *See* cyberattack elements; threats
  and attacks